MW01618690

From Caliphate to Secular State

From Caliphate to Secular State

Power Struggle in the Early Turkish Republic

Hakan Özoğlu

AN IMPRINT OF ABC-CLIO, LLC
Santa Barbara, California • Denver, Colorado • Oxford, England

Copyright 2011 by Hakan Özoğlu

All rights reserved. No part of this publication may be reproduced, stored in a retrieval system, or transmitted, in any form or by any means, electronic, mechanical, photocopying, recording, or otherwise, except for the inclusion of brief quotations in a review, without prior permission in writing from the publisher.

Library of Congress Cataloging-in-Publication Data

Özoğlu, Hakan, 1964–
From Caliphate to secular state : power struggle in the early Turkish Republic / Hakan Özoğlu.
p. cm.
Includes bibliographical references and index.
ISBN 978–0–313–37956–7 (hard copy : alk. paper) — ISBN 978–0–313–37957–4 (ebook)
1. Turkey—Politics and government—1918–1960. 2. Atatürk, Kemal, 1881–1938—Assassination attempt, 1926. 3. Political culture—Turkey—History—20th century. 4. Power (Social sciences)—Turkey—History—20th century. 5. Nationalism—Turkey—History—20th century. 6. Panislamism. 7. Secularism—Turkey—History—20th century. 8. Islam and politics—Turkey—History—20th century. I. Title.
DR590.O96 2011
956.1′023—dc22 2011005967

ISBN: 978–0–313–37956–7
EISBN: 978–0–313–37957–4

15 14 13 12 11 1 2 3 4 5

This book is also available on the World Wide Web as an eBook.
Visit www.abc-clio.com for details.

Praeger
An Imprint of ABC-CLIO, LLC

ABC-CLIO, LLC
130 Cremona Drive, P.O. Box 1911
Santa Barbara, California 93116-1911

This book is printed on acid-free paper ∞

Manufactured in the United States of America

To my children, Seren and Pelin

Contents

Preface

Working on a critical study on the early Turkish Republic poses a particular challenge for someone like me, who grew up and was oriented in the same political discourse as the subject of this study. The challenge is more visible when one realizes that my subject—the formative years of the Republic of Turkey—has always been regarded as "sacred" for an academic work. Being a product of such an intellectual and political environment had long prevented me from questioning the validity of information about the emergence of my own country, information that I was exposed to during my elementary, middle school, high school, and college education. I remember being upset with those who tried to do what I did in this book: simply read Turkish republican history under a more critical light. I regarded those individuals as people who harbored hatred toward my country. The irony is that there may be some people today who would regard this study as such and accuse me of having some ulterior motives. Let me begin by firmly stating that my only aim is to produce an academic study that would stand firm under the highest degree of scholarly scrutiny. Although I am aware that this study can be exploited by different and even diametrically contradictory political discourses, I know that I did not write it with any political purpose in mind. I am not naive to assert that my study is free of biases. However, I can safely state that they are unintentional, and I hope that the reader will judge it fairly.

In addition to overcoming mental blocks, in the process of working on this study, I had to cope with other, less painful obstacles, namely, finding and reaching reliable information. The reader should be informed up front that much information is still not fully available to researchers, and my research is not immune from these limitations. However, there is sufficient direct and indirect information to support my conclusions in this book. Another challenge was to maintain a critical eye on every piece of information obtained from all my sources, both primary and secondary. I hope this study will add another layer of scholarly brick on top of previous reputable works in the reconstruction of the early Turkish republican history.

This work from its conception to its production has taken over a decade. As new information became available, I tried to incorporate it into the text. The manuscript was read by several scholars who are specialists in their fields. They made very valuable comments. Although I benefited from their criticism and revised my text accordingly, I must accept full responsibility for the shortcomings of this work. Therefore, I must recognize the valuable input of the following scholars. I am deeply indebted to Professors Mete Tunçay, Şükrü Hanioğlu, Hamit Bozarslan, and Reşat Kasaba for their time in reading and commenting on the text. I am also grateful to Carole Gonzalez for proofreading it and to Eyüp Türker for his help in İstanbul during my research. I am most thankful for the grants provided by the University of Central Florida and the Pauley Endowment.

NOTES ON TRANSLITERATION AND TRANSLATION

Except for terms common in English, regardless of origin, all words used in the Ottoman context are spelled according to Modern Turkish orthography. Therefore, all Turkish proper names are rendered in Modern Turkish forms. Particular challenge emerged, however, for the names that end with soft/voiced consonants. Since there is a tendency in Modern Turkish to end words with hard/voiceless consonants, proper names such as Cavid, Receb, and Mehmed were spelled as Cavit, Recep, and Mehmet unless they are part of a direct quotation. Therefore, the reader might see both ways of spelling for some proper names that end with voiceless consonants. To provide a degree of uniformity, I omitted some diacritics for names and terms that were taken from Ottoman texts.

The Turkish system of alphabetization is also utilized for placenames in Turkey, such as Ankara and İstanbul, not Angora and Istanbul. Common Ottoman/Turkish and Islamic titles were spelled in English, such as sheikh, sayyid, qadi, and pasha. For uncommon titles, I utilized the Turkish transliteration, such as *mutasarrıf* and *kaymakam*.

1

Introduction

It is a known fact that after every successful revolution, an inevitable power struggle emerges. The Republic of Turkey was no exception to this proposition. Following the collapse of the Ottoman Empire after World War I, the political map of the Middle East changed significantly. Since many newly formed Middle Eastern states were still under the mandate of Great Britain and France, their internal power struggles were delayed until after the departure of the Western Powers. A notable exception was the Republic of Turkey, which almost immediately locked in an internal strife for the vision and the leadership of the state. An examination of this struggle is significant for it reveals clues about the radical transition from an empire, which housed the seat of the Islamic caliphate for over four centuries, to a secular state in which religion was confined to a private sphere.

As a secular nation, Turkey has often been cited as an example of a successful modern state in the Islamic world, which made serious commitments to the Western mode of government. However, circumstances that allowed such a drastic transition were not satisfactorily documented, examined, and explained. How did Turkey make such a radical transformation? Was there any internal opposition to the leadership and vision of the new regime? What were the methods employed to circumvent the opposition? These significant questions fall in the subject of the current study. This book aims primarily at explaining the process in which the opposition in the new republic was silenced. However, it also invites readers to rethink the early republican history in the context of a power struggle that helped shape the Turkish political identity. I hope that this line of thinking lends itself to the larger issue of the Kemalist vision in general. I propose that the nature of the new Turkish state was not a result of a predetermined vision but a pragmatic synthesis of political realities and opportunities to silence the opposition.

In order to guide the reader, the narrative must begin with an overview of the political situation in Turkey after World War I. As it is known, the Ottoman Empire lost the war and, in the period between 1918 and 1920, was waiting for its fate, which was to be determined by the victorious Allied Powers. Following the occupation of İstanbul[1] by the Allies and İzmir by Greece[2] after World War I, there were many competing visions for the future of the state within the empire. The dominant view among the Ottoman government officers, high-level bureaucrats, politicians, and the sultan was that the only way for political survival of the empire was to cooperate with the victors. This attitude was challenged by a group of nationalists who created the Anatolian Resistance Movement. This group, consisting mainly of individuals who believed that the empire could not survive by surrender, set its base in Ankara, a small town in central Anatolia. Led by able Ottoman military commanders and statesmen such as Mustafa Kemal (Atatürk), Kazım Karabekir, Ali Fuat (Cebesoy), and Rauf (Orbay), this new movement soon found itself locked in a power struggle with the İstanbul government for the future of the state.

In this context, the years between 1920 and 1924 were crucial in determining the fate of the Ottoman Empire and the direction of the emerging Turkish regime in Ankara. Despite many claims to the contrary, it should not be a forgone conclusion that the empire was destined to collapse after World War I, at least until the signing of the Treaty of Sevres in 1920. Many high-level bureaucrats and politicians, as well as the dynasty, were clinging to a desperate hope that the empire could survive, albeit with a substantial territorial loss. The members of the İstanbul Circle (the monarchists and associates)[3] were trying their best to spare the empire with a minimum loss of territory. Since they lacked the necessary military force to ensure the empire's security, the imperial government in İstanbul was hoping that cooperation with the Allied Powers would perhaps soften the blow to the very existence of the state. This tactic to protect the empire, however, was proven to be disastrous and played into the hands of the Nationalists (the Ankara Circle) since the Allies had no desire to allow the empire to survive in a meaningful way.

It must be remembered that in the pre–Treaty of Sevres period, the nationalist movement was not entirely outside the realm of the İstanbul government. The Anatolian resistance began in 1919 with the manifest goal of protecting the empire and the sultan. In other words, until after the Turkish War of Independence (1919–1922), the two sides, İstanbul and Ankara, differed on the method of saving the empire, not on the purpose. The opening of the Turkish Grand National Assembly (TGNA) in Ankara on April 23, 1920, expressly challenged the authority of the İstanbul government but registered its purpose as saving the empire and the caliph. This move was, nevertheless, a major challenge to the İstanbul government, as it attracted some İstanbul parliamentarians to Ankara. The final blow to the strained Ankara-İstanbul relations came after the signing of the Treaty of Sevres in 1920, which later proved to be the death sentence of the Ottoman Empire.

It is worth mentioning that during the War of Independence (1919–1922), the İstanbul government's reaction to Ankara was not monolithic. Some cabinet members in the post–Committee of Union and Progress (CUP)[4] governments sympathized with the resistance movement in Anatolia. However, as soon as Ankara rejected the authority of İstanbul, there emerged more of a unified tone against the nationalists, championed by Damat Ferit Pasha,[5] and many of his cabinet members. İstanbul governments under Damat Ferit Pasha's premiership accused the nationalist movement in Anatolia of harming the interest of the state and its citizens by provoking the Allies. The imperial government in İstanbul believed that World War I was lost and that any military action against the Allies was doomed for failure. These actions would provoke the superior military powers to harm the interest of the empire and adversely affect the upcoming peace negotiations.

However, there was another not well-articulated reason for the hostility of İstanbul toward Ankara. This reason fundamentally colored the perception and affected the attitude of the İstanbul Circle against Ankara. It was the alleged connection of the nationalists to their political nemesis, the CUP. Memoirs of the members of the İstanbul Circle reveal that the Damat Ferit Pasha cabinets and many members of the anti-CUP coalition sincerely believed that the nationalist movement in Anatolia was another deception by the CUP to replace their government of the Liberal Entente.[6] In their minds, there existed sufficient evidence to connect the Ankara Circle to the CUP, a fear that was justified by the CUP backgrounds of many nationalists, including Mustafa Kemal. Even more significant was that, at its inception, the Ankara movement did not have a clearly manifested political identity that separated it from the CUP. Many foreign observers also considered this movement first as an arm of and then as the custodian for the CUP.[7] This perception is significant in understanding the rivalry between İstanbul and Ankara and, later, Ankara's purges of İstanbul.

No doubt, by 1920, Ankara was resolute to break ranks with and to replace the government in İstanbul; however, one should be cautious to blindly accept the proposition that Ankara was determined to get rid of the monarchy and that the nationalists aimed at creating a new secular republic. Accepting such a proposition would mean reading the history only retrospectively. The Ankara movement could have stayed loyal to the sultan if he recognized the TGNA as the legitimate government of the Ottoman Empire. The turning point in Ankara's break with the sultan came with the realization that such recognition would never materialize. Consequently, the nationalists abolished the sultanate on November 1, 1922, forcing Vahdettin to flee from the empire on November 17, 1922. Although the deposed sultan claimed that he was leaving İstanbul only temporarily,[8] this was a great opening for the Ankara Circle to initiate a process in which the authority of the imperial government would be completely destroyed. Was the departure of the sultan from İstanbul devised and instigated by Ankara to get rid of the sultanate? This question cannot be answered definitively; however, one should not discount the possibility that Ankara was acting pragmatically and improvising its moves against the sultanate and the İstanbul government. A strong possibility exists that one of the main reasons for the abolition of the sultanate in 1922 was to replace the İstanbul government, for it was clear that the sultan would never recognize Ankara over İstanbul. Therefore, the office of the sultanate needed to be abolished, a decision that garnered overwhelming support in the TGNA.[9]

One can convincingly make the case that Ankara originally intended to get rid of the "office" of sultanate, not necessarily the sultan in person.[10] In other words, the main target for the abolition of the sultanate was the İstanbul government, not Sultan Vahdettin or the Ottoman dynasty. It is telling that Vahdettin was still the caliph until his escape on November 17, 1922. Vahdettin became the main target of many pointed attacks from Ankara as a traitor to the nation after his departure but not necessarily because of it.[11] Ankara accused the last sultan of treason only *after* his escape for his activities that took place prior to his escape. If Vahdettin in person were the main target for Ankara's historic move to abolish the sultanate, he could have been deposed as the caliph also on the date of the abolition of the sultanate. Conversely, if he did not leave the country, the possibility remains that he could have continued to be the caliph, and this could have changed the entire course of Turkish and Islamic history. This nuanced action demonstrates that Ankara did not have a clear plan as to how to deal with the dynasty as yet and was responding to the developments only pragmatically. The escape of the last Ottoman sultan provided Ankara with an opportunity to devastate the sultan's legitimacy and to build its own. As a result, Ankara felt increasingly confident to claim the sole authority to govern.

However, nationalists in Ankara knew that there were still able contenders for power. By 1923, until the republic was proclaimed, Mustafa Kemal alienated some of his close friends and respected figures in the Ankara Circle, such as Rauf Orbay, Ali Fuat Cebesoy, and Kazım Karabekir. In İstanbul, there were still the remnants of the old regime: the İstanbul Press, Ottoman politicians, the newly appointed caliph Abdülmecit Efendi (TGNA voted for his appointment on November 19, 1922) and the members of the Ottoman dynasty, many of whom were antagonistic toward Ankara and any of whom would pose danger to Ankara's bid to govern. These groups were required to be subdued. Mustafa Kemal judged that as long as the Ottoman dynasty resided in Turkey, the opponents of Ankara would be encouraged. Nationalists were keenly aware that the office of the caliphate still carried high esteem among the Muslim population of the empire and beyond.

After the departure of Vahdettin, Ankara hoped to have a "tamed" dynasty headed by Abdülmecit. However, soon it became evident that even this move was too risky for the well-being of the new regime. Unlike the abolition of the sultanate, the abolition of the caliphate targeted the entire Ottoman dynasty and sought their removal from Turkey. Ankara probably did not feel confident enough to make this move in 1922.[12] With a degree of reasonable confidence, one can state that the office of the caliphate was abolished mainly to eliminate the threat of the dynasty, not just the caliph, for Ankara's legitimacy. In other words, the office of the sultanate was abolished to eliminate the imperial government, not the Ottoman dynasty. On the other hand, the main target for the abolition of the caliphate was the Ottoman dynasty, not necessarily the caliphate itself.

A U.S. archival document[13] supports the claim that in fact one of the main reasons for the abolishment of the caliphate was to remove the dynasty, not necessarily to abolish the office of the caliphate as an Islamic institution. In this document, the U.S. source informs Washington that Kemalists were promising to support Seyyid Ahmet Sanussi for his bid for the caliph as long as he promised to support the Ankara government and reside outside Turkey. Seyyid Sanussi's private secretary, Osman Fahreldine (Fahrettin) Bey, reported to the U.S. embassy in İstanbul the following information:

> Shortly before the abolition of the Caliphate and the expulsion of Abdul Medjid last March, Moustapha Kemal Pasha in an interview with Sheik Senoussi offered him Turkey's support in Caliph on the condition that the seat of the Caliphate be outside of Turkey. This offer the sheik refused. He made it plain that he favored the retention of Abdul Medjid as Caliph with spiritual powers at Constantinople; . . . as a result, Ankara cancelled his allowance.[14]

If this is true, it shows that Ankara was more interested in uprooting the Ottoman dynasty than in the abolishing the caliphate.[15] Having a caliph who would be responsive to Turkish demands and—unlike the Ottoman dynasty—could not claim legitimacy to challenge the Ankara government would have been the best-case scenario for Mustafa Kemal.

In any case, the caliphate was abolished on March 3, 1924, and the caliph was hurriedly removed from Turkey the same night. Other members of the dynasty were given a little longer time to leave the country. When the dynasty was exiled, the next group to pose danger to the authority of Ankara became the supporters of the monarchy who were hostile toward the nationalists. The research for this book excludes the abolition of the caliphate but focuses on several other significant events.

GENERAL ARGUMENTS OF THE CHAPTERS

The present research is organized around three specific events between 1923 and 1926, after which Mustafa Kemal emerged as the sole leader whose authority was not challenged. Each chapter examines in detail the political and judicial maneuverings of Mustafa Kemal and his close associates to eliminate the opposition. As already suggested, the silencing of the opposition was not a painstakingly planned and executed political action. In fact, as mentioned before, the Kemalist governments in Ankara were improvising their action in response to the emerging political conditions. This pragmatic approach can be seen as the most valuable asset of the Kemalist regime in the early years of the republic.

Although there were many events to demonstrate the power struggle and the Kemalist success in silencing the opposition, I picked three to represent the others. I can categorize these events as (1) opposition to Ankara, (2) opposition in Ankara, and (3) opposition at large.

The first event that constitutes Chapter 2 deals with opposition to Ankara and focuses on the elimination of the political challenge to the authority of the Ankara government. This chapter examines the exile of the 150 so-called opponents of the Ankara Circle. This event, known as the "the Incident of 150ers" (*Yüzellilikler Olayı*), in Turkish Republican history represents the process in which the Ankara government established its legitimacy by exiling 150 members, many (not all) of whom were loyal to the old regime. This event can be seen as one of the earliest attempts of the Ankara government to insert its authority over the İstanbul Circle. More specifically, Chapter 2 sheds lights on three main questions: who were the 150ers, what did they do, and how were they silenced? This chapter demonstrates that the 150ers were indeed an eclectic group and included members of the monarchists, ulama, military, former high-ranking Ottoman statesmen, journalists, and anti-Ankara rebels. The Ankara Assembly selected them by employing very loose and incoherent standards to deter opposition to the legitimacy of Ankara. Chapter 2 also contains prosopographical information for the 150 people since in the current scholarship not much is recorded about their backgrounds. Therefore, this chapter is greatest in length. The first section of the chapter introduces and analyzes the issue, and the second section provides biographical information for the individuals who were selected on the list. Unfortunately, available information about them is uneven. The reader will find that we have significant biographical information on some. However, there is almost no information available for some other members on the list.

Chapter 3 continues to examine the process of silencing the opposition by analyzing some aspects of the Sheikh Said Revolt of 1925, a Kurdish/Islamist revolt, and the government's response to it. This rebellion became the main justification for the Kemalist government to silence the religious and other oppositional (such as the leftists) establishments in Turkey and hence paved the way for the secularization reforms to come. Equally significant was that this rebellion provided the pretext for the suppression of the opposition in Ankara. To understand the significance of the event, one needs to fully appreciate the political conditions of the period.

Let us first look at the political environment prior to the Sheikh Said Revolt. The regime in Ankara spent most of 1924 in restructuring the new state. After the signing of the Treaty of Lausanne on July 24, 1923, which formally recognized the Ankara government and the borders of the new Turkey, the Turkish government was still not content with the little authority afforded to the caliph and the suspicions of the legitimacy that the Ottoman dynasty still possessed. As discussed above, on March 3, 1924, the caliphate was abolished—a source of discontent for some in Ankara and for many outside Ankara. Kemalists were bracing themselves for the rise of reactionary rebellions by Islamic-minded groups among which the Naqshbandi Kurdish *tariqas* (mystical orders) were visible in the eastern territories of Turkey. Mustafa Kemal and his associates in Ankara were already extremely sensitive toward any sign of opposition and discontent in and out of Ankara. They were fully justified in their sensitivity since their unprecedented move of abolishing the caliphate could have made them the target of many in the Islamic world.

When the Sheikh Said Revolt commenced on February 13, 1925, the political party in power was the Republican People's Party (RPP). This party, which originally included almost all of those who formed the Ankara Circle, split in November 1924. Some of Mustafa Kemal's former close associates (such as Rauf Bey, Kazım Karabekir, Refet, and Ali Fuat Pasha) accused several RPP members of radicalizing the party and Mustafa Kemal of having autocratic tendencies. Suggesting that a fully functional democracy needed a political opposition, these former leaders of the RPP, whose charisma were second only to that of Mustafa Kemal, established the first opposition party in the Turkish republic and called it the Progressive Republican Party (Terakkiperver Cumhuriyet Fırkası [PRP]). One must take note that this party was established only three months before the Sheikh Said Rebellion. Therefore, the timing of this rebellion has lent itself to many speculations about the cause and the nature of as well as the instigations for the rebellion. As discussed in Chapter 3, entry of the PRP into the Turkish political arena made Mustafa Kemal and some members of his party (such as Recep Bey and İsmet Pasha) very agitated. They might have seriously concerned that this political movement would be the commencement of a counterrevolution in which their lives were on the line. Therefore, the RPP's reaction to the Sheikh Said Revolt was understandably but disproportionately harsh.

The rebellion, which contained in itself Kurdish nationalist tendencies but was overtly Islamist in nature, was suppressed in a relatively short period of time by the Turkish army. Sheikh Said and 47 of his associates were executed on June 29, 1925. Although the rebellion had ended, a political witch-hunt had just begun. This chapter examines specifically this process of silencing the political and intellectual opposition in Turkey. It seeks answers to the following questions: What political and judicial maneuverings were employed to eliminate the opposition in the Turkish Grand National Assembly? How were the critics of the Ankara regime, such as the journalists, silenced? What is the likelihood that the Sheikh Said Revolt was fomented by the RPP government to eliminate the opposition? And how was this rebellion manipulated and exaggerated to discredit the opposition and accomplish the radical Kemalist reforms within such a short time as three years?

Chapter 4 is the continuation of the previous chapter in that it examines the completion of the process of silencing the political opposition and the political consequences of an assassination plot against Mustafa Kemal in 1926. This event, known as "the İzmir Conspiracy," resulted in the removal of all members of the PRP from parliament. Furthermore, it went far beyond expectations and purged the potential opposition at large, which was embodied in the remnant of the CUP. There should be little doubt that higher-ranking officers of the former CUP could have challenged the RPP in the upcoming general elections in 1927. As foreign observers in Turkey reported, there was a good chance that a new party, manned by the former CUP leaders, would even attract a large group of former lower-ranking CUP members who were in the RPP. If such unification was realized, this would constitute a counterrevolution that Mustafa Kemal and his inner circle were afraid of. A document, dated October 15, 1923, and penned by Maynard B. Barnes, the American consul and the delegate of the U.S. high commissioner for Turkey, concluded that the RPP is a purely fictitious organization whose popularity depends heavily on that of Mustafa Kemal. "The rank and file of the [RPP] are still Unionists who will revert to their original party as the popularity of Kemal wanes and when strong Unionist leaders openly enter the political arena."[16]

Against this background, the trials for the İzmir Conspiracy in 1926 become more revealing to demonstrate how this threat was dealt with. After the İzmir Conspiracy trials first in İzmir and then in Ankara, there was no visible dissent left in and outside the TGNA. Laws passed with little or no discussion in parliament. Until the next election in 1927, no opposing vote was cast. Deputies showed their discomfort to a particular bill by not showing up for the voting. Newspapers refrained from making any comments that could be interpreted as critical to the government. Even after the 1927 general elections, the lack of a healthy opposition was so visible that even Mustafa Kemal recognized the harm it might have caused to the republican regime. Against this background, the reader can better understand Mustafa Kemal's desire for a tamed political opposition and hence the formation of the Free Party (Serbest Fırka) by the directives of Mustafa Kemal himself.[17] The current study does not interest itself with this political experience in 1930, which lasted only three months. However, this experience illustrates that the formation of an oppositional party stirred so much emotion among a considerable group of people (especially in İzmir and the Aegean region in general) that Mustafa Kemal asked the leader of the Free Party, Fethi Bey, his close associate in the RPP, to shut the party down.[18] The opposition remained mute until after the death of Mustafa Kemal. It was the post–World War II necessities that forced İsmet İnönü, the new president of the country after Mustafa Kemal's death, to allow the formation of new political parties in 1945. Therefore, understanding the political history of modern Turkey requires diligent scholarly examination of the period that has long been considered "sacred" and hence affected the unbiased scholarly production. Although politicians continue to make a growing number of references to the period under examination here, their references lack authority because of the limited number of objective studies available to them. The same problem also exists for the new generation of scholars, especially outside Turkey. The highly politically charged nature of the period caused many students to shy away from this extremely significant subject for Turkish and Middle Eastern studies.

STATE OF THE FIELD AND ARCHIVAL SOURCES

Compared to other subfields in Turkish studies, history of the early republican Turkey can readily be considered in the stage of infancy, particularly in the scholarship outside Turkey. When considering the current state of the field in the early Turkish republic, we need to separate the scholarship into two categories: the scholarship that has been produced inside and outside Turkey. The first category understandably is much greater in volume compared to the second. However, it is dominated by nonprofessional historians whose analysis of issues lacks academic discipline and thoroughness. These books, however, are great sources for academics, for they contain significant leads to recently available primary sources. For the "Incident of 150ers," for example, we have, among others, Kamil Erdeha, *Yüzellilikler Yahut Milli Mücadelenin Muhasebesi*; İlhami Soysal, *150'liler*; and Cemal Kutay, *150'lilikler Faciası*. These books are useful but lack scholarly rigor. In academia, there are a small number of master's theses: Şerife Özkan, "Yüzellilikler and Süleyman Şefik Kemali: A Legitimacy and Security Issue"; Şaduman Halıcı, "Yüzellilikler"; and Sedat Bingöl,

"Yüzellilikler Meselesi."[19] The last two are especially significant, for the authors utilize a number of primary sources that even today are not fully available to researchers. These works are limited in the sense that they report only the activities of the 150ers in exile and do not provide us with much biographical information. In addition, both are master's-level works that require academic maturity and benefit from a degree of objectivity. Although my conclusions differ from these sources, I have made use of them in reference to some archival sources that I did not have access to. There is no published academic work that exists on the subject of the 150ers in English or, to my knowledge, in any other language. For that reason, the current study fills a significant gap for those who cannot use Turkish as their research language or simply cannot access these secondary sources.

There is a considerably large body of scholarship that exists on the subject of Chapter 3 since this is one of the most controversial subjects in Turkish republican history. Therefore, the researcher must be cautious in examining them, expecting that their professional judgments would be colored by their political positions. On the subject of the Sheikh Said Revolt of 1925, there are a number of books in Turkish, including Metin Toker, *Şeyh Sait ve İsyanı*; Uğur Mumcu, *Kürt İslam Ayaklanması 1919–1925*; Behçet Cemal, *Şeyh Sait İsyanı*; and Nurer Uğurlu, *Kürtler ve Şeyh Sait İsyanı*. The available books in Turkish are mainly descriptive in and do make references to the period after Takrir-i Sükun. In English, Robert Olson's *The Emergence of Kurdish Nationalism: 1880–1925* and Martin van Bruinessen's *Agha Shaikh and State* provide useful information on the Sheikh Said Revolt. All secondary sources uniformly conclude—although differing in intensity—that the Sheikh Said Revolt initiated a period of political silence in Turkey. However, all of them neglect to demonstrate and document how exactly this was accomplished. Chapter 4 is unique in that it documents and examines the process of political intimidation.

I must recognize that there are a growing number of able Turkish scholars dealing with certain aspects of the process described above. For example, Ahmet Yeşil's *Türkiye Cumhuriyeti'nde İlk Teşkilatlı Muhalefet Hareketi: Terakkiperver Cumhuriyet Fırkası* is a great contribution to the field and updates Erik Jan Zürcher's *Political Opposition in the Early Turkish Republic: The Progressive Republican Party 1925–1925*, a classic on the first opposition party and its fate. I have greatly benefited from these sources when I examined the dissolution of the first organized political opposition in Turkey, the PRP. Although all of us may share similar conclusions, the present study brings in many other primary sources to make stronger arguments. Furthermore, this chapter examines the demise of the oppositional press and intellectuals. Although a growing number of memoirs have become available in recent years, no scholarly work has been done on the effect of the Takrir-i Sükun on the oppositional press and how they were muzzled.

Chapter 4 deals with a significant issue of purging the former CUP members. Erik Jan Zürcher has ably examined this subject in his *The Unionist Factor: The Role of the Committee of Union and Progress in the Turkish National Movement, 1905–1926*. However, since its publication in 1984, many other primary sources have become available. This chapter aims at updating Erik Jan Zürcher's work with available primary sources. Accordingly, our conclusions are similar with the exception that I emphasize the pragmatic nature of purging the opposition more than Zürcher does.

Throughout the book, in addition to Turkish and British archival sources, I make heavy use of U.S. consular reports. The main reason for this is to introduce these sources, which have not been fully examined by students of Turkish republican history. Lest I be accused of relying heavily on these sources in my conclusions, I must state that my conclusions are based on more than one collection of primary sources. The U.S. sources are displayed prominently in the text with my hope to demonstrate that these sources are in fact rich and detailed and can shed some light on early Turkish republican history. They provide us with some information that cannot be found in Turkish archives, the reliability of which, like any other sources, cannot always be vouched for.

Finally, let me make several comments on the accessibility of Turkish archives, which is still limited. For this study, I have consulted the Prime Minister's Republican Archives and the Institute of Turkish Republican History archives in Ankara. The Directorate of General Security Archives (DGSA) on the 150ers was transferred to the Prime Minister's Republican Archives. I was informed by the DGSA that this collection was in transit. However, the Republican Archives informed me that the collection was not cataloged and hence not open for researchers as of 2010. I had photocopies of several DGSA documents on this subject, and for the remainder, I relied on the previously mentioned works. The researcher must be warned that these documents, once recataloged at the Prime Minister's Republican Archives, might very likely have different reference numbers. Parliamentary minutes are in print and available to researchers in the TGNA library and other venues. I did not attempt to work on the ATASE archives of the

General Staff for the expected problems in accessing information and possibly very little return. I utilized published material from the Presidential Archives (Çankaya Arşivi) and the TGNA archives; on occasion, I collected information from secondary sources that included copies and reprints of some significant documents regarding the PRP.

After the implementation of a better cataloging system and easier access to some of these archives, future researchers may stretch our understanding of the period greatly. Other consulted primary sources are listed accordingly in the bibliography.

2

Opposition to Ankara: The Case of the 150ers

INTERNAL POWER STRUGGLE AND THE 150ERS: THE NARRATIVE

After the loss in World War I and the successful War of Independence, concluded in 1922, a power struggle emerged in the land that was to become the Republic of Turkey. There were several sides that were vying for power. For the purpose of this study, I will categorize them roughly as the İstanbul Circle and the Ankara Circle.[1] These circles were by no means monolithic and did contain very diverse ideological elements. However, their loyalty to their respected circles originated from their vision for the future of the state and, more important, their own positions in it.

Who constituted the İstanbul Circle? The short answer would be any Ottoman citizen who did not support the Ankara movement. Expectedly, the İstanbul Circle gathered around the sultan, Vahdettin, and the imperial government. This group consisted mostly of members of the Ottoman dynasty—including the *damats* or sons in-law; many ulama in the religious establishment; former high-level Ottoman bureaucrats and administrators who were hostile to their nemesis, the Committee of Union and Progress (CUP); and, finally, the pro-İstanbul Press. Many bureaucrats in the İstanbul Circle belonged to the Hürriyet ve İtilaf Fırkası, or the Liberal Entente (LE), a political opponent of the CUP.

The Ottoman caliph was theoretically the leader of the Sunni/Islamic world. Naturally, this traditional authority was a source of concern for the Allied Powers that occupied İstanbul, the seat of the sultanate and the caliphate, in 1919. But particularly for Britain, an empire that governed a large segment of the Islamic population in India, the office of the caliphate was always regarded as a potential threat for its authority over its own Muslim subjects. However, the same potential to agitate Muslims also formed a major challenge for the Ankara Circle, as its appetite to rule grew larger by the day. After the abolition of the sultanate in 1922, the caliph still remained the symbol for political power for many Muslims, a fact that concerned some secular-minded nationalists.

Next to the caliph, prodynasty ulama immensely distressed Ankara. As the students of the Ottoman Empire attest, the ulama were mostly integrated into the Ottoman system, and their interests were skillfully tied to the Ottoman dynasty. The fact that the ulama had the potential to mobilize masses, especially in the rural areas, also troubled the Ankara Circle. The ulama's support for the sultan/caliph would surely affect Ankara's bid for power, for religious functionaries were numerous, organized, and, in many instances, invincible. The people in the Ankara government were keenly aware of the danger that the ulama could pose if threatened. The problem was that since the ulama's incorporation into the Ankara administration would defeat its stand as secularists, it was inevitable that a clash would materialize with them.[2]

Another section of the İstanbul Circle included the members of the former Ottoman governments and high-level bureaucrats. Although this group was the counterpart to the Ankara administration, they were the least influential, as their power was eclipsed by their inability to govern and the loss of legitimacy after World War I. They were in an unwieldy position caught in between Ankara and the foreign occupiers in İstanbul. As they felt the need to accommodate humiliating demands by the Allied Powers, judging that good relations with them would bring the least harm to the empire, they jeopardized their own standing among the public. They were readily discredited by the government in Ankara as collaborationists. After World War I, with the fall of the CUP government, this group was united mostly under the LE.

The pro-İstanbul Press played a significant role also in the public relations aspect of the Ottoman Empire in the post–World War I era and, to some extent, in the early years of the Turkish republic. After the inauguration of the Turkish Grand National Assembly (TGNA) on April 23, 1920, the pro-İstanbul Press became even more suspicious of the political ambitions of the nationalists. As fresh newspapers emerged to carry out the message disseminated by Ankara, newspapers, especially in

İstanbul, felt threatened.[3] The reader should be warned that this group also contained many competing ideologies. For example, the anti-Ankara newspapers included the Islamist Press (such as Eşref Edip's *Sebilürreşat*) and modernists (such as Ahmet Emin Yalman's *Vatan* and Hüseyin Cahit Yalçın's *Tanin*) who admired the Western way of life.[4]

What united the diverse İstanbul Circle was their rage against the CUP and its sympathizers.[5] It is well documented that the İstanbul Circle originally judged Ankara as the reincarnation of the CUP.[6] This judgment or misjudgment colored their attitude toward the Ankara government. For example, Rıza Tevfik, a well-known member of the İstanbul Circle, states that the members of the Ottoman cabinet fiercely objected to his motion that Mustafa Kemal be appointed to the cabinet as the minister of war. He remembered the intense objection in the cabinet meeting: "the other cabinet members told me that Mustafa Kemal was a main figure in the CUP."[7] This hostility was personal at many levels. The LE members wished to avenge their sufferings and previous exiles. It is only natural that this rivalry spilled into the republican period. As many rank-and-file members of the former CUP became integrated into the new regime, they wished to single out the LE members as their opponents. This feud must have colored the selection process of the 150ers since many of the LE members were also part of this group.

Let us look at the Ankara Circle and their opposition in relation to İstanbul. First, it must be stated that although the Ankara leadership was not as diverse as the İstanbul one—at least politically they were by no means homogeneous either. The idealist members of the military were the backbone of this group. However, it also included minor religious functionaries, local notables, and, as mentioned, some lower-level CUP members. Many in this group in fact fought in the War of Independence to preserve the empire. Their support for the inauguration of the first Grand National Assembly in 1920 was not to challenge İstanbul's authority but rather to maintain an assembly away from the Allied pressure. By the end of 1922, however, the Ankara Circle was fully convinced that the old regime in İstanbul formed a great obstacle for its political authority and diplomatic success in the upcoming international peace conference. İstanbul's elimination from power became the next significant challenge for the Ankara Circle after the successful conclusion of the War of Independence in 1922.

This chapter discusses a significant but poorly studied aspect of early republican history, the *yüzellilikler* or, hereafter, the 150ers. These are 150 exiled persons, mostly from the İstanbul Circle. The 150ers included many well-known members of the İstanbul Circle who were clearly hostile to the Ankara government during the War of Independence. Some members were suspicious over the nature and intentions of the nationalist movement and were vocal about it. However, other than their political positions against the Ankara Circle, this was an eclectic group. Following is a discussion of the emergence of the idea of the 150ers, their selection, and their silencing.

The Idea of the 150ers

The general narrative about how the idea of the 150ers emerged is based on one source that is no longer available. All references directly or indirectly refer to the unpublished memoirs of Topçu İhsan (Eryavuz) Bey, the president of the Ankara Independence Tribunal. Currently, we have only a book written by a Turkish historian, Cemal Kutay, who reportedly read these memoirs and quoted them extensively in his *150'likler Faciası*.[8] In his book, Kutay informs us that the subject emerged on February 3, 1921, in İhsan (Eryavuz) Bey's house in Keçiören, Ankara. While discussing the İstanbul government's hostility toward the nationalist movement in Anatolia,[9] İhsan Bey warned Mustafa Kemal, stating that "we do not leave any document to history. As long as you continue to tolerate the people [who oppose us], history cannot judge them appropriately as traitors. . . .We need to record their misdeeds."[10] This suggestion was seconded by Dr. Adnan (Adıvar) Bey, interior minister. However, Adnan Bey pointed out the urgency of an archive only with concrete documents. In other words, Adnan Bey was favoring such a list only if it was supported by conclusive evidence.[11] He must have been suspicious that such a list could have been used to settle personal rivalries.

This conversation, however, did not progress into action until the fall of 1922. One day in September or October 1922, Mustafa Kemal raised the issue in a meeting attended by İhsan Bey, İsmet Pasha, Fevzi Pasha, Kazım (Özalp) Pasha, Ali Fethi Bey, Yusuf Kemal Bey, and Seyyid Bey. In the meeting, Mustafa Kemal turned to İhsan Bey and reminded him,

> If you remember, one day in a private meeting we talked about making a list of people whose presence in Turkey would cause trouble and disturb the well-being of the state. As far as I remember, you suggested that these names needed to be determined. Now, Yusuf Kemal Bey reminds us that every International Peace

> agreement would require an amnesty and warns us to be prepared for such a possibility. What preparations would you suggest we make?[12]

İsmet Pasha joined in the conversation, indicating,

> Some of these people of concern were overseas. There are some of them that still live in the country. However, for internal security, their residence in Turkey must not be allowed. If these people were caught by the Independence Tribunals, they would have been executed due to the crimes they committed against the state. In fact, some of these people were already tried in absentia. If there is a possibility of a General Amnesty, it is necessary that we determine the names of those who should not benefit from such an amnesty. But how do we determine these names?[13]

Discussions on the subject continued as more concrete questions arose, such as the following: What would be the effective time frame in which treason was committed? Would those who were responsible for the loss of the Balkan Wars and those who dragged the empire into World War I be included? What about those who signed the Treaty of Sevres or the Mudros Armistice; should they be included?[14] No definite decisions arose from the meeting at the time, except that a list was to be prepared. Meanwhile, rumors circulated that the Ministry of the Interior, the Office of the Prime Minister, and the Office of the Joint Chief of Staff were working on preparing lists.[15] It is interesting to note that when İhsan Bey noticed some of the names on these lists, he supposedly said, "Emotions seem to play a decisive role [in determining the names]."[16] This statement hints at possible biases in the process of naming. We know that on this subject, while conversing with Kazım (Özalp) Pasha, the minister of defense, İhsan Bey pointed out this subjectivity by stating, "How strange that . . . some people who deserve to be on the list are not on it."[17] This was exactly what Rauf and Adnan Bey feared earlier: the subjectivity of preparing such a list. In any case, until the Treaty of Lausanne, the issue remained on the back burner.

The Treaty of Lausanne and the 150ers

After the War of Independence that ended in 1922, Turkey and the Allied Powers turned their attention to the signing of a peace treaty that effectively would end the war. All sides were already weary of this massive war that not only cost those involved millions of lives but also drained their treasury. However, all sides were aware that the signing of the treaty was perhaps the trickiest stage of the war. World War I was far from being the war to end all wars. True, the peace treaty was significant to settle the military and political issues. However, this was also the greatest opportunity to gain more from one another, something that they failed to do on the battlefield. The new government was already proclaimed in Ankara, arguing to represent Turkey. The İstanbul government was already crippled and was in no position to effectively negotiate a peace treaty. It was not only Great Britain that was aware of the weakness created by the dual government. The Ankara government was also conscious of this weakness; and therefore it decided to exclude the İstanbul representatives from participating in the Lausanne Conference.

The reader should be informed that the beginning of the negotiations in Lausanne was a time of chaos for the İstanbul Circle, as it came only 19 days after the abolition of the sultanate (November 1, 1922) by the Ankara government's decree (*kararname*)[18] number 308 and only three days after the last Ottoman sultan's escape from İstanbul on a British battleship. Clearly, Ankara had the upper hand. Although Great Britain hoped to exploit the differences between the Ankara and İstanbul governments, they failed to do so, as the sultan had left the country and the İstanbul administration was declared null by Ankara.[19] The İstanbul government was plainly not in a position to make any demands from the conference, nor did it have the ability to manage Ankara. In fact, there was no government in İstanbul; the last one resigned on November 4, 1922, only 16 days before the Lausanne negotiations, and there was no replacement government.

When the Ankara delegates, under the leadership of İsmet Pasha, went to Lausanne, their legitimacy was not in question, as they represented the armed forces that defeated its enemies.[20] However, it would be a grave mistake to suggest that Ankara was fully confident in its ability to bring the remnant of the İstanbul government under its control. On the contrary, Mustafa Kemal was apprehensive about the opposition even in the TGNA (the Second Group).[21] While the negotiations were continuing, the Ankara government was looking for ways to isolate, if not eliminate, the rival power brokers of the İstanbul Circle. True, the sultanate was abolished, and the newly appointed caliph, Abdülmecit, and the dynasty were under close surveillance. However, as mentioned above, there were many other potential rivals that could harm Ankara's authority.

On November 20, 1922, the negotiations opened in Lausanne and subsequently were interrupted on February 4, 1923, because of disagreements on several significant issues (such as the future of Mosul, the question of the straits, the capitulations, the Ottoman Public Debt Administration, and the minorities).[22] On April 23, 1923, the conference resumed the negotiations. A significant change was the replacement of Lord George Nathaniel Curzon with Sir Horace Rumbold on the British side. In a sense, this was a victory for the Turkish side since Lord Curzon was not accommodating Turkish demands. Rumbold seemed to be more aware of the urgency of signing the treaty. In any case, the Treaty of Lausanne was signed on July 24, 1923, as all sides were weary of the exhausting negotiations. Only the decision on the Mosul boundary was postponed to a later date in 1926.[23]

Let us now look at the emergence of the 150ers at Lausanne. Among other more visible and substantial issues, a protocol, added to the General Amnesty clause, looked inconsequential to the Allied Powers. However, this protocol, which excluded 150 Muslims (the 150ers) from the General Amnesty, was in fact consequential for the legitimacy and internal power struggle between the İstanbul Circle and the Ankara Circle. It was a way that the Ankara government would proclaim its authority over the İstanbul Circle. Therefore, the Turkish representatives in Lausanne were insistent on such a protocol being added to the treaty.

It is customary that after every major war, the warring parties agree to issue a comprehensive amnesty to promote internal reconciliation. This principle was best explained by Cemil Birsel:

> If the deeds which are carried out during the war are prosecuted and punished after the peace, then the wounds of the wars would never heal but bleed continuously. The pain and suffering that should be forgotten once and for all between the warring countries would linger much longer; this may result in the renewal of war. . . . In order to erase the past sufferings, all past activities of individuals must be forgiven.[24]

In this context, the issue of the General Amnesty was discussed in one of the subcommittees in Lausanne. The proposed amnesty excluded ordinary crimes but targeted specifically political and military ones.[25] The related article in the proposed treaty stipulated that a general amnesty would be issued and would include persons in Turkey and Greece who were involved in political and military activities by cooperating with the enemy. The proposed period for this amnesty was between August 1, 1914, and November 20, 1922, that is, between the beginning of World War I and the opening of the Lausanne Conference.

It should be noted that there were disagreements in the subcommittee meetings regarding the scope of the General Amnesty. The Greek side wanted as comprehensive an amnesty as possible, yet the Turkish side asked to limit it only to non-Muslims.[26] A limited amnesty obviously would give more room to the Turkish side to get rid of collaborators and potential political rivals. Therefore, the Turkish delegation sought as narrow a General Amnesty as possible.

As for the Allied Powers, the tactic was simple. By using the general amnesty, they wished to weaken the authority and hence soften the demands of the Turkish side. One way to accomplish this was through special requests for the minorities. It was in the interest of the Allies to keep the definition of "minorities" as broad as possible; therefore, the definition of "minority" became a subject of a major controversy. While British and Greek delegates in the "Minorities Subcommittee" submitted that the minorities should include the ethnic ones (such as the Kurds), Dr. Rıza Nur, the Turkish delegate, fiercely objected to this proposal and stated that minorities in the Ottoman context and also in the republican one had always meant religious, not ethnic, minorities.[27] Therefore, a general amnesty should not include ethnic minorities. In other words, what Rıza Nur was proposing was that the Muslim population who collaborated with the enemy during the war should not be immune from prosecution. Rıza Nur clearly stated that "all Muslims should be excluded from the General Amnesty. The Turkish government cannot accept the betrayal of those Muslims to their own people."[28] To this, Sir Horace Rumbold, the British representative, objected, stating that as the representative of one of the largest Islamic states (referring to the Muslims living under the British India), he could not accept this exclusion."[29] We know, however, that this objection was not sincere. For example, in reference to Turkey's opposition to include Muslims of different ethnic origin under the term "minority," Forbes Adam, a member of the British delegation, reflected,

> The Turks maintain that all the Moslems of Turkey should be regarded for the purpose of minority protection as Turks, and the actual minorities to be protected should only be religious minorities. This attitude is, of course, quite illogical, as the basis of the other European minority treaties is the application to all

> minorities of race, language and religion. The Turkish attitude would lump in together Arabs, Kurds, Circassians and Turks.
>
> In practice, however, and except for the possible indirect effect which Allied acceptance of Turkish claim might have on our arguments as regards the Kurds in the Mosul Vilayet, the Allied delegations *did not consider it important to insist upon a refusal of the Turkish claim.*[30] (emphasis added)

As this document indicates, the British side was interested in the well-being of the Muslim population in Turkey only as it related to the British interests, especially in the Mosul province. In the end, the Turkish side consented to a general amnesty, including the Muslim subjects of the empire, worded as follows:

> Nobody residing in Turkey and mutually nobody residing in Greece will be disturbed and/or offended either in Turkey and Greece for his military or political behavior between the dates 1 August 1914–20 November 1922 and because of his assistance to a foreign country or citizens of such country that signs the Peace Treaty dated today by any kind of excuse either in Turkey or in Greece. In accordance with this Peace Treaty, nobody residing in lands that are separated from Turkey will be disquieted or offended, because of his political or military behavior against Turkey or for Turkey within the period of time between dates 1 August 1914–20 November 1922 or because their nationalities will be determined in compliance with this treaty. In respect to all of crimes which were committed within the same period of time and with the clear connections with the political events which took place within this period, the Turkish government and the Greek government will announce a complete and unconditional amnesty mutually.[31]

Noticeably, Muslim ethnic minorities were not mentioned as separate groups in the article. In fact, throughout the document, they were referred to as the "Muslim population." The Allied negotiators were successful in including the Muslim population in the general amnesty.

However, in return, the Turks managed to include a protocol into this agreement that gave them the right to name 150 people of Muslim origin for the exclusion from the general amnesty:

> It has been decided that, while the first paragraph relating to the notice concerning the General Amnesty remained in force, the Turkish government reserves the right to prohibit 150 persons

> included in the category of persons stipulated in this article be able to enter to Turkey and to reside there. As a result, the Turkish government can expel the persons among the mentioned persons that lived in the country and can prohibit those living in foreign countries from returning to Turkey.[32]

We know that the Turkish side during this time was working on a list of people whose entry into Turkey was considered harmful to the interests of the new regime. For that reason, the Turkish delegates pushed for this additional protocol to prohibit 150 names from entering the country. The protocol, signed on July 24, 1923, was significant not only for the banning of the entry of those who opposed the new regime but also for the authority granted to it by an international body to expel those living currently in Turkey. Since the protocol excluded only the non-Muslim population of Turkey, the Ankara government was free to include on this list any Muslim it wished and to exile them from their own country. Another significant but often omitted feature of this additional protocol was that it was not reciprocal. None of the other countries did request such exclusion. On the session dated January 11, 1923, Rıza Nur informed the British delegates about the number 150, stating that "Turkish government does not act against these people with the feeling of revenge. However, it is in the high interest of the Turkish government that those Muslims who left the country not be allowed to return."[33]

No doubt, the Ankara regime intended to use the protocol against its internal rivals for power, mainly the İstanbul Circle.[34] At this point, we can justifiably ask about the significance of this number. Surely, the supporters of the İstanbul government numbered more than 150. Where did this number come from? Rıza Nur, a Turkish delegate in Lausanne, sheds some light on this issue. In his memoir, he suggests that this number is arbitrarily determined:

> Finally one day we received the news from Ankara. They authorized us about the General Amnesty. However, exclusions must be made. We did not know the exact number of these exclusions. Most of them have already left the country. Even if you begged them, they would not come back. We did not know exactly how many they were. . . . We were asked to request a protocol to the General Amnesty to exclude a certain number of people whose names are to be [later] determined by us. . . . But Ankara determined this number as 150.[35]

It is interesting to note that, on another occasion, Rıza Nur remembers the determination of the number 150 differently:

> I had personal meetings with the British about a protocol of excluding 150 Muslims, who committed treason, . . . from the General Amnesty. The British used these men and did not protect them. I determined the number [of 150], but not the names.[36]

This contradiction was perhaps a lapse of memory. No corroborating evidence exists for this claim. In fact, İsmet Pasha, the head delegate of the Turkish side, states that this number was determined in Ankara even before they went to Lausanne. "While coming to the second portion of the Conference, "we were prepared on this subject in Ankara. In our proposal, we asked for and received the protocol excluding 150 people."[37]

The Allied Position Toward the List

It must be stated that Britain was suspicious of the Turkish side's intentions to punish those who cooperated, especially with Britain and Greece. For example, on the subject of the 150ers at the Lausanne Conference, several telegrams were exchanged by İsmet Pasha and the Office of the Prime Minister (Heyet-i Vekile Riyaseti) in Ankara. For example, an interesting telegram indicates the British interest in the list of 150ers. Sent by Prime Minister Rauf (Orbay) to İsmet Pasha on January 8, 1923, the telegram requests information regarding the news, which appeared in the British press, suggesting that Ethem the Circassian (one of the supporters but later an opponent of Ankara) and some other Circassian people living around Adapazarı, should benefit from the general amnesty.[38] Coincidentally, in a session one day later, Lord Curzon asked İsmet Pasha the reason for Turkey's insistence on excluding the Muslim population from the amnesty. Curzon stated that Circassians around northwestern Anatolia (including Adapazarı and Bursa) interacted closely with the Allied forces. Would the revenge against these Circassians be the primary reason for the Turkish position?[39] This question was rather insightful since we know that later, two-thirds of the 150ers were selected from those of Circassian origin. Sedat Bingöl points out that Curzon's question only "indicates [the pro-Allied] attitude of the Circassians in the region."[40] However, it also indicates that the British were aware that Ankara would act against these Circassians, who could further create problems for the new government with their militia. We do not know whether the

British representatives were concerned about the potential or the intention that the protocol could be used against any member of the İstanbul Circle. We do know that the Allied Powers did not attempt to protect the members of the former İstanbul cabinets.

Another telegram dated May 19, 1923, informs us that the Allied Powers already consented to the protocol to exclude 150 Muslims from the general amnesty.[41] The Italian delegate Giulio Cesare Montagna and the French delegate Maurice Pelle registered two requests for those yet-unnamed 150 people: (1) give them a 12-month period to sell their belongings in Turkey and (2) issue the list of names as soon as the general amnesty was declared.[42]

We know that the Turkish side was confident in receiving the concessions regarding the issue of the 150ers as early as January 1923. İsmet Pasha, in a telegram dated January 12, 1923, requested from his government that it should start naming the 150ers.[43] It is worth repeating that the protocol on the 150ers was a flexible one for the Allied negotiators, as it did not directly threaten their position. Even before the conference broke down in February 1923, the Allies seemed to make concessions on the issue. Expectedly, as indicated above, the protocol was signed and added to the treaty. This was the extent of the foreign involvement in the 150ers. They managed to include all non-Muslim and most of the Muslim population in the amnesty, and that was enough. As for the Turkish side, another protocol that was signed on January 30, 1923, stipulated a massive population exchange of non-Muslim (mainly Greek Orthodox) minorities.[44] In this way, Turkey was able to expel 1 million to 2 million Greek Orthodox citizens who lived in Anatolia and received approximately half a million Muslim Turks from abroad. Retrospectively, one can see the success of the Turkish negotiators in expelling "unwanted" groups from Turkey.

In any case, as for the unwanted Muslim population, the issue before Turkey now was to determine these names; this was not an easy task. To examine this issue, we can now look at discussions in the TGNA regarding the preparation of the list.

Discussions in the TGNA

On December 26, 1923, the TGNA passed an amnesty law (number 391). This was done for the occasion of the declaration of the republic. It was a partial amnesty for nonpolitical crimes and stipulated that previously given sentences be reduced to half (article 1) and that death sentences be converted to 15 years in prison (article 2). However, article 4 made it very clear that this amnesty did not include the 150 people.[45]

This amnesty was not the agreed-on general amnesty stipulated by the Treaty of Lausanne. That had to wait until April 16, 1924. To fulfill its promise regarding a general amnesty in the Treaty of Lausanne, the TGNA passed another law (number 487). When the Turkish declaration of intent (*beyanname*) at the Lausanne Conference and the actual general amnesty (law number 487) are compared, one can see that the former is more detailed than the latter. The main reason that the two documents were not identical—one can only speculate—may be that the vagueness of definitions would suit the Turkish side better. The most eye-catching difference between the two was that while the manifesto specifically named Greece several times as the opposite side to reciprocate, the actual law defined it as any foreign country that had a signature on the Treaty of Lausanne. This obviously gave Turkey more leverage against Great Britain and France, in addition to Greece, since there may have existed collaborators with the Kemalists in countries such as Iraq and Syria. We do not know who in fact the supporters of the Kemalists were or how many of these people on the Allied side benefited from such an amnesty. However, since the war was fought mostly in Turkish territories, one can assume that the amnesty benefited many more individuals supporting the Allies in Turkey than the reverse. In any case, it should also be mentioned that article 3 of the law excluded 150 people from the amnesty.[46] In this way, Turkey emerged as a country fulfilling international responsibilities.

After the law was signed, the TGNA began discussing the names of the 150ers on April 16 and again on April 22–23, 1924, in closed sessions over 15 months, after İsmet Pasha's original request in his previously mentioned telegram to determine the list of 150ers. It was also almost three years after the original idea emerged in Topçu İhsan Bey's house.[47] One reason for this delay was that the Turkish government was waiting for the ratification of the Treaty of Lausanne by Great Britain, Japan, and Italy.

Who was to be included on this list? This was the provocative question in everyone's mind. We know that the Ministry of Interior and the Directorate of Security prepared a list of 600 names. These names were later reduced to 300.[48] The task remained that 300 names had to be cut in half. This was not an easy undertaking, for everyone in parliament had a list in mind. However, there was also a list that was finalized by the government. It was the subject of session 39 on April 16, 1924, to confirm the names of the proposed 150 people. Parliamentary minutes of these sessions give us a clear picture concerning the mindset of the members of parliament.[49]

On April 16, 1924, the president of the chamber opened the session and gave the floor to (Ahmet) Ferit (Tek) Bey, the minister of interior, to introduce the list. Ferit Bey stated that the protocol, added to the Treaty of Lausanne, allowed them to exclude 150 names from the general amnesty. Acknowledging the difficulty of selecting 150 names out of many others who deserved to be on the list, Ferit Bey continued that at first glance 600 names were readily identifiable. Therefore, the first list included these 600 people. However, because of the looming requirement to reduce these names further, the Directorate of General Security arbitrarily[50] cut the list to 300.

The interior minister, Ferit Bey, then asked the question of how to reduce these names to 150 and introduced the government's reasoning. Ferit Bey stated that the members of the Ottoman dynasty were already taken off the list since they were dealt with by another law that was passed earlier (March 3, 1924). This well-known law, number 431, was about the abolition of the caliphate and the exile of the Ottoman dynasty. This law cleared much needed space in the list of the 150ers. Only several of Sultan Vahdettin's close associates needed to be included on the list.

The other group, according to Ferit Bey, that the government took out included some members of the 300 list—those who were already serving in the Greek military. The government signed a decree (*kararname*) to strip them of their citizenship with the accusation of violating the *Tabiyet Kanunu* (Nationality Law).[51] This law stipulated that any Ottoman citizen who served in the military of a foreign country may be stripped of his citizenship by the government. Since there were many individuals who served the interest of the occupying forces, these names could be taken off the list. This action also helped reduce the number of names. It must be mentioned that some people who were accused of collaborating with the occupying forces were still included in the 150ers. The government seemed to be tying a double knot to make sure that these people (such as Ethem the Circassian) were forced out of the country.

Nevertheless, all these measures were not sufficient to allow the government to come up with objective criteria to determine the list of 150 people. At this point, Topçu İhsan Bey, who was credited with coming up with the original idea of a list, stated the following:

> Dear Friends, the number of those who committed the act of treason is surely greater than 500, 600 and 1000. They are more

numerous than these numbers. Since we cannot exceed the number 150, based on our commitment at Lausanne, . . . we should focus on those who potentially can harm us in the future.[52]

In other words, İhsan Bey was suggesting that if all else was equal, the TGNA should not fall in the trap of avenging the past but rather should choose those people who would potentially challenge and undermine the new regime. This was in fact the very reason that the idea of the 150ers emerged. Eliminating the supporters of the ancien régime and hence the possible opposition to the emerging one was of utmost importance. If the number 150 was not enough to include all the opposition, it was certainly a start.

The discussion in parliament continued with members requesting names to be included on the list. Requesting to speak, the representative from Aydın, Mazhar Bey, first acknowledged that there were many other names that deserved to be on the list, yet it was impossible to include all of them. Therefore, "it is not beneficial to drag the discussions on this list." He suggested, "Let us endorse the list that was prepared by the cabinet as a whole."[53] On the contrary, heated discussions followed. The minutes of the closed session reveal that in the session on April 16, 1924, 36 members of parliament participated in the discussions without any result. The closed session ended at 5:15 P.M. with the understanding that the list was to be reexamined by the government in light of proposed new names and be brought before parliament once more.[54]

One of the reasons for the abrupt ending of the session was the argument between Ferit Bey, the interior minister, and Süreyya Bey of Karesi. It was clear that until this session, the members of parliament did not have sufficient information about whether non-Muslims would be included on the list. Şükrü Bey of İzmir asked directly, "Please say clearly, does [the treaty] state that [we cannot] expel the Greeks, the Armenians, or the Jews?" Süreyya Bey interjected, "Clear answer, yes or no." To this, Ferit Bey responded, "The Director of the General Security went [and asked this question] to the legal counselors (*hukuk müşaviri*) who were present at the meetings. They stated that 'yes, we made written and oral commitments [not to include non-Muslims].' "[55] Süreyya Bey, asserting that the interior minister was making contradictory statements, pressed on:

> I am convinced that [Ferit Bey] is lying[56] . . . The Minister, when he failed to show this in the Treaty of Lausanne, said that there were secret protocols. He failed to give a direct answer to Şükrü

> Bey's question. He mentioned Venizelos' position [to exclude the Greeks from the list], yet failed to clarify İsmet Pasha's response. . . . [Therefore] I call the Interior Minister a liar![57]

Upset with the accusation, Ferit Bey reacted, "You need to learn manners." "No, you need to learn manners," shot back Süreyya Bey, "everybody in the country knows who you are."[58] After this exchange, the president of the assembly called for a motion to end the session.

It is interesting to see that members of parliament were uninformed about the stipulations of the Treaty of Lausanne even when they were discussing the list of the 150ers. It is possible that the government wanted to get approval of the list from parliament without much debate and released the specifics only on an "as-needed" basis. However, as the members showed great interest in the names to be included on the list and wanted to insert names they came up with, some specifics of the subcommittee meetings, such as the positions of non-Muslims in the meetings, became available to them.

Another significant point that can be made here is related to the last comment made by Süreyya Bey that "everybody in the country knows who you are." If one examines the names of the ministers who signed the decree (*kararname* number 544) on the list of 150 people on June 1, 1924,[59] one realizes that the signature of the interior minister belonged to Recep (Peker) Bey. Ferit Bey, who represented the government in the discussions as the interior minister, had already resigned on May 21, 1924. The sole reason for his resignation was a telegram in 1919 that Ferit Bey sent to Refet (Bele) Bey (later Refet Pasha), who was an associate of Mustafa Kemal. As it was known, Ahmet Ferit Bey was the minister of public works in the Damat Ferit Pasha cabinet prior to the collapse of the İstanbul government in 1922. In this specific telegram, Ferit Bey was criticizing Mustafa Kemal for not favorably responding to İstanbul's recall of him from Anatolia:

> He [Mustafa Kemal] does not return. He is making a mistake. The British are insisting on his return to İstanbul. If he wants to serve the country, thank God, he is not the only commander in the military. Since his return has become a matter of international importance, he should have returned leaving someone else back as his representative.[60]

This telegram, which was sent in 1919, was published in newspapers on April 28, 1924.[61] When asked, Refet (Bele) confirmed the telegram by stating that "at that time, Ferit Bey was trying to prevent the British occupation of İzmir (Smyrna) and he was against the national struggle [hence Mustafa Kemal]."[62] This was the final blow to Ferit Bey's standing as a member of the cabinet. As mentioned above, he resigned from the post on May 21, 1924, 10 days before the decree was signed. After this, Ferit Bey left parliament to join the Foreign Ministry as an ambassador and spent considerable time overseas.[63]

This story is significant in that the very minister who was in charge of preparing a list of the 150 people who were against Mustafa Kemal was in fact at one time against him. This example plainly demonstrates the arbitrariness of the list. Evidently, he did not fall into the category of those who would continue to or would pose a threat to the new regime. Yet some writers have argued that many members of the 150ers were also far from being a threat to Ankara.[64]

Continuing with the examination of the significant discussions in the parliamentary session dealing with the 150ers, we can point out that Recep (Peker) Bey submitted a motion to the TGNA, the exact text of which is missing.[65] We know about it because of Recep Bey's introduction to it in the TGNA:

> The government should make a "Black List" in addition to the list of the 150ers. All the other names [that are not part of the 150ers] should be included on this list. We do not need to publish it in the newspapers.... This "Black List" should be distributed to all security forces of the state, especially in the seaports, [and] to the busiest sections of İstanbul ... and it should contain their pictures. The security forces should know that when the nation was in danger some of its citizens wished to harm her. These people were not included in the 150ers because of the limited space on this list. When conducting surveillance of those who continue to live in the country, there is no need to harass them. They will have to avoid [harming us] and isolate themselves to a corner knowing that the security forces of the nation is watching them as a member of the "Black List." Those who are overseas will know that there is no breading room for them [in Turkey].[66]

As seen, Recep Bey wanted an additional list that would name other people who were considered harmful for the future of the new regime and intimidate them. This list would identify many oppositional figures without forcing them into exile and put them on notice. When the president of the Turkish parliament, Fethi (Okyar) Bey, opened the floor for voting, this motion was probably recognized as a form of overt intimidation and out of line since we know that the TGNA voted it down. No doubt, such an additional list would have led to a further "witch-hunt."[67]

Süreyya Bey raised another significant question concerning the time frame of the amnesty. The Treaty of Lausanne stipulates that Turkey must declare a general amnesty for those who betrayed the country (read the Ankara government) between August 1, 1914, and November 20, 1922. "However, are we required to forgive those who continued to commit the High Treason even after 1922? There are Circassian bandits in the [Greek] islands that today continue to work against Turkishness. . . . We do not need to include them on the list. They were the traitors of yesterday and they continue to be the same today."[68] This is an interesting take on the issue, for it would allow prosecuting many more people who opposed the Ankara government during the dates indicated in the treaty. This line of reasoning would have readily cleared the way for the prosecution of those who did not candidly shift their political positions in favor of Ankara. On this subject, Ferit Bey showed apprehension on legal grounds. He gave the example of Ethem the Circassian[69] and warned that if the TGNA excluded him from this protocol and if one day he wished to come back to Turkey, the government could not stop him in doing so. In order to stop his entry into Turkey, the prosecution could clearly prove that he worked against Turkey overseas. According to Ferit Bey, this could not be done with hearsay; solid proof would be necessary.[70] In other words, the protocol to exclude 150 names from the amnesty was legally the safest way to get rid of main oppositional figures.

It should be noted here that the government, by invoking the Ottoman Citizenship Law (*Tabiyet-i Osmaniye Kanunnamesi*, law number 1044) that was enacted on February 19, 1869, the government planned to clear some names off the list by revoking their citizenship. Süreyya Bey described the related article of the law in the discussions as the following: "The Imperial government reserves the right to strip an individual off his/her citizenship if the named person assumes a citizenship of another country or serves the military of a foreign country."[71] This is significant because some names on the 600 list did not enter the 150 list because this law was invoked, and these individuals were stripped of their citizenship.[72] At this point, the case for Ethem the Circassian becomes more important, for one of the accusations against him was that he served the Greek military interests. If proven, this accusation would clearly give the government the right to revoke his citizenship and block his return to Turkey. Considering that almost two-thirds of the list consists of people of Circassian origin, some of whom were Ethem's associates, such a move would have spared considerable room for other nominees for the list. The fact that Ethem and his associates remained on the list of the 150ers indicates that the government saw them as a major threat and did not want to gamble on his exile on legal grounds. It may also indicate that the government did not have convincing evidence against them and their service to the Greek military.

The second parliamentary session on the subject of the 150ers took place on April 22, 1924, and ended after midnight. In this session, the members of parliament debated the issue further. There were still requests to include certain names on the list; however, the debates were not as confrontational as they were in the previous session. Twenty-nine members actively participated in the discussions, but statements were very brief. The closed session ended at 1:55 A.M. on April 23, 1924. However, this did not mean that the discussions were long-winded; speakers stated their positions for the record and accepted the result. There was a clear understanding that the list must be approved soon, as the general amnesty law was already signed by the president, Mustafa Kemal. In the end, three names on the previous list were replaced by Madanoğlu Mustafa, Osman Nuri, and Refik.[73] By the majority of votes, the list was approved by parliament at the forty-fourth session on April 23, 1924. However, because of the death of one member on the list, the number went down to 149. On June 1, 1924, another name was added to the list by the government and approved by Mustafa Kemal. Finally, the list was published in the *Resmi Ceride* on January 7, 1924.[74] Soon after, those who were still in Turkey were asked to leave, and the Prime Minister's Republican Archives indicate that the government funded the transportation cost of some of the 150ers.[75]

Revoking the Citizenship of the 150ers

Three years into the exile of the 150ers, the Turkish government decided to strip them of their citizenship, initiated by the law 1064 on May 28, 1927.[76] The second article of the law specified that by losing their citizenship, the 150ers also lost the right to own property (*hakk-ı temellük*)[77] and to receive any inheritance (*hakk-ı tevarüs*) in Turkey. This law may be considered the Turkish government's attempt to cut off the 150ers from their financial sources in the country and to limit their overseas activities. However, we know that the government already issued a decree (*Kararname*) on November 10, 1925, that stipulated that since there is no specific instruction in the Treaty of Lausanne as to what happens if the 150ers fail to liquidate their property within the requested nine months, the government reserves the right to liquidate these properties.[78] The nine-month period began with the declaration of the 150 names on January 7, 1924, and should have ended on October 7, 1925. However, we know that another governmental decree on August 26, 1925, forbade the 150ers to communicate with people in Turkey in 1925.[79] No information exists on the following dilemma: if the government already forbade the 150ers to have any kind of communication with Turkey, how did it expect them to sell their property?

These actions by the government are indicative of the sensitivity of the regime toward the activities of a small number of the 150ers, for the Turkish government was well aware that a great majority of the 150ers were not politically active in exile. It must have been decided that collective punishment would be more effective to deal with anti-Ankara activities in exile.

Was there any resistance in parliament to revoke the citizenship of the 150ers? Kamil Erdeha points out the lack of opposition to the law "which may have contradicted the Constitution" in parliament.[80] Neither the press nor the deputies in parliament showed any opposition to it, and the bill quickly became law. Erdeha concludes that the reason for the lack of opposition was to allow the government to flex its muscles against the 150ers who were involved in anti-Ankara activities overseas. Pointing out the earlier intense debates in parliament for less controversial issues, he states that "there is no other way of explaining the lack of opposition in parliament."[81] In fact, there is. As Mahmut Goloğlu—another Turkish researcher—argues, after 1926 there was no visible opposition left in parliament. Goloğlu correctly observes that the only expression of opposition after 1926 materialized as being absent from the voting. Indeed, in the period between 1926 and 1927, a great majority of the laws passed with unanimous vote, cast only by less than half the members of parliament.[82] Those who did not want to vote for a particular bill simply did not show up rather than speaking against it.

Amnesty for the 150ers

In 1938, 11 years after the law stripping the 150ers of their citizenship and just before the death of Mustafa Kemal Atatürk, the government granted the 150ers a limited amnesty. This amnesty not only reinstated their citizenship but also pardoned them for their past anti-Ankara activities. The limitations were the following: (1) those among the 150ers who earned a government pension because of their past public service could not claim this right; (2) the 150ers would be forbidden to be employed in public service for eight years; (3) those former civil servants who were banned from government positions were forgiven, but they could not accept paid appointments for a period of two years; and (4) discharged military personnel among the 150ers could not be appointed back in former positions. Perhaps the most significant caveat related to the 150ers was stated in article 5, which declared that the cabinet reserved the right to revoke their citizenship yet again if it deemed necessary.[83] The government simply did not want to leave anything unchecked.

Cemal Kutay, in his *Yüzellikler Faciası*,[84] tells of the emergence of the idea of the amnesty in the following way. On June 1, 1938, Mustafa Kemal Atatürk informed his close associate Ali Fethi Okyar (then the ambassador to Paris) that he was asking the government to prepare an amnesty law for the 150ers. This date must be incorrect, for we know that the bill was already discussed in parliament on May 23, 1938.[85] In any case, during this period, the government was headed by Celal Bayar, who, unlike the previous İsmet İnönü governments, was favorable toward such an amnesty. In fact, this move was the third attempt by Mustafa Kemal Atatürk since 1933 to forgive the 150ers. According to Tevfik Rüştü Aras, the minister of foreign affairs, the earlier attempts were blocked by the İsmet Pasha governments.[86] However, Celal Bayar was determined to prepare a bill as quickly as possible and passed it in parliament to honor Mustafa Kemal's last wish from the government, as it became apparent that the latter's health was deteriorating rapidly. Kutay suggests that Mustafa Kemal's health may have made him sensitive to the suffering of the 150ers and therefore wished to forgive them.[87] Kamil Erdeha emphasizes the fact that the 150ers were not able to pose any threat to the regime anymore, and this was the underlying reason for Mustafa Kemal's decision.[88]

The government stated its reasoning for the amnesty bill (number 6/2171) as the following:

> A regime that is based upon such strong principles should not fear from those who opposed or betrayed it. The Republic which prevails over injustice surely shows forgiveness towards the poor and helpless. . . . [The children and relatives of the 150ers]

> carry with them the stain and the embarrassment [of being associated with the 150ers]. As our citizens, they expect compassion from the Republic to free them from the spiritual pain they have been exposed to. There remains no reason for the Kemalist regime to deny its compassion to the 150ers.[89]

In other words, the government acknowledged that the 150ers posed no threat to the regime, and their forgiveness stemmed from the government's desire to lift the shame of being associated with the 150ers from their relatives and children. Expectedly, it did not acknowledge any wrongdoing.

The bill was adopted on June 29, 1938, and was put into effect on July 16, 1938, as law number 3527. The second article of the law stated, "People whose names were registered in the list of 150 which was referred to in the General Amnesty protocol and declaration in the Treaty of Lausanne on 24 July 1924 are forgiven."[90] It should be noted that this bill did not pass without controversy. Emin Sazak of Eskişehir showed his frustration regarding the law by stating,

> Divine justice for these kinds of people [the 150ers] is the Ali Kemal style [lynching] death.[91] They must die the way Ali Kemal did. I want to kill them myself by biting off their flesh with my own teeth. I consent to their arrival only if they will be lynched by the people.[92]

Newspapers also joined in the controversy and published articles praising or complaining about the amnesty. Yunus Nadi, in his daily *Cumhuriyet*, claimed that this amnesty defeats the purpose of deterrence and stated that "our vote for the amnesty is an enormous 'nay.' "[93]

It should be noted that not many of the 150ers would benefit from the amnesty simply because many were already deceased by this date.[94] As the following section demonstrates, some chose not to return, and those who had no political ambition left and wished to die in Turkey. This tumultuous period experienced the passing of a generation—a generation whose loyalty to the empire was challenged by the emergence of the nation-state.

The following sections examine the backgrounds of the 150ers with the aim of discovering any possible pattern in their inclusion on the list. Among others, it will shed light on the following questions: Who were the 150ers, and why were they chosen? Were they ever a threat to the emerging regime? Why did they oppose the new regime? The reader must be warned that we have considerable information on some of the 150ers; however, almost no information exists about many others.

CATEGORIES AND MEMBERS OF THE 150ERS: THE PROSOPOGRAPHY[95]

The list contained 150 names under 10 categories: Former Sultan Vahdettin's entourage (8 people), members of the former Ottoman cabinets who had responsibilities in the *Kuvva-yi İnzibatiye* or the caliphal army (6 people), delegates who signed the Treaty of Sevres in 1920 (3 people), members of the caliphal army (7 people), people from the Ottoman civil service and military (32 people), Ethem the Circassian and his associates (9 people), those who participated in the Circassian Congress as delegates (18 people), police officers (13 people), journalists (13 people), and other people (41 people).

Vahdettin's Entourage

The first category, Vahdettin's entourage, consisted of eight names of people who were not members of the dynasty and, therefore, were not expelled earlier based on law number 431, which was enacted on March 3, 1924. As we will see later, this law, called the Law on the Abolishment of the Caliphate and the Exile of the Ottoman Dynasty (Hilafetin İlgasına ve Hanedan-ı Osmani'nin Türkiye Cumhuriyeti Memaliki Haricine Çıkarılmasına Dair Kanun), included 155 members of the dynasty. Certain members of Vahdettin's entourage, however, were in İstanbul making the Ankara Circle nervous about their political future. Many other names could have been included on this list; however, the government selected the following names.

(1) Kiraz Hamdi: According to Tarık Mümtaz Göztepe, Hamdi Pasha had a nickname *kiraz*, "cherry," because of his good looks.[96] He graduated from the Ottoman Military Academy and became a general during the reign of Abdülhamit II. However, because of his disagreements with the CUP he was forced to retire. After World War I, when the LE[97] came to power, he was brought back from retirement as an army corps commander. It was during this time that Hamdi Pasha received his honorary title as aide-de-camp to the sultan (*Yaver-i Fahri*).

In 1920, Hamdi Pasha became a founding member and the chairperson of the secret Tarikat-ı Salahiye,[98] which aimed at supporting pan-Islamist movements in and outside the Ottoman Empire. With the rise of the Ankara government, he left the country in 1922. According to Tarık Mümtaz Göztepe, Hamdi Pasha established this organization only to get money from the exiled Vahdettin but in reality was not active.[99] The most relevant aspect of the organization was its opposition to Mustafa Kemal and the Ankara regime. Hamdi Pasha was included on the list because of his visible opposition to Ankara.

One of the most significant sources of information about Hamdi Pasha comes from the Directorate of General Security Archives (DGSA). According to these sources, Hamdi Pasha began working for Turkish intelligence (with the code name 686) in 1925 and collected intelligence about the other members of the 150ers in exile. For his service, he was on the payroll of Ankara; this was his only income.[100] During his exile, we do not have any evidence that he worked to undermine the Ankara government. He died in Köstence, Romania, in poverty on January 18, 1935, before the amnesty for the 150ers became a reality in 1938.

(2) Commander of the Special Guards Unit Zeki: Zeki was the commander of Vahdettin's special guards and also the brother-in-law of the former sultan. When Vahdettin left the country, Zeki accompanied him to Malta, Hijaz, and his final destination in San Remo, Italy. As one of Vahdettin's closest associates, he was included in the 150ers; however, he too worked for Turkish intelligence, providing Ankara with information about the activities of Vahdettin and his entourage in exile.[101] Needless to say, this information must have been very valuable for Ankara. Furthermore, after the death of Vahdettin in 1926, Zeki requested from Ankara that he be sent to Nice, France, where the exiled former caliph Abdülmecit lived. A letter sent from Turkey's ambassador to Rome to the minister of interior informs us that after the death of Vahdettin, Ankara's interest of the exile community shifted from San Remo to Nice. The letter indicates that Zeki Bey received an invitation from the exiled last caliph, Abdülmecit Efendi, and Zeki Bey would accept this request only if approved by Ankara.[102]

Clearly, Zeki Bey never posed any danger to the Kemalist government. Was Ankara aware of this fact? This is hard to determine; however, Rıza Nur indicates that Zeki Bey was trying to establish contacts with Ankara as early as 1923.[103] If the relationship between Ankara and Zeki Bey originated in 1923, it raises the question as to why he was included on the list. As an operative of Ankara, at least his handlers in Turkey should have known about Zeki Bey's service to the new regime. It is possible that Ankara considered his inclusion of the list a cover for his intelligence activities. Surely, being a member of the 150ers, Zeki Bey would give him a layer of cover and hence protection. Nevertheless, we lack conclusive evidence to suggest that he was included on the list solely to spy on the other 150ers. However, we have conclusive evidence to suggest that Zeki Bey worked for the Ankara government for most of his life in exile abroad.

Zeki Bey was initially unable to go to Nice, as he was arrested by the Italian police. He was a suspect in the killing of Vahdettin's physician, Reşat Pasha. The charge was not proven, and finally the released Zeki Bey managed to go to Nice and remained in the service of Ömer Faruk, the son of Abdülmecit. Turkey's Nice consulate informed Ankara of Zeki Bey's suicide on November 24, 1928, adding that lately the other exile community members were becoming suspicious of him.[104]

Like (Kiraz) Hamdi Pasha, Zeki Bey was an operative for the Turkish (Ankara) intelligence. Therefore, it is difficult to believe that he posed any danger to the Ankara regime, a charge that was a determining factor in finalizing the list of the 150ers. Unlike Hamdi Pasha, we do not have any evidence that he was actively involved in undermining the Ankara government even before his exile.

(3) Inspector of Imperial Treasure Kayseri'li Şaban Ağa: He was originally in the CUP but later shifted his loyalty to the LE. Şaban Ağa was first exiled by the CUP after the assassination of Şevket Pasha in 1913 but returned to İstanbul after World War I. He was appointed to the Inspectorate of Imperial Treasure (*Hazine-yi Hassa*) by the anti-CUP Damat Ferit Pasha government. As a significant member of the LE, he remained close to the palace.

After the War of Independence, like Zeki Bey, Şaban Ağa left the country with Sultan Vahdettin on the British battleship *Malaya* and was with the deposed sultan until his death. Şaban Ağa died in Alexandria, Egypt, in 1928.

(4) Tütüncübaşı Şükrü Bey: He also belonged to the inner circle of Vahdettin and belonged to his entourage in San Remo. Şükrü Bey remained in San Remo until 1929. Sedat Bingöl points out that Şükrü Bey sent 14 letters to a Turkish intelligence officer, suggesting that he was in contact with Ankara and possibly collecting intelligence for the new Turkish government.[105] Based on a report sent by Turkey's Jerusalem Consulate,[106] we learn that after 1936 he was contacted by Ankara to collect information on the activities of Celadet Bedirhan, a Kurdish nationalist and a sworn enemy of the Ankara government, and Nizamettin Kibar, another oppositional figure.[107] It is significant to note that neither Celadet nor Nizamettin were part of the 150ers despite the fact that they spent their lives in opposition to Ankara. In a closed session of the TGNA, when the names were discussed, Ferit Bey, the interior minister, reasoned that his inclusion (and that of Zeki Bey) on the list was that Vahdettin paid close attention to his advice.[108]

Tütüncübaşı Şükrü Bey spent his later life in Damascus and must have died after 1956 since we know that in 1956 he gave an interview to Feridun Kandemir, a Turkish author and journalist.[109] We know that he was in Damascus in 1937 and in 1958.[110] However, Sedat Bingöl claims that Şükrü Bey returned to Turkey in 1938 with the amnesty for the 150ers. We do not know when and where he died.

(5) Head Court Chamberlain (Ömer Pasha): He graduated from the military academy in 1884 and rose to the rank of a three-star general. During the CUP rule, Enver Pasha forced him into retirement. During World War I, he was in İzmir, where he was not involved in politics. After the CUP era, however, Ömer Pasha was recruited by the third Tevfik Pasha cabinet and became the minister of war on January 31, 1919. Because of his refusal to eliminate CUP supporters from the military, he was asked to resign. On March 31, 1919, Ömer Pasha was appointed to the position of head court chamberlain (*Serkarin*). In July 1920, the Ankara Court of First Instance sentenced him to death in absentia.[111] Two years later, he fled the country with Vahdettin, but on the way to Hijaz, he left Vahdettin in Egypt. Ömer Pasha died on February 4, 1931, in Beirut.

(6) General Staff Colonel Tahir: He was a general staff officer not on good terms with the CUP. After the Young Turk revolution in 1908, he left the empire for Morocco and taught classes in the Moroccan army. Later, Tahir moved to Egypt. After World War I, when the CUP leaders left the country, he became an aid to Vahdettin during the second government of the LE. Grand Vizier Damat Ferit Pasha raised Tahir's rank to colonel and appointed him to the caliphal army (Kuvva-yı İnzibatiye), which was formed on April 18, 1920. Since he was listed on the list of the 150ers under the category "Vahdettin's Entourage," we can assume that his activities in the caliphal army were not the primary reason for his inclusion in the list. In fact, Ferit Bey, the interior minister of the Ankara government, stated his proximity to the sultan as the reason.[112] When the Ankara government established itself, Tahir left the empire with Damat Ferit Pasha for Paris on September 22, 1922. A list prepared in February 1933—on the activities of the 150ers by the Directorate of General Security

Archive—informs us that he received income from the Serbs, as he opposed the Albanian government and this was his main income.[113] Since he was also on another list,[114] we know that he died after 1937, but when and where we do not know.

(7) First Aide-de-Camp Avni Pasha: A graduate of the Ottoman Military Academy, he served in the first Damat Ferit Pasha government as the minister of public works and was an interim minister of war (March 4–10, 1919). In the Second Damat Ferit Pasha government, he was appointed as the minister of the navy on April 2, 1919, and for the second time between May and July 1919. After that, he became first aide-de-camp (*başyaver*) to Sultan Vahdettin.

After the War of Independence, Avni Pasha left the country for Egypt and joined the sultan in San Remo. In the 1933 report, his location was listed as Damascus, but we do not see his name in the 1937 report, which indicates that he died before 1937. Kamil Erdeha suggests that Avni Pasha may have died in 1935 in Cairo, Egypt; however, Şaduman Halıcı gives the date as 1934 and the place as Lebanon.[115]

(8) Former Director of Imperial Estate and of the Imperial Revenues Refik: He was one of the bureaucrats who advised Vahdettin on financial matters. With his knowledge of financial affairs, Refik served as the director of imperial estate and the director of imperial revenues. After his exile from the empire, he spent time in France with the ousted caliph Abdülmecit. Refik Bey was one of the very few members of the 150 who did not have great financial difficulties. According to a letter from the Interior Ministry to the Foreign Ministry, Refik Bey was in close contact with Tashnaksutyun Armenians in Bulgaria for the preparation of an assassination attempt on the life of Mustafa Kemal.[116] We do not know the accuracy of this information; however, we do know that he returned to Turkey after the amnesty for the 150ers in 1938. The year of his death is unknown.

As mentioned above, there were eight names in this category, all of whom served and advised Vahdettin at some point in their careers. As far as we can ascertain, however, only Refik Bey may have been involved in anti-Ankara activities in exile. On the contrary, several members of this category worked for the Turkish intelligence, gathered information, and submitted it to authorities in Ankara. This is significant since the sole reason for their inclusion in the list was their potential to harm the new regime.

Also significant was the information that several of these people were active members of the LE, a party that is known for its opposition to the CUP. This fact may support the suspicion that former CUP members in the Ankara regime wished to settle scores with their former political rivals.

Members of the Former Ottoman Cabinets Who Took Responsibilities in the Kuvva-yi İnzibatiye

In this category, we have six names. This group consisted of Ottoman cabinet members who assumed responsibilities in the anti-Ankara caliphal army. The caliphal army was founded on April 18, 1920, by Damat Ferit Pasha, the infamous grand vizier of Vahdettin who was known for his hostility toward Ankara. The main purpose of this military unit was to counter and destroy the Ankara forces. In addition, the caliphal army was tasked to support the rebellions against the Ankara government and its militia known as the "*Kuvva-yı Milliye*," or the nationalist forces, and to win the loyalty of the locals for the İstanbul government in northwestern Anatolia (Düzce, Hendek, and Adapazarı). This organization was to be responsible to the Ministries of War and Interior and would consist of three infantry regiments and an artillery battalion. It was estimated to be around 4,000 men strong.[117]

The first commander of the caliphal army was Süleyman Şefik Pasha (see below), who was listed under the 150ers. However, under him, there was another local militia commander, Ahmet Anzavur, who was a sworn enemy of Mustafa Kemal. For his service to the İstanbul government, by rebelling against Ankara several times between 1919 and 1920, Anzavur received the title of pasha and enjoyed considerable autonomy in using his militia.[118] Soon after assuming his appointment as commander of the caliphal army, Süleyman Şefik Pasha realized the impossibility of working with Anzavur and resigned from his post, which he held only 12 days.[119] The caliphal army had several other appointees as the commander, but Anzavur became the last one. The caliphal army was a concern for the Ankara government, which utilized the forces of Ethem the Circassian to counter Anzavur. In the end, the Anzavur forces were defeated, and the caliphal army was dispersed by the İstanbul government on June 25, 1920. Anzavur was not on the list of the 150ers simply because he was killed on April 15, 1921 by the nationalists. If he had survived, he surely would have been included on the list.

When one examines the names under this category, one sees that not all commanders of the caliphal army were included. Interestingly, the list starts with someone from the ulama class.

(9) Mustafa Sabri Efendi, former Sheikh al-Islam (1869–1954): With a great interest in politics, he personified the ulama class that agitated the Ankara Circle. He received his religious education in Kayseri and became *müderris*, or madrasa, professor. Later he became the imam of Fatih and Beşiktaş Mosques. Mustafa Sabri soon got involved in politics and in 1908 joined the CUP. However, soon he found himself on the opposite side of the late Ottoman political spectrum. He first formed the Ahali Fırkası (Liberal Union Party) and in 1911 joined the LE. According to Ali Birinci, an author of a book on the LE, Mustafa Sabri was one of the oppositional figures that made the CUP very nervous because of his great oratory skills.[120] After the CUP regime, he became the sheikh al-Islam in the first Damat Ferit Pasha cabinet on March 3, 1919. As a member of the *Şura-yı Saltanat*, or the Imperial Council, he opposed the nationalist war in Anatolia. However, since his views were in the minority during the War of Independence in the imperial circles, he resigned from his post. Nevertheless, on July 31, 1920, he became the sheikh al-Islam for the second time. He remained in this post until September 29, 1920.

After Vahdettin's departure from the empire, Mustafa Sabri realized that staying in Turkey would be too dangerous, and he left for Egypt and later Lebanon, Greece, and Romania. In Greece, he published a newspaper, *Yarın*, in which he continued to attack the Ankara government. In an article in *Yarın* on July 29, 1927, Mustafa Sabri published a long poem criticizing Ankara's "anti-Islamic" activities in the name of Turkish nationalism. The title of the poem, "İstifa Ediyorum," or "I Am Resigning," includes the following verses:

> Henceforth, let the entire world witness that,
> To remain only a human and a Muslim,
> I resign from being a Turk
> With all my honor and dignity before God.[121]

There was no doubt that Mustafa Sabri despised Ankara and its dealings with Islam and the ulama class. Among other members of the 150ers, he was one of the most vocal ones. Because of the diplomatic pressure applied by the Turkish government to the Greek government, Mustafa Sabri was asked to leave the country for Cairo. He did not return to Turkey after the amnesty in 1938 and died in Egypt on March 12, 1954.

Mustafa Sabri was listed under this category because he served in the Damat Ferit Pasha cabinets, during which time the caliphal army was established. However, he could have been listed under several other categories as well, such as "Vahdettin's Entourage," for he spent time with the former sultan in exile.

(10) Former Justice Minister Ali Rüştü: Born in Bosnia, he received a madrasa education. Later he became a judge (*kadı*) and rose to the rank of justice minister on April 5, 1920, in the fifth Damat Ferit Pasha cabinet. When the cabinet resigned on October 17, 1920, his position came to an end. Like other members of the Damat Ferit Pasha cabinets, he was a member of the LE. When the list was discussed in the TGNA, Ferit Bey, Ankara's interior minister, suggested that during the War of Independence, Ali Rüştü praised the invading Greek army as "our military."[122]

Ali Rüştü was a staunch opponent of Ankara and was involved in the formation of the caliphal army. For this reason, he left the country for Egypt, where he died in 1936.

(11) Former Minister of Agriculture and Commerce Cemal: He was born in 1862 and graduated from the College of Civil Service (*Mülkiye*). As a bureaucrat, he served different parts of the empire and became the governor of Elazığ on September 4, 1912. However, the CUP forced him into retirement in 1915. Cemal was a member of the LE and rose to the rank of interior minister in the first Damat Ferit Pasha government in 1918. Interestingly, for his disagreements with Damat Ferit Pasha, Cemal was removed from office the next year. We later see him receiving appointment in the office of the governor in Konya, a central Anatolian town, on May 14, 1919. Because of the proximity of this location to Ankara, Cemal's appointment was significant for the Kemalists. However, Cemal was involved in aiding the anti-Ankara rebellions in the Konya region (such as Bozkır), for which he was forced to flee from Konya back to İstanbul on September 26, 1919. He later became the minister of agriculture and commerce in the fifth Damat Ferit Pasha government.

Cemal Bey had the nickname of "Artin" (a common Armenian name). for he accused the CUP of massacring 800,000 Armenians. During the TGNA discussions, the government asked that he not be listed as Artin Cemal because the term would diminish the seriousness of the issue.[123] This was a move that clearly illustrates his disdain for the CUP, a political party some members of which were part of the Ankara government. Cemal was also a member of İngiliz Muhipler Cemiyeti, or the Society for the Friends of Great Britain, which surely secured his place in the list of the 150ers.

In his exile, the Directorate of General Security Archives indicates that Cemal Bey was not involved in any political activities. In fact, as early as 1925, Cemal sent requests for amnesty to Ankara.[124]

After the amnesty in 1938, he returned to Turkey, received the last name of Keşmir, and died in Turkey. His son, Halit Nazmi Keşmir, became the minister of finance in the sixteenth republican government (1947–1948). We do not know the exact date of his death.

(12) Former Minister of Marine, Hamdi (known as "*Cakacı*," or ostentatious): He was of a Kurdish and military origin. He graduated from the military academy and rose to the rank of a divisional general, or *Ferik*, in the Ottoman military. However, like many of his co-list members, he was forced to retire by the CUP government. After the fall of the CUP government in 1918, more specifically on May 12, 1920, Hamdi Pasha became the chief of general staff and assumed the political office of minister of the navy (July 31–October 17, 1920).

Hamdi Pasha was also the secretary-general of the Kürdistan Teali Cemiyeti, or the Society for the Advancement of Kurdistan (1918–1920).[125] In the TGNA, Ferit Bey suggests that he was not listed with the nickname "Kurd" but did not object to "*cakacı*," indicating that the government was sensitive to ethnic labeling. As discussed above, this is understandable since the government downplayed the significance of ethnic division in Turkey at the Lausanne Conference. Also significant to note was the fact that he was listed among the 150ers not because of his involvement in the Society for the Advancement of Kurdistan, which was a Kurdish nationalist organization, but because of his appointment in the imperial government and in the caliphal army.

During the War of Independence, Hamdi Pasha left the country for Greece and in 1929 was in Albania. The DGSA contains a report in 1933 indicating that Hamdi Pasha was not involved in any anti-Ankara activities overseas.[126] We know that he did not return to Turkey after the amnesty in 1938 but stayed in Albania. However, we do not know in which year he died.

(13) Former Minister of Education Rumbeyoğlu Fahrettin: He was born in İstanbul in 1867 and graduated from the School of Civil Service in 1887. After becoming a diplomat, he served in Vienna, Rome, Athens, and Petersburg. In 1912, he received the rank of ambassador. Fahrettin became the minister of education on April 5, 1920, and occupied that post until July 30, 1920. During the Paris Peace Conference in 1918, he was part of the Ottoman delegation. He was instrumental in the formation of the caliphal army, for which he was listed under the 150ers and left the country. He spent his exile years in France, but after the amnesty, he returned to İstanbul, where he died in 1942.

(14) Former Agriculture and Commerce Minister Kızılhançerci Remzi: Remzi Pasha was of a military origin, and like many of his contemporary military officers on the 150ers list, he was forced to retire by the CUP government. What is known about him was that he established an anti-Ankara Kızılhançer (Red Dagger) organization in 1919. This organization was in close contact with the caliphal army, and its sole purpose was to destroy the Kemalists/nationalist Ankara Circle. During the fourth Damat Ferit Pasha government, he served in the cabinet as the minister for agriculture and commerce (April 5–July 30, 1920). When he left the country as a member of the 150ers, he went to Munich, Germany, where he spent the rest of his life away from politics. He died on September 30, 1934. His son, Şevket Mocan, a well-known anticommunist, served in the Republican parliament as a member of the Democrat Party in the 1950s.

As discussed above, members of this group of the 150ers came from high posts in the Ottoman governments and were almost uniformly anti-CUP. This fact is significant to demonstrate that the rivalry between the CUP and LE continued even after both parties ceased to exist. To these former ministers, the Ankara government represented the CUP ideology. They did not differentiate the two; therefore, they were hostile to Ankara. As repeatedly stated, at its inception, there was not much evidence that drew a distinction between the Ankara (nationalist/Kemalist) movement and the CUP. One can suggest, therefore, that their opposition to Ankara was fueled by the belief that the Anatolian movement was another trick initiated by the CUP.

Another commonality was that members of this group were not involved in anti-Ankara activities in exile. One of the reasons for this was their ages. In the 1920s, most of them were in their sixties and seventies. Another reason is that they realized the new regime was not the continuation of the CUP movement despite the fact that it was born out of it. Many of the members—if they were alive—returned to Turkey after the amnesty in 1938. There are two members of this group, Remzi Pasha and Cemal Bey, whose sons served in the republican parliament.

This group was formed based on their affiliation of and support for the caliphal army. However, they were selectively chosen. Some of the other cabinet members who bore various responsibilities in the formation and the actions of the caliphal army were not included on this list, such as Cemil Pasha (Topuzlu), the minister of public works, and Ahmet Reşit (Rey), the minister of interior.[127]

Delegates Who Signed the Treaty of Sevres

The Treaty of Sevres was signed on August 10, 1920, and was practically the death sentence for the Ottoman Empire. It stipulated that the Ottoman territories, with the exception of Central Anatolia, be divided among the Allied Powers. The treaty had four signatories: Rıza Tevfik, Grand Vizier Damat Ferid Pasha, Hadi Pasha, and Reşid Halis. The Ankara government fiercely objected to the treaty and declared that it would fight against the implementation of it.

In fact, previously the Anatolian movement (which later formed the backbone of the Ankara government) already proclaimed the National Pact (Misak-ı Milli) on February 17, 1920.[128] Basically, this pact drew the current boundaries of present-day Turkey with the exception of the Mosul province. Inherently, the Treaty of Sevres and the National Pact were in conflict regarding their stipulation of the boundaries of the empire. It should be noted that although the Treaty of Sevres was signed, it was never ratified in the Ottoman parliament, as the parliament was shut down prior to the vote. However, it gave the nationalist movement a much-needed advantage over the İstanbul government in the eyes of ordinary citizens. This was a significant boost for the Kemalist movement since the Muslim population of the Ottoman Empire had already lost their faith in protecting its citizens, a sentiment that began to sink in with the occupation of İzmir (Smyrna) on May 15, 1919, and İstanbul (for the second time) on March 15, 1920. The establishment of the TGNA on April 23, 1920, was a clear indication of the resentment of the Anatolian movement over the İstanbul government. The signing of the Treaty of Sevres in August was the final blow to İstanbul's authority over the nationalists in Anatolia and hardened the resolve of the nationalists to establish an alternate assembly in Ankara. One can see it as the formal commencement of the power struggle between the Ankara Circle and the İstanbul Circle. It moved the Anatolian movement farther away from İstanbul government though not necessarily from the sultan. Therefore, it should be no surprise that signatories to this treaty were placed on the list of the 150ers. The only exception was Damat Ferit Pasha, who had already passed away on October 6, 1923, in France. The other three members were on the list. In a closed meeting discussing the list in the TGNA on April 16, 1924, Ferit Bey, the prime minister, stated that although the Directorate of General Security suggested that they should be put on the list of those who were eligible for the revoking of their citizenship, these people should be on this list just to be safe.[129]

(15) Former Education Minister Hadi: He was born in Baghdad in 1861 and graduated from the military academy in 1882. He rose to the rank of pasha and became a divisional general. In 1911, Hadi Pasha served as the joint chief of staff but was forced into retirement by the CUP in 1914. After the CUP regime, he was brought back from retirement, like many of his colleagues, and was appointed to the post of the joint chief of staff on August 12, 1919. After a month, Hadi Pasha was appointed to the Ayan Chamber (Ottoman Senate). Between May 2 and 12, 1920, we see him occupying the post of the joint chief of staff. He was also a member of *Şura-yı Saltanat* (Imperial Council), which discussed and voted for the Treaty of Sevres.[130] In the meeting of the Imperial Council, Hadi Pasha supported the treaty and, therefore, was on the blacklist of the Ankara Circle. After the collapse of the Ottoman government, he left the country for Albania but died in Beirut in 1932.

(16) Former President of the Ottoman Ayan Chamber (Senate) Rıza Tevfik: Rıza Tevfik (Bölükbaşı) was born in the Ottoman Edirne[131] in 1868 and graduated from the medical school in 1899. In 1907, he joined the CUP and in 1908 became a member of parliament. After that, in 1911, he switched his loyalty to the opposition party, the LE, blaming the CUP for its despotic methods and for the loss of the Balkans. Ali Birinci, an expert on the LE, estimates that Rıza Tevfik's membership in the LE did not last more than six months.[132] He was very much interested in philosophy and was also known as Rıza Tevfik, the Philosopher. The languages he spoke included Hebrew, Spanish, English, Italian, Albanian, Armenian, and French,[133] and he was an accomplished poet. As a Renaissance man and a critic of the CUP, he captured the attention of Sultan Vahdettin and was offered the position of education minister, a post he accepted in 1918. In addition, he served as the deputy minister for mail and telegram (November 11, 1918–January 12, 1919). During the Damat Ferit Pasha governments after World War I, Rıza Tevfik participated in governmental meetings to discuss the upcoming Treaty of Sevres. During this time, he was appointed to the Ayan Chamber and twice became the president of this chamber (first May 24–June 18, 1919, and later July 31–October 21, 1920).

Rıza Tevfik, in his memoirs, claimed that he suggested that Damat Ferit Pasha appoint Mustafa Kemal as the minister of war, a proposal that was strongly rejected by the cabinet with the accusation that Mustafa Kemal was an important member of the CUP.[134] However, he later objected to the appointment of Mustafa Kemal to Anatolia as a military inspector in 1919. He was clearly a significant member of the

İstanbul Circle and was highly suspicious of Ankara. He even implies in his memoir that the Ankara movement indirectly served the interest of Great Britain by forcing Vahdettin to leave the empire.[135]

Rıza Tevfik became a member of the 150ers first and foremost for having signed the Treaty of Sevres (August 10, 1920). After the Kemalist victory, he escaped to Egypt on November 15, 1922, and joined Vahdettin's Hijaz trip. Later, Rıza Tevfik accepted the invitation from the king of Jordan to become director of the National Museum and Library in 1925. During his exile, he lived in the United States, Cyprus, Hijaz, Jordan, and Lebanon. He did not return to Turkey immediately after the amnesty in 1938 but waited until 1943 and died on December 30, 1949, in İstanbul.

(17) Former Bern Ambassador Reşat Halis: He served as undersecretary in the Ministry of Education from March 4 to May 18, 1919. During his appointment, he was appointed to Bern as an ambassador by Damat Ferit Pasha. His inclusion in the 150ers is solely for having signed the Treaty of Sevres, not because of his opposition to the Ankara Circle. During his exile in Paris, he married Şaziye Sultan[136] from the Ottoman dynasty. For this reason, he could not return to Turkey after the amnesty.

The only commonality of the members of this group is that they signed the Treaty of Sevres, and, as such, this group seems to be most objectively defined. Only Rıza Tevfik was on record criticizing Mustafa Kemal's appointment as the inspector general to Anatolia. He can be categorized more pro-İstanbul than anti-Ankara. The other members of this group were bureaucrats and soldiers who were not politically active and never posed any danger to the new regime.

Members of the Caliphal Army

(18) The Commander of the Caliphal Army Süleyman Şefik[137]: He was born in 1866 and graduated from the Military Academy on May 16, 1886, with the rank of first lieutenant.[138] Süleyman Şefik (Söylemezoğlu) rose to the rank of general and was forced into retirement by the CUP in 1914.[139] After this date, he was brought back from retirement several times.[140] When the CUP regime was replaced by the LE after World War I, on August 13, 1919, he was appointed to the post of minister of war by Damat Ferit Pasha. After the formation of the caliphal army, he became the first commander, a post he retained for only 22 days (April 29–May 21, 1919). In a letter sent to Tarık

Mümtaz Göztepe, Süleyman Şefik explained that his appointment to the post of the commander of the caliphal army was requested by Damat Ferit Pasha and approved by the sultan. "Since I was the highest ranking aide-de-camp to the Sultan (*yaver-i ekrem*), I could not refuse the Sultan's request. . . . I requested the authority to communicate with the nationalist forces (*Kuvva-yı Milliye*) and to give immunity to those members of the Anatolian movement without requesting permission from İstanbul."[141] Things clearly did not go as planned, and just over three weeks after accepting the post, Süleyman Şefik resigned from his post, citing his disapproval of Ahmet Anzavur, the lower-ranking commander of the militia under the caliphal army.[142]

By now, it should not be a surprise to the reader that like many other 150ers, Süleyman Şefik was a former member of the CUP and shifted his loyalty to Damat Ferit Pasha, a sworn enemy of the CUP.[143] Tarık Mümtaz Göztepe, another member of the 150ers, claims that when Süleyman Şefik was appointed as the minister of war in the Damat Ferit Pasha cabinet, he was an unknown figure in the LE circles; he was someone who was a friend of the infamous Enver Pasha and hence considered a CUP member.[144] He was indeed a sworn member of the CUP, and this was known in the cabinet. Ali Fuat Türkgeldi, an eyewitness to the period, wrote that Damat Ferit had confidence in him and was willing to give him a chance in the cabinet.[145]

We know that prior to his appointment as the minister of war, Süleyman Şefik clearly showed his disdain with the nationalist forces in Anatolia. In an interview to daily *İkaz*, Süleyman Şefik warned, "Mustafa Kemal Pasha is responsible for the current situation in Anatolia. He openly rebelled against the government. These kinds of actions ruin the country."[146] It was not just the statements that earned Süleyman Şefik his place on the infamous list of the 150ers. His deeds also attested to the fact that he was someone determined to crush the Anatolian movement. It is known that Mustafa Kemal Pasha was released from his post as the inspector general by Ali Kemal, the minister of interior, on July 8, 1919, and that he resigned from the Ottoman military on the same date. This was the clear indication that the nationalist movement headed by Mustafa Kemal rejected the authority of the İstanbul government, which was apprehensive about the size and strength of the nationalists. In order to prevent the nationalists from communicating with one another, Süleyman Şefik, as the minister of war, issued an order on August 18, 1919, instructing army corps commanders to not to use encrypted messages among themselves.

The only exception is the communication between the ministry and the army corps commanders.[147] Süleyman Şefik was aware of the necessity for encrypted telegrams among the army corps to mobilize the nationalist movement in Anatolia. This would, for example, hinder the cooperation between Ali Fuat Pasha, the commander of the 20th Army Corps in Western Anatolia, and Kazım Karabekir Pasha, the commander of the 15th Army Corps in Eastern Anatolia. In return, the nationalists after the Sivas Congress decided to cut all communication with İstanbul on September 12, 1919.[148]

Another of Süleyman Şefik's actions against the nationalists was a telegram sent to Ali Galip, the governor of Elazığ, on September 3, 1919. This telegram, signed by Süleyman Şefik and Interior Minister Adil, instructed the governor of Elazığ to prevent the nationalist convention from convening in Sivas by all means. We know that Mustafa Kemal had a copy of this telegram and was aware keenly aware of Süleyman Şefik's hostility.[149]

For all these reasons, Süleyman Şefik knew that the nationalist victory posed a great danger to his personal security. Therefore, he took refuge in the British protection and left the country for Egypt in 1922. Next, we see him on February 2, 1926, in Mecca, where he worked for King Ibn Saud as a bureaucrat until retirement in 1929. During his exile, Turkish intelligence sources collected much information about his activities abroad. Reports indicate that Süleyman Şefik was trying to form an oppositional organization in exile. The name of this organization would be the Society for Revenge (Öç Cemiyeti), which would work to topple the nationalist regime and restore the sultanate in 1928.[150] In another document, we see that Süleyman Şefik was planning for another organization, the Society for the Ottomans (Osmanlı Cemiyeti), in 1939 at the age of 73.[151] Seemingly, this document relates to his activities in Turkey and indicates that he was still interested in bringing the Ottoman dynasty back. The program of the Society for the Ottomans included 16 articles that carried an anti-Kemalist tone. For example, a police report noted the following statement by him:

> Turkey is very near an abyss and destruction. They will divide Turkey and the leaders of the Republic will escape the country. Their luggages are ready and their money is in the European banks. Didn't their older brothers, the CUP group, follow the same path?[152]

It is possible that the Ankara government did not take him seriously and allowed him to reside in Turkey after the amnesty despite the fact that he continued to be critical of the Ankara government. Even in 1940, he was closely watched, and his moves were recorded.[153] A document in the police archives (DGSA 12222/18) indicates that Süleyman Şefik visited Fethi Okyar, the minister of justice in the republican government, on May 4, 1940. The same document also indicates that Süleyman Şefik sent a letter to İsmet Pasha, then the president of Turkey. We do not know the content of the letter and of his meeting with the minister of justice. However, it is interesting to note that although he was an ardent opponent of the republican regime, he interacted with the republican government at the highest levels. Since there was no action to back his rhetoric and perhaps because of his old age, Süleyman Şefik was not prosecuted.

The exact date of his return to Turkey is not known. We know that he was in Turkey in 1940. A document from the Prime Minister's Republican Archives locates him in Lebanon in 1939.[154] Therefore, his return must have taken place in this period. He died in İstanbul on February 16, 1946.

(19) Süleyman Şefik's Adjutant Tahsin the Bulgarian: He graduated from the military academy and rose to the rank of captain and served Süleyman Şefik as his adjutant. Tahsin was from Filibe and therefore was known as Tahsin the Bulgarian. He was a member of the Society of Military Guard, or Nigahban-ı Askeri Cemiyeti, which was anti–National forces.[155]

(20) Chief of Military Staff for the Caliphal Army Colonel Ahmet Refik: He had a military academy background but resigned just before achieving the rank of general and joined the CUP. Like many others, Ahmet Refik switched his loyalty to the LE and accepted the post of general staff officer in the caliphal army. Damat Ferit Pasha was impressed by Ahmet Refik's hostility toward the nationalist forces of Ankara. He tried actively to recruit anti-Ankara officers to the caliphal army. However, after the collapse of the Ottoman Empire, Ahmet Refik left for Bulgaria, where he died in 1930. Emin Karaca informs us that his brother remained in Turkey and became the director of religious affairs and that his son served the republican government as a high-level bureaucrat.[156]

(21) Commander of the Machine Gun Unit of the Caliphal Army and Damat Ferid Pasha's Aide-de-Camp Tarık Mümtaz (Göztepe): He was born in 1893 in İstanbul. He was of military origin and served as aide-de-camp to several ministers of war, including Damat Ferit Pasha. He was also known as an author whose books contain valuable information about the late Ottoman and early republican eras.[157] After

World War I, he published a literature journal called *Ümit*. After the collapse of the Ottoman Empire, he left the country and joined Vahdettin in San Remo. He was an eyewitness to Vahdettin's life in exile and remained with him until Vahdettin's death in 1926.

Tarık Mümtaz was included in the list of 150ers under the section of the caliphal army as he took responsibilities as the commander of the machine gun unit in this anti-Ankara military force. While abroad, he taught in Turkish schools in Bulgaria and published newspapers in Syria, such as the Circassian-language *Marc* (1928–1931). When he returned to Turkey after the amnesty, he worked for newspapers such as *Yeni Sabah* and *Zafer*. Like many of his co-list members, after his return, he refrained from making remarks against the government and died in İstanbul on January 24, 1977.

(22) Former Commander of the Caliphal Army and of the İzmir (17th) Army Corps Ali Nadir: Ali Nadir Pasha was a graduate of the Ottoman military academy and better known in the military as "the commander who surrendered Salonika to the enemy"in the Balkan Wars (1912–1913).[158] Although he was forced to retire after this, Ali Nadir Pasha was appointed as a member to the first Martial Law Court on December 16, 1918.[159] As the commander of the 17th Army Corps, he was held responsible for surrendering İzmir to Greek forces on May 15, 1919. Ali Nadir was included in the list because of his appointment as the commander of the caliphal army. Although there is conflicting information about the place of his death, it is very likely that he died in poverty in Nice in 1930.[160]

(23) Member of the Caliphal Army and of Nemrut Mustafa's Court Martial, Sub-governor (*Kaymakam*) Fettah: He was of military origin and rose to the rank of lieutenant colonel before he was forced to retirement by the CUP. However, on April 5, 1920, he was appointed as a member of the First Court Martial, which was also known by the public as "the Court Martial of Nemrut Mustafa," who presided over the court and was famous for his prosecution of sympathizers and members of the Ankara Circle and the nationalist circle.

After the War of Independence, Fettah left the country for Egypt and later Syria. Since he was of Kurdish origin, Kamil Erdeha claims, he became involved in Kurdish nationalist activities in Aleppo and worked to stir up a Kurdish rebellion in Turkey.[161] Fettah died in Syria before 1933.[162]

(24) Member of the Caliphal Army Çopur Hakkı: He was of military and Circassian background and was a sworn enemy of the Ankara Circle. Hakkı was a founding member of the Nigehban-ı

Askeri Cemiyeti (Society of Army Watchmen), which was formed in January 1919 to eliminate the CUP. By claiming that the Ankara Circle was the extension of the CUP, this organization was also hostile toward the Kemalists. Çopur Hakkı also served in the caliphal army, for which he was listed among the 150ers. It should be noted that his name was added to the list with the insistence of the members of the Turkish parliament.[163]

After leaving Turkey, Çopur Hakkı went to Greece and became a Greek citizen and worked tirelessly against Ankara.[164] We do not know when and where he died. However, we do know that in 1937 he was in İskeçe, Greece.[165]

As can be seen, this group was almost exclusively of military background, and many of them were ethnically Circassian. They were included in this list under the caliphal army, but some of them could have been included in the list under different categories.

People from the Civil Service and the Army

(25) Former Bursa Governor Gümülcüneli İsmail: He was born in 1877 in Gümülcine (in present-day Greece) and entered politics as a CUP member of the Ottoman parliament in 1908 from his place of birth. Soon after, he left the CUP and formed the Ahali Party, which later, on November 21, 1911, merged with the LE. After the killing of Mahmut Şevket Pasha, İsmail left for Paris. However, on the LE's revival in 1919, he returned. On March 13, 1919, he was appointed to Bursa as the governor. In Bursa, he became an ardent opponent of the CUP. Like many of his colleagues, he considered the Ankara Circle as an arm of the CUP and was hostile toward it. When he was released from his post on July 29, 1919, for bad behavior, he emerged in Gümülcine, where he remained until June 1920. In the second half of 1920, he was in İstanbul. However, when the nationalist government controlled İstanbul in 1922, he went to Romania and later San Remo. Sources describe him in exile as a lowlife who cheated many of his close friends and even the former sultan Vahdettin.[166] After the amnesty in 1938, he did not return and remained in France. He died in 1942, possibly in Greece.

(26) Member of the *Ayan* (the Ottoman Senate) Konya'lı Zeynelabidin: He was one of the founders of the Ahali and the LE. After the nationalist victory, he left for Egypt and then joined Vahdettin in Mecca. Later, he lived in Syria and worked as a trader. In his later years, he emerged in Iraq working as a clerk. Şaduman Halıcı claims that he died after 1939.[167]

(27) Former Cebel-i Bereket Sub-governor (*mutasarrıf*) Fanizade Mesut: He was born in 1889 in Adana and was a member of a well-known family migrating to Adana from Süleymaniye (present-day Iraq). As we will see, the family was of Kurdish origin and had other two members on the list. Mesut studied law and became the sub-governor of Cebel-i Bereket, a town in Adana, during the French occupation, earning him a place among the 150ers. Immediately after the Kemalist victory, Mesut left for Syria and later France, where he completed his doctorate. Interestingly, his dissertation was on the Kurds, aiming to dispute Kurdish nationalist claims. During his research and after his graduate work, he contacted the Turkish consulate for financial support.[168] In 1933, he returned to Antakya (then in French Syria) and worked as a teacher in a local high school.

After the amnesty, Mesut returned to Turkey and worked as a lawyer. He also published a book on Mustafa Kemal praising his success.[169] Clearly, Fanizade Mesut was impressed by the accomplishments of the Ankara government and in his later life remained an admirer of Mustafa Kemal. He died in İstanbul on November 15, 1979.[170]

(28) One of the leaders of the LE, Colonel Sadık: Born in 1860, Sadık Bey was of military origin. In 1906, he became a member of the CUP in Manastır (present-day Bitola in Macedonia). However, Ali Birinci, a scholar of the LE, claims that he was always kept away from the inner circle of the CUP, paving the way for his departure from the party.[171] He later joined the LE and became the deputy chair for it. Like some other figures in opposition to the CUP, after the Mahmut Şevket Pasha's assassination in 1913, he left the empire for France until 1919. In 1920, Sadık became the chairman of the LE, and in 1921 he was elected to the presidency of the Association of the Friends of England in Turkey (Türkiye'de İngiliz Muhipleri Cemiyeti), which claimed to be working to preserve the empire by collaborating with England.[172] In reality, this organization was a pawn for the British interests in the empire and was a strong opponent of the CUP. Convinced that it would harm the goodwill of England toward the Ottoman Empire, Sadık was also a vocal opponent of the nationalists in Ankara. For this reason, he left Turkey in 1924 for Romania, where he remained for the next 16 years.[173] He died in İstanbul in 1940, the same day that he arrived from exile.

(29) Former Malatya Sub-governor Bedirhani Halil Rami: He was one of the sons of Bedirhan Pasha,[174] a famous Kurdish notable, and was the *mutasarrıf* (sub-governor) of Malatya during the War of Independence. Mustafa Kemal mentions Halil Rami several times in his *Nutuk* in the context of his efforts to raid the Sivas Congress in September 1919 and to kill Mustafa Kemal.[175] In addition, the British secret agent Major Edward W. C. Noel's contact with Halil Rami to organize Kurdish tribes against the Kemalists was well documented.[176] Therefore, it was not a surprise that he was listed among the 150ers. What is surprising is that he was not in the original list but was included by the request of Halit Bey of Kastamonu in the TGNA.[177]

Halil Rami was captured in İstanbul in 1925 and sent to exile in Beirut, where he became involved in Kurdish nationalist activities. Turkish police archives indicate that he died on December 8, 1932.[178]

(30) Former Manisa Sub-governor Girit'li Hüsnü: He studied law and became Manisa sub-governor (*mutasarrıf*) on February 19, 1919. Kamil Erheda claims that Hüsnü was of the opinion that the Greek forces were too superior to fight against when Manisa was under Greek military occupation and therefore chose to collaborate with them. However, he went so far in his collaboration and worked for the Greek forces as a Greek officer that people gave him the nickname "Hüsnüyadis."[179]

After the Turkish victory, Hüsnü left the country with the withdrawing Greek forces. He became a Greek citizen and lived in Athens. The remainder of his life, he worked for the Greek National Bank as a legal consultant.[180] After the amnesty, he did not return, and he died in Greece.

(31) Former Chief of the Court Martial Nemrut Mustafa: He was of military origin and became a general. During the CUP period, Nemrut (Kürt) Mustafa Pasha was forced into retirement. After the fall of the CUP on December 16, 1918, he became a member of the First Court Martial, which prosecuted the CUP members. When he became the chief justice for the same court in 1920 after assuming several other administrative appointments in Anatolia, he worked tirelessly against the Ankara Circle and sentenced many of its members, including Mustafa Kemal, to capital punishment. During the Tevfik Pasha government (October 21, 1920–November 17, 1922), he was accused of misusing his authority and sentenced to seven months in prison. However, he was pardoned by Sultan Vahdettin on February 7, 1921.

During the War of Independence, Mustafa Pasha left for Damascus on June 28, 1921, and later Baghdad, where he became involved in Kurdish nationalist activities. He remained a devoted opponent of the Ankara government in Iraq, where he died on January 29, 1936.[181]

(32) Uşak Mayor Hulusi: After he left the country, he lived in Greece and died there on April 5, 1930. There is no record of his anti-Ankara activities in exile.[182]

(33) Former Adapazarı Sub-governor Mustafa the Traitor: He graduated from the School of Civil Service in 1907 and consequently served as sub-governor (*kaymakam*) in several towns. He was appointed to Adapazarı in 1919, and when the Greeks occupied the region, he remained in his post under the Greeks. As a member of the LE, Mustafa was an ardent opponent of the Ankara government.[183] We know that he was in Salonika, Greece, in 1937. However, when and where he died is not known.

(34) Former Tekirdağ Mufti Hafız Ahmet: He worked as a lower-level religious functionary in Edirne until the Greek occupation and later became the mufti of Tekirdağ. He left the country with the Greek forces for Salonica. He died in Cangaza on July 16, 1931, and was not part of any anti-Ankara activities.[184]

(35) Former Afyonkarahisar Sub-governor Sabit: He spent his exile years in Greece, where he died in 1926.

(36) Former Gazi Ayıntap Sub-governor Celal Kadri: He served as a sub-governor of Gaziantep during the French occupation and left the country with them for Aleppo, where he worked for the French intelligence. He also published a newspaper called *Doğru Yol* in Syria. The police reports indicate that after 1935, he also worked for the Turkish intelligence and returned to Turkey after the amnesty.[185]

(37) LE General Secretary (*Umumi Katip*) Adana'lı [Fanizade] Zeynelabidin: He was born in Adana in 1884 and was a notable member of the LE. He was known as the spokesperson of the party and became its general secretary. He presented the view of the LE in the Imperial Council (*Şura-yı Saltanat*), which was assembled on May 26, 1919, to discuss the difficulties of the empire.[186] After the War of Independence, he left for Egypt and later went to Baghdad, where he died.

(38) Former Member of the Ayan Chamber and the Minister of Pious Foundations Vasfi Hoca: He was one of the few members of the ulama class in this group and worked as a judge in several towns in the empire. In 1908, he entered the Ottoman parliament from Balıkesir. He was a founding member of the LE. He served as the minister of imperial pious foundations (*Evkaf-ı Hümayun*) between March 4 and May 17, 1919, and the minister of justice between May 19 and July 20, 1919. On September 18, 1919, he was appointed to the *Ayan* chamber. After his inclusion in the list of the 150ers, he went to Romania and later Egypt, then returned to Romania, where he died in 1926.[187]

(39) Former Harput Governor Ali Galip: He was born in 1871 in Kayseri. Having graduated from the Military Academy in 1895, Ali Galip rose to the rank of lieutenant colonel.[188] On April 14, 1911, he left the military for politics in the LE. In May 1919, Damat Ferit Pasha appointed him to Harput as governor. It is in this appointment that he became engaged in the Kemalist groups and is remembered as the leading figure in the "Ali Galip Incident." When Ottoman Interior Minister Ali Kemal's order came to Ali Galip for the arrest of Mustafa Kemal and his associates during the Sivas Congress in September 1919, he unsuccessfully proceeded to execute the order with a British agent, Major Noel, and some Kurdish notables. Nationalists were well aware of this attempt to break the Sivas Congress and to arrest the nationalists. Mustafa Kemal devotes a section for this incident in his *Nutuk* and informs the TGNA that Ali Galip failed in his attempt to stop the nationalists and left for İstanbul via Aleppo.[189]

After the declaration of the 150ers list in 1924, Ali Galip left country for Romania, where he died on November 15, 1932. In exile, he became a merchant, first producing and selling cheese to local schools in Köstence and later buying and selling of animals to İstanbul. There is no record that he was involved in politics against Ankara in his exile years.

(40) Former Deputy Governor of Bursa Aziz Nuri: Because of his fervent opposition to the CUP, he was exiled to Egypt by the CUP regime. On his return after the CUP's fall from power, he became the chairperson for the LE in Bursa, where he also tried to establish an anti-Ankara organization. When Bursa was under Greek occupation, Aziz Nuri was named the deputy governor of Bursa by the Greeks. After the Kemalist victory, he left for Egypt and then Greece. From Turkish intelligence sources, we know that he was in Amman, Jordan, in 1933 and Pire, Greece, in 1937.[190] He did not return after the amnesty; however, he wished to establish contact with Mustafa Kemal before his death.[191]

(41) Former Bursa Mufti Ömer Fevzi: He was of ulama background and an LE politician. After the Treaty of Sevres in 1920, he became the mufti of Bursa, where he opposed the nationalist struggle. Along with Aziz Nuri (see above), Ömer Fevzi tried to form an anti-Ankara organization but failed. The nationalists arrested him and exiled him to Kütahya. After the Greek occupation of Bursa, he returned and worked for the Greek military forces. He died in Egypt before 1933, for his name was listed as "deceased" by a Turkish intelligence report.[192]

(42) Former Advisor to the Qadi of İzmir Ahmet Asım: He spent his exile years in Gümülcine and İskenderun and died in Greece on June 14, 1928.[193]

(43) Former İstanbul Guardian Natık: According to daily *Tan*, he was one of the first (and most stubborn) opponents of the CUP, which exiled him to Salonika, Greece.[194] After the CUP fell, he returned and became the guardian of İstanbul. He died in Egypt before 1933.

(44) Former Minister of Interior and member of the Ayan Chamber Adil: He was born in 1867 in İstanbul and died in Bucharest. We do not know when he died.[195]

(45) Former Minister of Interior Mehmet Ali: He was a graduate of Galatasaray Mekteb-i Sultanisi, a school that produced many high-level Ottoman bureaucrats. After graduation, Mehmet Ali was appointed to the sub-governorate (*mutasarrıflık*) of Beyoğlu, İstanbul. After World War I, he was instrumental in the reestablishment of the LE, and when Damat Ferit Pasha formed his first government, he became the mail and telegram minister. After the ministry was abolished, he became the minister of interior. It has been rumored that his British wife played a role in this appointment.[196] He was given credit for convincing Damat Ferit Pasha and Vahdettin to appoint Mustafa Kemal to Anatolia, an event that marks the beginning of the Turkish War of Independence in 1919. There are plenty of references to the friendship of Mehmet Ali and Mustafa Kemal prior to the War of Independence.[197] However, soon after the formation of the Anatolian movement that culminated in the Ankara government, Mehmet Ali became hostile toward Mustafa Kemal and the Ankara Circle. He became an honorary member of the Association of the Friends of England.[198] According to Sedat Bingöl, Mehmet Ali Bey was the leading figure abroad in the opposition to Ankara.[199] Bingöl arrives at this conclusion based on the bold statements that Mehmet Ali invoked to refer to Mustafa Kemal, such as "illegal leadership" (gayri kanuni riyaset) and "dictator."[200] In fact, when in Paris, Mehmet Ali published a newspaper, *La Republique Enchainee* (The Republic in Chains), where his attacks on Ankara were more pronounced.[201] Turkish intelligence sources report that even as late as 1937, Mehmet Ali was conspiring to stir up a rebellion among lower-ranked officers in Turkey against the regime.[202] Interestingly, despite all his misgivings against the Ankara government, Mehmet Ali took advantage of the amnesty and returned to Turkey, where he died on October 16, 1939.

(46) Former Deputy Mayor [of İstanbul] and Governor of Edirne Salim: He was born in Varna in 1867 and graduated from the School of Civil Service. He became a member of the LE and was appointed to Edirne as the governor. Salim carried the administrative title "pasha." In Edirne, he took an anti-Ankara stance. Kamil Erdeha informs us that after a community meeting on October 6, 1919, with regard to Edirne's position toward the nationalist forces, sensing the great support for the nationalists, he secretly left that night for Karaağaç under Bulgarian occupation.[203] Between April 18 and December 2, 1920, he served as the deputy mayor of İstanbul.

(47) Sub-governor of Kütahya for the Greeks Hoca Rasihzade İbrahim: He was included in the list for he agreed to serve as sub-governor (*mutasarrıf*) of Kütahya. We know that he was on the island of Midilli in Greece in 1933 and 1937. According to police records, with his wife he owned a grocery store in a poor neighborhood of Midilli and was quite poor and in need.[204] His name was listed under those who returned to Turkey after the amnesty.[205]

(48) Adana Governor Abdurrahman: He was born in Baghdad and served as the member of the city council of Adana in 1919. He became a governor of Adana under French occupation and served from June 1 to December 20, 1920. In this capacity, Abdurrahman tried to silence the nationalist resistance in the area. However, when the French withdrew from the region, he left with them. In 1933, he was in Paris, and in 1937, the police reports locate him in Beirut.[206] After the amnesty, he returned and took the surname "Paksoy." Abdurrahman returned to İstanbul after the amnesty in 1938 but died in Adana.

(49) Former Karahisar-ı Şarki Representative Ömer Fevzi: He was a member of LE in the 1908 parliament and was exiled by the CUP after the infamous Mahmut Şevket Pasha assassination in 1913. After the CUP period, he entered the Ottoman parliament from Tokat. As an experienced LE politician, he opposed the Ankara government, for which he was listed among the 150ers. After the War of Independence, he left for Egypt. In 1937, he was in Syria.

(50) Lieutenant Adil the Torturer: He was a graduate of the Military Academy and was known his torture sessions inflicted on the members of the nationalist forces in İstanbul. After the Kemalist victory, he was spotted in Gümülcine (Komotini), Greece, in 1937, and his name was not listed under those who returned after the amnesty.

(51) Lieutenant Rıfkı the Torturer: Coming from the same background as Adil, he too was involved in the torture of Kemalists. He was a caricaturist, drawing for *Aydede* magazine, which was in opposition to Ankara. His drawings were always anti-Ankara. In 1933 and 1937, he was in Cairo working for a newspaper also as a caricaturist and making a good living.[207] He died in Cairo, possibly in 1944 or 1945.[208]

(52) Former Kırkağaç Sub-governor Şerif: He was born in 1883 in Manisa and graduated from the School of Civil Service in 1907. After several administrative appointments, he became the sub-governor (*kaymakam*) of Kırkağaç. He was placed on the list because of his cooperation with the Greek forces when Kırkağaç was under Greek occupation in 1919. In 1933, Şerif was reportedly in Rhodes, and his name does not appear on the list of those who returned to Turkey.

(53) Former Çanakkale Sub-governor Mahmut Mahir: He was born in 1858 in Berat to a family of Albanian origin. Having graduated from the School of Civil Service in 1888, he served in several low-level administrative and teaching posts. During the Second Constitutional period (1908–1918), he became a sub-governor; however, the CUP forced him into retirement. After the CUP regime fell, he returned to civil service and became sub-governor of İzmit on March 9, 1919, and later of Afyonkarahisar. During his appointments in Anatolia, he opposed the nationalist forces. On September 17, 1919, Mahir was arrested by the Ankara forces and was released. He was on the list because of his cooperation with the enemy as sub-governor of Çanakkale. Later, he escaped to Albania, where he died before 1933.

(54) Former Head of the İstanbul Central Command Emin: A graduate of the Military Academy, Emin was forced for retirement by the CUP when he was at the rank of full colonel. However, Damat Ferit Pasha brought him back from retirement and appointed him to the post of the İstanbul Central Command with the rank of brigadier general. The İstanbul Central Command was the place for the persecution and torture of Ankara supporters. Therefore, he was included in the list with the insistence of the members in the TGNA. Emin Pasha was among those who left the country for Egypt. He died on December 20, 1931, in Alexandria.

(55) Kilis Sub-governor Sadullah Sami: He was a medical doctor and served as a sub-governor under the French occupation, after which he left for Aleppo. We know that after the amnesty, he applied to return to Turkey several times. The latest police report indicates that he was given permission to enter Turkey on June 11, 1957. However, we do not know if he did go or where he died.[209]

(56) Former Counselor for the Ministry of Interior and Bolu Sub-governor Osman Nuri: He was born in Bulgaria and studied law. During and after World War I, Osman Nuri served as an administrator in different parts of western Anatolia. His appointment to Dersim on

September 8, 1919, was prevented by Mustafa Kemal. The Kemalist forces sent Osman Nuri back to İstanbul. On April 29, 1920, he was appointed to Bolu, where he supported the anti-Ankara rebellions of Düzce. Furthermore, he organized a militia 2,000 strong to attack the nationalist forces and later helped organize the caliphal army in Bolu. However, when the Bolu-Düzce rebellion that he supported failed, Osman Nuri escaped to İstanbul on May 24, 1920. After the War of Independence, he left for Bulgaria, where he published articles in a number of Turkish-language newspapers. He returned to Turkey after the amnesty, but the year of death is unknown. Interestingly, his name was not in the original list of the 150ers that was prepared by the government. However, he was included in the list as a result of the warning from some deputies.

This group of people were mainly middle- and high-level administrators who did not support the Ankara movement. Some of them collaborated with the Allied Powers as local administrators. Many of them came from an LE background and were staunch opponents of the CUP and later the Ankara movement. However, most of them remained neutral in exile and returned home after the Amnesty.

Ethem "The Circassian" and His Associates

(57) Ethem the Circassian: He was born in 1887 in Bandırma. Coming from a Circassian family, he grew up in a farm and did not have a formal education. After a brief military training, he became a warrant officer (*gedikli erbaş*). He entered the service of the Secret Organization (*Teşkilat-ı Mahsusa*), Ottoman special forces, under the Ministry of War. During the War of Independence, he joined the nationalist forces and was regarded highly for his military service to Ankara. His one-time "hero" status sets him apart from other members of the 150ers. Ethem was in fact a valuable member of the Ankara Circle, instrumental in suppressing many rebellions against the Kemalists in Western Anatolia and destroying the caliphal army.

His standing changed with his refusal to submit to the authority of Ankara's regular army, which was formed on November 8, 1920, and to go under the command of İsmet Bey (İnönü).[210] On May 9, 1921, Ethem and several of associates were tried by the Independence Tribunals for his rebellion against the Ankara government and sentenced to death in absentia.[211] There is much literature produced about his rebellion against the Ankara Circle and subsequent defeat by the nationalists on January 22, 1921.[212] A controversial account of his activities is his alleged service to the Greek army. As mentioned above, however, the government was not confident that this charge would be proven without a doubt.[213] Therefore, as opposed to revoking his citizenship based on his service to the Greek military, he was put on the list of the 150ers.

Ethem left Turkey before the publication of the names of the 150ers. We know that he participated in the Circassian Congress of İzmir in 1921. He must have left Turkey by the end of 1922 with the withdrawal of the Greek army.[214] After Athens, Ethem resided in Germany and Lausanne during 1923–1924. Afterward, he was on the move, living briefly in Athens and Mosul. In 1926, Sedat Bingöl, referring to the Directorate of General Security Archives, claims that Ethem was in Baghdad, Kirkuk, and Aleppo, working closely with French and British authorities, to incite rebellion among the Kurds in Turkey.[215] As mentioned before, his anti-Ankara activities are a matter of controversy.[216] After the amnesty, Ethem refused to return to Turkey and died in Amman, Jordan, on September 21, 1948.

(58) Ethem's Brother Reşit: He was Ethem's older brother. Unlike Ethem, he graduated from the Military Academy and joined the CUP. Like his brother, he was recruited for the special forces. At the end of World War I, he resigned from the army and became a farmer. However, he was elected to the Ottoman parliament from Saruhan (Manisa) on January 12, 1920. After the dissolution of the Ottoman parliament, he joined in the TGNA. After his brother's revolt against Ankara, Reşit was sent to Ethem to convince his younger brother to submit to the authority of Ankara. However, he joined in his brother's rebellion. Therefore, he was expelled from parliament on January 8, 1921.

After the suppression of the Çerkez Ethem rebellion, Reşit followed his brother and left for Greece and later Jordan. However, unlike his brother, Reşit returned following the amnesty in 1950 and died in Bandırma on September 10, 1951.

(59) Ethem's Brother Tevfik: He was born in 1879 and graduated from the Military Academy in 1902. He was a member of the CUP; however, after World War I, Tevfik retired to his family farm with his brother Reşit. When İzmir was occupied by the Greek forces on May 15, 1919, he joined his younger brother Ethem and worked for the formation of the nationalist forces (*Kuvva-yı Milliye*). Tevfik was one of the commanding officers in Ethem's irregular mobile forces (*Kuvva-yı Seyyare*) and remained loyal his brother against the Ankara government during Ethem's rebellion. With his brothers, he left

Turkey after the suppression of the rebellion and spent his exile years in Greece and Jordan. After the amnesty, he returned immediately to Bandırma, where he died on June 20, 1946.

(60) Kuşçubaşı Eşref: He was born in 1873 in İstanbul and graduated from the Military Academy in 1898.[217] He took responsibilities in the special forces under the CUP and served in India, Central Asia, the Balkans, and the Arabian Peninsula. During World War I, Eşref (Sencer) participated in the failed sabotage attempt against the British interests in the Suez Canal in February 1915 and was captured by the British forces when he was fighting against the Arab forces on the Arabian Peninsula in January 1917. After his internment in Malta, he returned to Turkey in 1920 and joined the nationalist forces. He was instrumental in providing a safe passage for the nationalists in their flight from İstanbul to Ankara and the transformation of weapons for the nationalist forces.

Eşref collaborated with Ethem and left the country with Ethem and his brothers for Greece. Because of his association with the Ethem forces, he was listed among the 150ers. However, a document in the Prime Minister's Republican Archives reports that on July 5, 1921, Eşref and associates were cleared from the charge of supporting Ethem's rebellion.[218] This information seems to contradict the charges against him, but nevertheless he was included on the list. In exile, Sedat Bingöl points out that Eşref and Ethem had their own differences in the 1930s.[219] In exile, Eşref sent several letters of forgiveness to Mustafa Kemal and İsmet Pasha in 1936.[220] After the amnesty, he returned to Turkey in 1955 and died there in 1964.

(61) Kuşcubaşı Eşref's brother Hacı Sami: He was the younger brother of Eşref and did not have a formal education. Like his brother, he worked for the special forces in Afghanistan, Turkistan, Kirgizstan, and the Sinjan region of China. After World War I, he joined Enver Pasha in Tajikistan. When Enver Pasha was killed by the Bolshevik forces on August 4, 1922, Sami took charge of the Turkish forces in Central Asia.[221] Emin Karaca claims that Sami wanted to return to Turkey in 1924 but was not allowed to because he was on the list of 150ers. He then left for Greece and joined his brother.[222] Karaca points out the inconsistency of Sami's inclusion in the list by stating that Sami was in Central Asia fighting against the Bolsheviks from 1914 to 1924 and hence was not in a position to collaborate with the enemy, concluding that his former rivals in Turkey unjustifiably included him on the list.[223]

Kamil Erdeha claims that Sami was killed on August 27, 1927, in Madran (in Aydın) when he entered Turkey to assassinate Mustafa

Kemal. Emin Karaca suggests that the assassination claim was only a fabrication planted by the Greek government and gives the date of his killing as August 3, 1927.[224]

(62) Former Akhisar Commander Captain Küçük Ethem: He was under the command of Ethem in the mobile forces and left for Greece with him. In September 1934, he became a Greek citizen but returned after the amnesty.

(63) Düzce'li Sami "Aço Fumpat": He was of Circassian origin and a graduate of the Military Academy. He was aide-de-camp to Ethem's brother Tevfik. After the amnesty, he returned to Turkey and died in Düzce on April 17, 1946.

(64) Burhaniye'li Halil İbrahim.

(65) From Susurluk Demirköprü'lü Hacı Ahmet: Both Halil İbrahim and Hacı Ahmet left the country with Ethem for Greece and died before the amnesty in Syria.

Delegates in the Circassian Congress

This group was listed in the 150ers because of their participation in the Circassian Congress in İzmir on October 24, 1921. This congress brought together many notable people of Circassian origin who stated their secessionist intention in a Declaration for the Association for Providing the Rights of Near Eastern Circassians (Şarki Karib Çerkesleri Temin-i Hukuk Cemiyeti)[225] to the Great Powers and the world. The anti-Ankara sentiments can clearly be observed in this declaration.[226] For example, the declaration claims that Turkish misgovernment was responsible for the stagnant Circassian population in the Ottoman Empire. The document suggests that the 2 million Circassians should have been 6 million. Because of the forceful Turkification policies of the CUP, the Circassian population did not grow to its potential. The nationalists in Ankara also forced and manipulated the Circassians to join them. However, as soon as the Circassians realized the Kemalist's antihumanitarian actions and defective politics (*gayri insani harekat* and *sakim siyaset*), they turned against them and united under the protection of the Greek government with the goal of living in peace under the "civilized government" of the Greeks.[227] The society was as critical of the Circassians who were in the service of the İstanbul government as they were of those who served Ankara (such as Rauf Orbay). Therefore, the member of the society was included in the 150ers not because of their service to the İstanbul government but because of their association with the Greeks and their potential to revolt against Ankara.[228] In this section of the 150ers list, there are 15 names out of 17 who were the founders and administrators of the Association for Providing the Rights of Near Eastern Circassians. Only Colonel Ahmet and Sefer Hoca were among the 150ers but were not listed as the founders and administrators for the society. Conversely, 10 of the founders of the society were not included in the list. We do not know why all the founders of the Circassian society were not part of the list and where the other two names came from. We do know that the president of the society, Talustan Bey, was not included in this list. Other than their mundane activities, not much useful information exists on the members of this group in the DGSA archives.[229]

(66) Bağ Osman.
(67) Former İzmit Sub-governor İbrahim Hakkı.
(68) Brau Sait.
(69) Berzek Tahir.
(70) Maan Şirin.
(71) Hüseyin, son of Koca Ömer.
(72) Bağ Kamil.
(73) Hamete Ahmet.
(74) Maan Ali.
(75) Harun-ür-Reşit.
(76) Eşkisehirli Sefer Hoca.
(77) Bigalı İsa, son of Nuri Bey.
(78) Kazım.
(79) Lampaz Yakup.
(80) Kumpat Hafiz Sait.
(81) Retired Lt. Colonel Ahmet.
(82) Attorney Bazadurug Sait.
(83) Şam'lı Ahmet Nuri.

Police

This group of people was selected mainly because of their cooperation with the occupying forces as police. They were instrumental in arresting and prosecuting the members of the nationalist forces in their regions.

(84) Former İstanbul Chief of Police Tahsin: He was born in Kalkandelen and was a member of the LE. Damat Ferit appointed him to the post of İstanbul's chief of police. In this post, he worked closely with British authorities against the nationalists, for which he was known as Gavur Tahsin, or Tahsin the Infidel. In 1933, Turkish intelligence reports locate him in Paris, being married to woman of Dutch origin. In 1937, he was in Holland. After the amnesty, he returned to Turkey on July 30, 1938, but went back on August 13, 1938. We know that he was stripped of his citizenship in 1939 and became a Dutch citizen in 1965.[230]

(85) Former İstanbul Deputy Chief of Police Kemal.

(86) Deputy Director for General Security Isparta'lı Kemal.

(87) Former Director of First Division (Political Crimes) of İstanbul Police Şeref.

(88) Former Inspector in the First Division (Political Crimes) of İstanbul Police Hafız Sait.

(89) Former Arnavutköy Police Officer Hacı Kemal.

(90) Police Inspector Namık.

(91) Şişli Commissar Nedim.

(92) İzmit Police Officer, Edirne Police Chief and Yalova Sub-governor Fuat: He left Turkey for Egypt in 1921. He was in Syria in 1922, working for French authorities. According to a police report dated November 12, 1936, he approached the Turkish consulate in Aleppo and requested employment in the Turkish intelligence, and he was hired to collect information about the 150ers in exile.[231]

(93) Adana Chief of Police Yolgeçen'li Yusuf.

(94) Former Unkapanı Police Officer Sakallı Cemil.

(95) Former Büyükdere Police Officer Mazlum: After Ankara's success, he took refuge with the British and lived in Greece. After working for British intelligence for some time, he moved to Java under the Dutch mandate. After the amnesty, Mazlum did not return.

In Şaduman Halıcı's MA thesis, there is some additional inconsequential information available on these former police officers.[232]

(96) Former Beyoğlu Deputy Commissar Fuat.

Journalists

Journalists in this group were vocal in their suspicion and, subsequently, opposition to the Ankara Circle. Their loyalty to the İstanbul regime was considered a threat by Ankara, and consequently these journalists were included in the list. This group clearly demonstrates the arbitrariness of the selection process, as many other oppositional journalists were not part of it.

(97) The Owner of *Serbesti* Newspaper, and the Member of the LE Mevlanzade Rıfat: He was of Kurdish origin from present-day Iraq, but he spent most of his life in exile. He was first exiled by Abdulhamid II with the suspicion that Rıfat was loyal to former sultan Mehmet Reşat V and returned from his first exile in Yemen in 1908 when the CUP reestablished the constitutional monarchy. On his return to İstanbul, he published *Serbesti*, a newspaper in which he published articles criticizing the CUP. His second escape from the empire comes on April 22, 1909, when the March 31 Incident[233] took place. This time, his place of exile was Paris, where he took part in the anti-CUP Islahat-ı Esasiye-yi Osmaniye Cemiyeti (Society for the Reform of the Fundamentals of the Ottoman Empire). We know that he also spent time in Egypt and Greece.[234] His return from his second exile coincides with the formation of the LE, which he joined. Halil Menteşe, in his memoirs, states that Rıfat was sued by Mustafa Kemal with the accusation that he insulted him.[235]

Mevlanzade Rıfat was involved in Kurdish nationalist activities after World War I; however, his inclusion in the list was due not to his Kurdish nationalist activities but rather to his stand against the Ankara movement. Mevlanzade Rıfat was critical of the CUP and the Kemalists in his *İttihat Terakki İktidarı ve Türkiye İnkılabının İçyüzü*.[236] This opposition earned him a place among the 150ers, and he left Turkey for the third time for Aleppo, Syria.

From Ottoman and British sources, we know that Mevlanzade Rıfat was involved in Kurdish nationalist activities, especially during the final years of the Ottoman Empire.[237] Some sources also report that he visited Sultan Vahdettin in San Remo as a Kurdish revolutionary.[238] However, Turkish intelligence reports surprisingly indicate that he was employed by Turkish intelligence. Sedat Bingöl, in his study of the 150ers, points out a document that clearly indicates his activities as a spy for Turkey. In 1930, Mevlanzade Rıfat informed Turkish authorities (possibly the Turkish consulate in Athens) that he planned to write pro-Turkey articles on the activities of the 150ers in exile, of the Kurdish nationalist Hoybun organization, and of the Armenians. However, the Turkish authorities asked him not to publish such articles, as it would blow his cover as a Turkish agent.[239] However, Mevlanzade Rıfat died before he received this information on September 12, 1930.

(98) The Owner of the Turkish Language *İstanbul* Newspaper Sait Molla: Born in 1882, he was of madrasa origin and from the ulama class. He became a member of the *Şura-yı Devlet* (Council of State) and was an active member of the LE. In May 1919, Sait Molla became the chairman for the Association for the Friends of England and published numerous pro-England articles in his newspaper *İstanbul*. When his letters to Rahip Frew, a British agent, were confiscated by the Kemalists, he was accused of being a British agent, a charge he refused.[240]

After the conclusion of the War of Independence, in 1922 Sait Molla left the country with a British passport for Romania and later Egypt. He was reported to send letters to Turkey informing Turkish authorities of the activities of the fellow 150ers in Egypt.[241] In May 1925, he was in Cyprus, where he continued to publish articles criticizing the Ankara regime and corresponding with Britain. In one of the letters, Sait Molla described the Ankara regime as a "poisonous snake" in the Islamic world.[242] On June 6, 1930, he left Cyprus for Paris but arrived in Athens three days later. His reason for this diversion seems to be his desire to meet with Venizelos, the Greek prime minister, for giving permission to his fellow 150ers stay in Western Trace. However, Venizelos did not meet with him. Sait Molla did not have a chance to proceed to Paris and died in Athens on July 14, 1930.

(99) The Owner of and Columnist for the *Müsavat* Newspaper in İzmir and the Member of the Council for the Sheikh al-Islam, İzmir'li Hafız İsmail: Born in İzmir, he received a madrasa education and became a Quran reciter (*Hafız*). His appointments in the Ottoman bureaucracy included head clerk of the Immigration Directorate and of the Council for the Sheikh al-Islam. He remained in this post until November 4, 1922. He was a sympathizer of the LE and published articles critical of Ankara. In 1919, in a sermon in the famous Ayasofya Mosque, he reportedly described the CUP as "those who do not fully embrace Islam" and "those who was responsible for forced migration and killings."[243] No need to state that Hafız İsmail Hakkı considered the Ankara movement a part of the CUP. After Ankara's success, he left for Egypt, where he continued to publish his newspaper, *Müsavat* (Equality). He died before 1933.

(100) The Owner of *Aydede* Newspaper and Former Director of Mail and Telegram General Directorate Refik Halit: He was born on March 2, 1888, in İstanbul.[244] His father, Mehmet Halit, was a known member of the Mawlawiyya (Mevlevi) Sufi *tariqa*.[245] He studied at the Galatasaray Lycee and trained as a lawyer. During several lower-level bureaucratic appointments in the Ministry of Finance and the İstanbul Municipality, Refik Halit stood apart among his CUP-oriented coworkers. Because of the assassination of Mahmut Şevket Pasha, a CUP-backed prime minister, on June 11, 1913, he was sent to exile to Sinop and later to Çorum until 1918. On his return, he officially entered the LE, and consequently, during the third Damat Ferit Pasha government on March 12, 1919, he was appointed as director of the Mail and Telegram General Directorate.[246] After a brief interval, because of a cabinet change, he was appointed to the same post for a second time on April 5, 1920.

Refik Halit was better known as a journalist and author. He worked for and published several newspapers, including *Servet-i Fünun, Tercüman-ı Hakikat, Son Havadis, Muhit, Fecr-i Ati, Kalem, Vakit, Tasvir-i Efkar, Zaman, Cem, Şerah, Alemdar, Peyam-ı Sabah, Peyam,* and *Aydede*. His publications always carried a tone of opposition, first to the CUP and then to Ankara. However, he became a target for the Ankara Circle when he, as the director of the Mail and Telegram Directorate, refused to send the telegrams of the Anatolian resistance movement. This move gravely hindered the communication among the nationalists and became one of the reasons for his inclusion in the list of 150ers. His newspaper articles very clearly demonstrated his opposition to Mustafa Kemal and the disdain for the Ankara Circle. In his mind, the Ankara movement was the CUP. In one of his articles, he likened Mustafa Kemal to the CUP leaders; he wrote, "Cemal is gone," referring to the CUP leader Cemal Pasha, "but Kemal has emerged."[247]

As the Kemalists gained upper hand in the War of Independence and pushed toward İstanbul and especially after the killing of his close associate Ali Kemal, a former interior minister who was a keen opponent of the Ankara movement, Refik Halit left the country on November 9, 1922. When the list for 150ers were declared in 1924, he was already abroad. His exile years began in Beirut. In Aleppo, he continued to publish anti-Ankara articles. However, his articles in *Vahdet*, which began publication on May 18, 1928, became gradually more pro-Ankara and Kemalist reforms. His pro-Ankara articles in Hatay (Antioch) were instrumental in the transfer of this area from French-controlled Syria to the Turkish republic in 1939. It has been suggested that Refik Halit's activities in Hatay were the main reason for the amnesty law for the 150ers in 1938.[248] Refik Halit was one of the 150ers who openly admitted his opposition to Mustafa Kemal and the Ankara movement and apologized for it.[249] He returned to İstanbul in 1938 and remained there until his death on July 18, 1965.

(101) The Owner of *Adalet* Newspaper in Bandırma Bahriyeli Ali Sami: He was of a military origin, reaching the rank of full colonel. During the reign of Abdülhamit II (1876–1909), he became the photographer for the Ministry of Navy. After the March 31 Incident (1909), he escaped to Egypt until the fall of the CUP. Some writers suggest that Ali Sami was a member of Abdülhamit's secret police.[250] On his return, he settled in Badırma and published a newspaper, *Adalet*. In it, he published bold articles condemning and insulting Mustafa Kemal. For example, in one of his writings, titled "Anadolu İslamlarına Hitap" (An Address to the Anatolian Muslims), Ali Sami states that "Mustafa Kemal, who thinks nothing but to harm Islam, continues to drink the blood of Muslims."[251] Naturally, he was included in the list of 150ers. He chose Greece as his exile residence and was still alive in 1937, living in Athens. His name was not included in the list of those who returned to Turkey in 1938. Kamil Erdeha claims that Ali Sami plotted an assassination of Mustafa Kemal but failed.[252] Emin Karaca suggests that he converted to Greek Orthodox Christianity with his family.[253] He died in Athens on February 24, 1943.

(102) The Owner of the *Temin* Newspaper in Edirne and of *Hakikat* in Salonika, Neyyir Mustafa: He was born in 1883 in Edirne and graduated from the School for Civil Servants (*Mülkiye*) in 1907. He worked as sub-governor (*kaymakam*) in several places, including Adapazarı. In 1919, Neyyir Mustafa was appointed to the post of the director of statistics in Edirne and became a member of LE. As such, he was an ardent opponent of the nationalists and published anti-Ankara commentaries in his newspaper *Temim*. After Thrace was occupied by Greece on July 25, 1920, he entered the Greek parliament as a representative from Edirne.[254] Until 1941, he remained in Greece and published *Hakikat*. While in Greece, he became involved in the organizational activities of the Turks in Western Thrace, and his son Muammer was killed in the Greek civil war by the Greek militia. Following this event, Neyyir Mustafa returned to Turkey in 1941. The Democrat Party in Turkey courted him for the membership of parliament during the transition to the multiparty system after 1946, an offer he refused. He shied away from politics until his death in 1948.

(103) Former *Köylü* Newspaper Chief Columnist Ferit: He was from Crete and the editor of the *Köylü* newspaper. After the War of Independence, he left Turkey for Greece. We know that in 1937 he was in Athens and converted to Orthodox Christianity with his wife. He and his wife changed their names to Mihail Mihalisko and Marya, respectively. He remained in Greece and died there in 1945.

(104) The Owner of *Alemdar* Newspaper Refii Cevat: He was born in 1890 and was a son of Ali Muhittin Pasha, a high-ranking Ottoman civil servant. Refii Cevat (Ulunay) graduated from the Mekteb-i Sultani (Galatasaray Lycee), after which he became a journalist. Interested in politics, Refii Cevat joined the LE. During this time, he published the *Alemdar* newspaper. With the rise of the CUP and after Mahmut Şevket Pasha's assassination, he was exiled to Sinop and later Çorum along with some other LE members. When the CUP regime collapsed and its leader left the empire, in 1918 Refii Cevat returned to İstanbul and became an opponent of the Ankara movement.

After the War of Independence, he left for France. He spent his exile years in poverty and immediately returned to Turkey after the amnesty. After his return, he shied away from politics and wrote apolitical articles for newspapers. He died on November 4, 1968, in İstanbul.

(105) Pehlivan Kadri from *Alemdar* Newspaper: He did not have a formal education but worked as a reporter in several newspapers. Later, he became involved in politics and joined the LE. In 1912, he became a manager in the *Alemdar* newspaper, which was known for its support for the İstanbul Circle. After the assassination of Mahmut Şevket Pasha, he was sent to exile by the CUP along with several other LE members in 1913.[255] After the Mudros Armistice in 1918, he returned to İstanbul and continued working in *Alemdar*. He died before 1933.

(106) The Owner of the *Ferda* Newspaper in Adana, Fanizade Ali İlmi: He was born in 1878 and was one of three brothers of the Fanizade family who was included in the list of 150ers.[256] He received education in the field of literature. During 1918–1922, he published *Ferda*, an anti-Ankara and pro-French newspaper, in Adana.[257] He left Adana for Antakya (at the time, a region controlled by the French) in 1922 and returned to Adana after the amnesty in 1938. Ali İlmi died in İstanbul in 1964.

(107) One of the Owners of the *İrşat* Newspaper in Balıkesir, Trabzon'lu Ömer Fevzi: Ömer Fevzi (Eyüboğlu) was born in Sürmene, Trabzon, in 1884 and was trained as a lawyer. He was a member of the Trabzon Müdafa-yı Hukuk Cemiyeti (Society for the Protection of Rights, Trabzon), which was one of the original organizations revolting against the Allied invasion of the Ottoman Empire. He later joined in the Erzurum Congress (July 13, 1919), which contributed to the formation of the Ankara movement. However, Kamil Erdeha alleges that at the Erzurum Congress, he objected to Mustafa Kemal's leadership for his own ambition and greed.[258] A letter sent to the TGNA on April 15, 1925, by Ömer Fevzi explains his views of the nationalists. In the letter, Fevzi claims that he was included in the list for two reasons. First, he did not agree with some of the decisions taken at the Erzurum Congress. These disagreements were simply differences of opinion about how to form a strong resistance against the Allied invasion and the İstanbul government. Second, he published two or three articles in *İrşad*, condemning the bloody actions (*kanlı icraat*) of some bands that joined the nationalist movements before the formation of the regular army. These few articles, insisted Ömer Fevzi, were far from being evidence for this treason.[259]

We know that Ömer Fevzi left Trabzon in 1919 for İstanbul. After this date, he lived in Balıkesir. We do not know when he left Turkey for France. He wrote the previously mentioned letter from Marseille in 1925. He spent most of exile years in Paris and published *Rehber-i İnkilab* (Guide for Reforms). After the amnesty in 1938, he returned to Turkey, where he died in 1951.

(108) The Owner of the *Doğru Yol* Newspaper in Aleppo, Hasan Sadık: Although he was listed under the category of journalists, he was included in the list because of his service as police chief and public prosecutor in Gaziantep under the French occupation. In his exile in Aleppo, he published the newspaper *Doğru Yol* (The True Path) and was critical of Ankara. He died in İstanbul in 1949.

(109) The Owner and Director of the *Köylü* Newspaper, İzmir'li Refet: He was the last person added to the list because of his anti-Ankara publications. He spent most of his time in exile in Greece and several times requested amnesty from Ankara, and he returned after the amnesty in 1938.

Other Persons

This group includes many names that could not be placed in any other category. Most of these people were regarded as replaceable in the sense that, in the TGNA discussions, if any significant name were being proposed to be included in the list, the government would take someone from this group off the list. This is an indication that their threat was not considered as great as the others.

(110) Tarsus'lu Ramilpaşazade Selami.
(111) Tarsus'lu Kâmilpaşadaze Kemal.
(112) Süleymaniye'li Kürt Hakkı.

(113) İbrahim Sabri, the son of Mustafa Sabri Hoca.
(114) Industrialist Bursalı Cemil.
(115) British Spy Çerkes Ragıp.
(116) Haçin'li Kazak Hasan who serves as a French Officer.
(117) Bandit Chief Süngülü Çerkes Davut.
(118) Colonel Çerkes Bekir.
(119) Necip who is the brother-in-law of Industrialist Bursalı Cemil.
(120) Former İzmir Supervisor of Islamic Affairs Ahmet Hulusi.
(121) Madanoğlu Mustafa in Uşak: His name was added to the list by the insistence of some members of parliament. He was from Uşak and of landowning background. He was appointed to the sub-governorate of Eşme by the Greek occupation forces. After the War of Independence, he was arrested by the Ankara government and jailed. Later, in 1924, he was sent into exile because his name was included among the 150ers. He was the father of General Cemal Madanoğlu, who was part of the military coup on May 27, 1960.
(122) Remzi, son of Yusuf from Tuzakçı, Gönen.
(123) Zühtü, son of Hacı Kasım from Bayramiç, Gönen.
(124) Şakir, son of Kocagöz Osman from Balcı, Gönen.
(125) Koç Ali, son of Koç Ahmet from Muratlar, Gönen.
(126) Aziz, son of Mehmet from Ayvacık, Gönen.
(127) Osman, son of Balcılı Ahmet from Keçeler, Gönen.
(128) İzzet, son of Molla Süleyman from Ayyıldız, Susurluk.
(129) Kara Kazım, son of Hüseyin from Muratlar, Gönen.
(130) Arap Mahmut, son of Bekir from Balcı, Gönen.
(131) Gardiyan Yusuf from Rüstem, Gönen.
(132) Eyüp, son of Ömer from Balcı, Gönen.
(133) İbrahim Çavuş, son of Talustan from Keçeler, Gönen.
(134) Hüseyin, son of Topal Şerif from Balcı, Gönen.
(135) İdris, son of Topal Ömer from Keçeler, Gönen.
(136) İsmail, son of Kurh from Bolca Ağaç, Manyas.
(137) Canpolat, son of Muhtar Hacıbey, from Keçeler, Gönen.
(138) İshak, son of Yusuf from Kayapınar, Marmara.
(139) Sabit, son of Alibey from Kızlık, Manyas.
(140) Selim, son of Deli Hasan from Balcı, Gönen.
(141) Osman, son of Makineci Mehmet from Çerkes, Gönen.
(142) Kamil, son of Kadir from Degirmenboğazı, Manyas.
(143) Galip, son of Hüseyin from Keçidere, Gönen.
(144) Salih, son of Çerkes Sait from Hacı Yakup, Manyas.
(145) İsmail, brother of slained Şevket from Hacı Yakup, Manyas.

(146) Deli Kasım, son of Abdullah from Keçeler, Gönen.

(147) Kemal, son of Corporal Hasan from Çerkes, Gönen.

(148) Kazım Efe, brother of Kamil, son of Kadir from Değirmenboğazı, Manyas.

(149) Kemal son of Yallaç from Kızlık, Gönen.

(150) Mehmet, son of Tuğ from Keçeler, Gönen.

Many of these names are from the area where the caliphal army was active and where the Circassians were abundant. Madanoğlu Mustafa was included in this section, but he could have been included in the section that listed other sub-governors (section II.e). This section seems to include the least consequential names about whom almost no information is available.

CONCLUSION

In discussing the "opposition to Ankara," this chapter focused on a significant event, the 150ers, in early Turkish republican history and examined the backgrounds of these people who were labeled as traitors to their own people. The event is significant in that it demonstrated the nature of the earliest power struggle in the post–World War I era, after which the Ottoman Empire, the seat of the Islamic caliphate for over four centuries, collapsed and a new secular nation emerged. The conclusions of this chapter can be delineated as follows.

First, this study concluded that although some of the members on the list did oppose the Ankara movement, none of them possessed any meaningful political or military power to challenge the authority of the nationalists. In fact, some of them established contacts with Ankara and spied on its behalf in exile. This was a significant discovery because the main reason for the selection of the group members was that they posed a potential danger to the new regime. Turkish intelligence reports during their exile years clearly confirm that many of the 150ers were having a hard time making ends meet and did not have any real potential to topple the nationalist government. More important, Ankara was aware of the inability of some of them to pose any threat. Why, then, were these people selected? It is fair to say that the most significant aim for the Ankara government in making such a list was to set an example and to deter those wished ill on the new regime from conducting oppositional activities. The issue of who should be on the list was of secondary importance to the fact that such a list did exist.

This brings us to the next issue, that is, how the members of the list were selected. This study concluded that, in many instances, the list was arbitrary and that the number 150 was randomly chosen. No doubt, the opponents of the Ankara movement were much more numerous than 150. The number must have been seen by Ankara as respectable enough not to receive protests from the Allied negotiators yet sizable enough to capture the attention of the opponents of the new regime. One of the by-products of the Treaty of Lausanne for Ankara was the Allied recognition and confirmation of Ankara's authority over İstanbul. In this context, symbolically choosing 150 people would demonstrate that the Allied Powers could not protect the İstanbul Circle from Ankara.

The 150 names were categorized under 10 subsections. However, the only cohesive and objective section of the list was the delegates who signed the Treaty of Sevres.[260] For the other categories, many names were chosen hastily. No doubt, no name in the list was friendly toward Ankara in the intertreaty period (1918–1923). However, one can make a case for many other people who were opponents of the Kemalist regime and who wished its destruction. For example, some Kurdish nationalist leaders, such as Kamuran and Celadet Bedirhan and Seyyid Abdulkadir, were not included in this list.[261] However, some inconsequential Circassian nationalists were indeed part of it. Does this mean that Ankara considered Circassian nationalism more of a potential threat than Kurdish nationalism? We do not know for sure; however, ethnicity does not seem to play a large role in the preparation of the list. After all, the Kurds were more numerous and potentially more harmful for the nationalist nature of the new regime. The reason for a large Circassian group being included in the list may be that the Circassians were traditionally close to the Ottoman palace and that the Ankara Circle was nervous about their potential to ally themselves with foreign powers.

Another significant conclusion was about the labeling of these people. The list members, by definition, cannot be branded as traitors, for they were never part of the regime to betray. They subscribed to a more conventional remedy, that is, protecting the empire by cooperation with the victors after it was certain that World War I was lost. One should remember that these people were more the opponents of the nationalist movement than they were the proponents of the Allied invasion of the Ottoman Empire. In their eyes, the nationalists were the traitors to the Ottoman Empire. Therefore, a better term for these people could be the "opponents" of the emerging regime, not "traitors" of the nation.

Many in this group were highly suspicious of the possibility that the nationalists could defeat the Great Powers. Some, such as Refik Halit (Karay), immediately changed their opposition when they realized that the nationalist success was not a utopia.

When one examines the backgrounds of the 150ers, one notices that preexisting political—and, to an extent, personal—rivalries also contributed to the selection and prosecution of the 150ers. The reader who is familiar with the rise of modern Turkey readily admits the role of the CUP in the success of the new regime. Many in the Ankara Circle had past associations with the CUP, including Mustafa Kemal and other notable leaders. It is, therefore, not surprising that many 150ers came from the political platform of the LE, the main rival of the CUP on the Ottoman political scene. For example, many generals in the list were once pushed aside for retirement by the CUP government prior to World War I. Hence, they were already bitter about the CUP.

Many civilian members of the 150ers also carried with them a similar bitterness as they were sent into exile by the CUP after the CUP coup in 1913. These former civil servants of the Ottoman state lost their prestigious appointments in the state because of the CUP policies. It was inevitable that when the CUP lost power after World War I, these exiled LE members, who now manned the Ottoman government and bureaucracy, would be hostile toward those who were associated with the CUP. A study of the backgrounds of the 150ers clearly demonstrates that many of them considered the emerging nationalist movement as the "CUP in disguise." Those who were in the government were convinced that the Anatolian movement was designed by the CUP to topple the LE government. Therefore, it was almost reflexive to oppose it. They were not aware that the Ankara Circle consisted of an eclectic group of people and that the Ankara leadership, particularly Mustafa Kemal, also felt threatened by the hidden power of the CUP. As Chapter 4 will demonstrate, Mustafa Kemal would not hesitate to silence even his closest associates in Ankara (Kazım Karabekir, Ali Fuat, Refet, and Rauf) and to eliminate his potential rivals in the defunct CUP (such as Kara Kemal and Cavit).

We must also point out that the nationalists were keenly aware of the sentiment of the İstanbul Circle in recognizing Ankara as a part of the CUP. At the first session of the Sivas Congress on September 4, 1919, the issue was discussed. One of the participants in the Congress, İsmail Fazıl Pasha, pointed out that "those who oppose the nationalist movement portray us as part of the CUP; we cannot deny that such an accusation has harmful effects nationally and internationally. Therefore; I propose that the members of the Congress should swear on his honor and God's name that . . . he will not work for the restoration of the CUP."[262] Interestingly, during the deliberations, there were heated discussions about keeping the word "CUP" in the text. The decision was by no means unanimous, yet the majority wished not to mention the CUP by name in the swearing text, indicating that a degree of loyalty to the CUP existed among certain members of the congress.[263]

The issue of the 150ers represents the first stage in a process in which political opposition to the new government was silenced. This stage represents the successful elimination of the threat to the *legitimacy* of the Ankara government. It played a major role as a deterrent against vocalizing any opposition to the legitimacy of the Ankara government. However, when opposition to Ankara was silenced, opposition in Ankara commenced. The next chapter examines the power struggle within the Ankara Circle and the elimination of the political threat to the TGNA and of the intellectual threat posed by the journalists who were not part of the 150ers.

3

Opposition in Ankara: Transition to the Single-Party System

Thinking of all that he had gone through in the hard days, it was almost touching to see Mustafa Kemal Pasha's exuberant joy.

"After you take Smyrna, Pasha, you will rest, you have struggled so hard."

"Rest; what rest? After the Greeks we will fight each other, we will eat each other."

"Why should we?" I said. "There will be an enormous amount to do in the way of reconstruction."

"What about the men who have opposed me?"

"Well, it was natural in a National Assembly."

He had been talking in a bantering tone, but now his eyes sparkled dangerously as he mentioned the names of two men from the second group (the name of the opposition party in those days).

"I will have those lynched by the people. No, we will not rest, we will kill each other."

Halide Edib Adıvar, *The Turkish Ordeal*, 355[1]

This conversation, which must have taken place in 1922 between Halide Edib (Adıvar), one of the most influential women in the War of Independence, and Mustafa Kemal (Atatürk), the founder of the new Turkish Republic, was indicative of the period of the power struggle that was to follow the War of Independence. Mustafa Kemal was keenly aware of this fact and was readying himself for another battle on the political front. Halide Edib informs us that in that conversation, Mustafa Kemal, named Hafız Mehemmed (Mehmet) Bey, the ex-commissioner of interior, was executed in İzmir in 1926 by the new regime's Independence Tribunals. Halide Edib continues,

> Though I did not take these words seriously, they were symptomatic. We were at the beginning of the final realization of our dream. Was he going to use his power, a power achieved at the cost of such national sacrifice, for petty grudges? He deserved the highest price he could ask from the nation for his services; but his desire for revenge for political purposes expressed so early was nauseating. I looked at İsmet Pasha. He was eating his dinner quietly.
>
> "When the struggle ends," he continued, "it will be dull; we must find some other excitement, Hanum Effendi."[2]

Indeed, one of the most significant and consequential developments that shaped the nature and future of the Turkish state stems from the power struggle that took place in the early years of the new regime. As the above quotation indicates, Mustafa Kemal was conscious of this possibility. Among the respected figures who led in the War of Independence that ended in 1922, he was one of the earliest leaders who positioned himself for such a power struggle. There is not any doubt that Mustafa Kemal emerged as the supreme leader of the new state after an initial and relatively short period of a power struggle that lasted only five years between 1920, when the Turkish Grand National Assembly (TGNA) was inaugurated, to 1925, when a law called Takrir-i Sükun (Law on the Maintenance of Order) was passed. This law virtually eliminated any and all future opposition to Mustafa Kemal and to his inner circle. Throughout republican history, it has been regarded as the most significant example of authoritarianism that the Kemalists demonstrated during the early years of the republic. In the light of conclusive evidence, the Kemalists did not question the undemocratic and extrajudicial nature of the early Turkish Republic. Instead, they developed counterarguments suggesting that such heavy-handed policies were necessary to protect the infant regime.[3]

There are many questions, however, that remain unanswered. The most significant of these is the suspicion that events leading up to the Takrir-i Sükun and its immediate aftermath were manipulated or even perhaps manufactured by the Kemalists to silence the opposition. At the present, there exists no evidence to suggest that either the Sheikh Said Revolt of 1925, which seemingly paved the way for the Takrir-i Sükun, or the İzmir assassination attempt of Mustafa Kemal in 1926 was manufactured. But did the Kemalists manipulate or exaggerate the Sheikh Said Revolt to silence the political, intellectual, and possible popular opposition?

This chapter examines this question within the context of the Takrir-i Sükun. It also examines the consequences of this law preventing political opposition from taking root in Turkey. The lack of political opposition in Turkey, particularly in the years leading up to the death of Mustafa Kemal in 1938 and even until the transition to the multi-party system in 1946, proved to be significant for the adoption of the Kemalist reforms—reforms that gave the new regime its character.

For a more complete treatment of the subject matter, one should begin the investigation with the period prior to the Takrir-i Sükun. There were other laws in the Turkish penal code that helped silence the political opposition. Among those enacted in this vein, the most significant one was the Law on High Treason (Hıyanet-i Vataniye Kanunu), which was passed by the newly formed parliament six days after its formation. Let us briefly look at this law.

CREATION OF OPPOSITION AND LEGAL MANEUVERINGS TO ELIMINATE IT PRIOR TO THE TAKRIR-I SÜKUN

As a newly formed regime, the most immediate need for the TGNA was to establish its authority in the country. In order to achieve this, the TGNA immediately passed a law forbidding any opposition to the authority of the newly formed parliament.

The Law on High Treason (Hıyanet-i Vataniye Kanunu)

This law, number 2, was enacted by parliament on April 29, 1920, and remained in effect until 1991. The original stated intention of the law was to protect the office of the sultanate and the caliphate as well as the Ottoman territories. The law had 14 articles, but the first three reveal the nature of the law very clearly:

Article 1.

> Those, by means of publication, active participation or public speech, who oppose and undermine the legitimacy of the Grand National Assembly, which was formed to save the office of the exalted Caliphate and Sultanate and the Ottoman state, from the hands of foreigners are considered traitors.

Article 2.

> Those who commit the act of high treason will be executed by hanging . . .

Article 3

> Those who, by means of public speeches and religious sermons openly incite and encourage various people for high treason and those who commit these acts by these kinds of encouragement and other various venues, face temporary imprisonment. If these incitements result in disturbances, the inciters face the capital punishment.

Clearly, this law intended to establish the authority of the TGNA, which described itself as the defender of the office of the caliphate and the sultanate. The main aim of article 1 was to silence the political opposition outside the TGNA. For this reason, the bill passed parliament quickly and became the second piece of legislation that was enacted by this legislative body. After the new parliament established itself in Ankara—at the expense of the imperial İstanbul government—and especially after the separation of the office of the caliphate from that of the sultanate and finally abolition of the sultanate, the TGNA amended article 1 of the Law on High Treason on April 15, 1923. The new law, number 334, stipulated the following:

Article 1

> The first article of the Law on High Treason was amended as below.
>
> Those, by means of publication, active participation or public speech, who oppose and undermine the legitimacy of the Grand National Assembly . . . and those *who contest the law dated November 1, 1922 concerning the abolition of the sultanate,* [emphasis added] are considered traitors.

This amendment is the first indication that the emerging regime was readying itself for the offensive to eliminate not only the old regime but also, more important, those who criticized its decisions.[4] In other words, the original article 1 was limited in the sense that it included only those who questioned the legitimacy of the TGNA. The amendment broadened the scope of the opposition to parliament; it now included those who accepted the legitimacy but criticized its decisions. This is a significant departure, for it signaled the era that the TGNA protected its decisions by classifying any opposition as high treason.

Law number 334 was the last piece of legislation of the first TGNA; the next day, it dissolved itself. As it is known, the first TGNA afforded political opposition to its members and contained two opposing groups. The First Group was formed by Mustafa Kemal and his close associates, some of whom, after the collapse of the Second Group, formed a weak opposition in the second TGNA. The Second Group included more conservative-minded members and distinguished itself by openly challenging what they regarded as Mustafa Kemal's "one man leadership."[5] During the campaign season in the spring of 1923, Mustafa Kemal asked the First Group members to base their own campaigns on the Nine Principles (*Dokuz Umde*), which included the affirmation of the abolition of the sultanate yet confirmed its loyalty to the office of the caliphate.[6] Some people have suggested that the amendment made it impossible to challenge the First Group's program, for doing so could readily be interpreted as a crime that was described in the amended article 1.[7] This could be true only for the Second Group politicians, who wanted to base their campaign on the revival of the sultanate. However, not all Second Group politicians were in favor of the sultanate, as not all members of the First Group were anti-sultan. The Second Group members could have challenged the First Group on other grounds and campaigned over many other issues. It might be a contributing factor, but it seems unjustified to put the blame for the failure of the Second Group members in the elections entirely on the amendment in the High Treason Law.

This is not to say, however, that Mustafa Kemal Pasha did not push for the election of the First Group nominees. On the contrary, he was actively involved in the process through the speeches he made and the alliances he formed.[8] Mete Tunçay describes this election as "the guided elections" (*güdümlü seçimler*).[9] There is no question that Mustafa Kemal tried to control the election process and to influence the outcome. Nevertheless, this should not suggest that the elections were fixed since Mustafa Kemal hoped to defeat the Second Group at the ballot box.[10] Yet it is fair to state that the Second Group candidates suffered from the lack of a nationally organized party and a charismatic leader who demanded respect, as did Mustafa Kemal.

The elections for the second TGNA were clear indicators that Mustafa Kemal wished to have a parliament in which the opposition to his vision was minimal to say the least. For that reason, many First Group candidates were nominated by Mustafa Kemal himself. Maynard B. Barnes, an American consul and a delegate of the U.S. High Commission in Turkey, cites a conversation with an unnamed "prominent Turk" regarding the elections in Turkey. "You know of course," the unnamed Turks states, "that we do not really have elections in Turkey, instead we have nominations."[11] This statement hints at Mustafa Kemal's growing influence on the political landscape of Turkey.

In the end, virtually all members of the Second Group lost their seats; only three independent candidates were elected as the opposition. This election result enabled the Kemalist faction (the First Group) to control the TGNA entirely, and this also afforded Mustafa Kemal an extraordinary power, a kind that he did not possess during the tenure of the first TGNA. However, until the Takrir-i Sükun in 1925, some form of opposition, in addition to the three independent deputies, still existed within the ruling party, albeit it was less prominent than that of the Second Group.

The backbone of the opposition in the second TGNA came from the members of the First Group (later became Republican People's Party [RPP]). The inner-party disagreements finally resulted in the emergence of the first political party in the opposition under the name of the Progressive Republican Party (PRP; Terakkiperver Cumhuriyet Fırkası).

The Creation of the PRP as the First Opposition Party[12]

Differences in the second TGNA generally stemmed not from the content or the spirit of the laws discussed in parliament but rather from the methods employed to pass them. This was the main difference between the opposition in the first and the second TGNA. Most (though not all) members of the group that formed the PRP shared a political vision similar to that of Mustafa Kemal for the modernization of the state. Yet they were more responsive to the demands of the public and hence can be described as evolutionists. On the other hand, the other group, often regarded as the revolutionists, believed that there was no time to waste in introducing and promoting new reforms. People needed to be led, and the reforms, if possible, had to be forced top down for the good of the country. This line of thinking reminded the opposition in and out of parliament of the Young Turk period, in which the slogan "for the people, by the people" was replaced with "for the people, despite the people."[13]

The most visible example for the disagreement in parliament was, without a doubt, the declaration of the republic. As it was known, the republic was proclaimed on October 29, 1923, without any substantial discussion in the TGNA. The fact that such a significant decision as the labeling of the new regime was acted on by Mustafa Kemal and a small group of his ardent followers caused frustration and disappointment among many members of the opposition. Opposition leaders, such as Kazım Karabekir Pasha, Rauf Bey, and Ali Fuat Pasha, were not present or even informed of parliament's decision. Rauf Bey, a former prime minister and a political rival of Mustafa Kemal,[14] learned of the proclamation in İstanbul from the press. Upset that he was kept uninformed, he gave an interview to two İstanbul daily newspapers, *Vatan* and *Tevhid-i Efkar*, on this subject and criticized the government for acting hastily without proper consultation and discussions.[15] In response, the RPP called its members to a meeting in which Rauf's statements were discussed and Rauf himself was asked to explain his position. The general accusation that was leveled against Rauf Bey was that he was anti-republican and pro-sultanate, which continued to be the main slogan to taint his loyalty to the new regime.[16] When asked to state his position on record regarding republicanism, Rauf stated, "I am in favor of people determining their faith without any condition. [If] this is called republicanism and I am a republican (*Cumhuriyetçiyim*)."[17] Here, Rauf's qualification of republicanism based on the will of the people hints at his dissatisfaction with Mustafa Kemal and the radical elements who evoked democracy and republicanism but, Rauf feared, paid only lip service to them. It was not long after that Rauf became fully convinced of Mustafa Kemal's authoritarian tendencies.

In an editorial published in *The Times* of London, Rauf did not spare the word "dictator" to describe Mustafa Kemal. In a response to the accusations Mustafa Kemal leveled against Rauf Bey and his colleagues in PRP as traitors, Rauf wrote,

> To the editor of The Times
>
> Sir, I have read all the dispatches of your Correspondent in Constantinople concerning speech of the President of the Turkish Republic, Mustapha Kemal Pasha, who is at the same time the leader of the People's Party, and in all of them the Ghazi not only speaks of Kiazim Kara Bekir Pasha, Refet Pasha, Ali Fuad Pasha, and myself as persons who have not served during the struggle for independence, but also accuses us of having created difficulties and of having upheld the Sultanate, and thus tried to lead the country into anarchy. And he further accuses the Progressive Party, which we had formed with the express desire of establishing s serious democracy and of preventing a *personal dictatorship* [emphasis added], which at all times and at all places ends in

> national disaster, of being reactionary and of being the cause of the Kurdish Revolt [Sheikh Said Revolt of 1925].
>
> Mustapha Kemal Pasha, who has led the Turkish Army to victory in the struggle for national independence, has used the prestige and glory attached to his name to establish a *dictatorship* [emphasis added], and I see with regret that, in order to excuse and to show the necessity for the atrocities and corruptions of the last few years, he has falsified important historical events. I intended eventually to publish documents which will throw light on these events as they actually occurred. To-day there is no freedom of speech or conscience in Turkey; but if the Dictator will allow me to publish these documents and will publicly promise that the persons mentioned in them will neither be prosecuted nor killed, I shall be glad to do so in the Turkish press.[18]

These statements were made in 1927, when Mustafa Kemal had already established himself as the supreme leader with the authority to govern single-handedly. We do not know exactly when Rauf became convinced of Mustafa Kemal's "dictatorship."

In any case, the PRP was formed on November 17, 1924, by Mustafa Kemal's former close associates, including such prominent names as Ali Fuad Pasha (Cebesoy), Refet Pasha (Bele), Rauf Bey (Orbay), and Dr. Adnan Bey (Adıvar). Kazım Karabekir, not Rauf, became the president of the party. It is worth mentioning that just over a year earlier, on November 22, 1923, in the previously mentioned meeting in which Rauf Bey's loyalty to republicanism was questioned, he strongly stated that forming an opposition party was against the interest of the new state and that he would not establish any opposition party:

> I do not understand; do they [my opponents] wish me to establish an opposition party? I will not form an opposition party, because forming such a party conflicts with the high interest of the state. . . . Friends, I will not form a party. If you expel me from the party [RPP], I will go . . . but I will not form a party.[19]

Again, we do not know exactly when Rauf changed his mind before he fully committed himself to the establishment of an opposition party. The minutes of the Ankara Independence Tribunal that tried former CUP members in Ankara regarding the infamous İzmir assassination attempt of Mustafa Kemal in 1926 includes the testimony of Ahmet Emin Bey (Yalman), the head columnist of *Vatan*. In responding to a question, Ahmet Emin Bey mentioned that Rauf visited him on

October 15, 1924, and told him that he was interested in forming an opposition party.[20] However, the idea must have been discussed among the founders of the PRP earlier than this date.[21] There is no reason to believe that Rauf entertained the idea of forming a party prior to 1923. What is noteworthy here is the total reversal of his decision and of his reasoning within one year. This indicates his frustration with the rank and file of the RPP.

Mustafa Kemal's Attitude toward the Creation of the PRP

Historical records contain contradictory information regarding Mustafa Kemal's attitude toward the new opposition party. In their memoirs, some members of Mustafa Kemal's inner circle claim that he welcomed the idea of having an oppositional party in parliament, for it served the interest of democracy. For example, Kılıç Ali, a close associate of Mustafa Kemal, remembers that "the Ghazi responded positively to the emergence of an oppositional political party in the TGNA. However, he was suspicious of the intention of several high ranking military commanders when they together entered the politics."[22]

Mustafa Kemal may have been suspicious of the activities of his political rivals. However, we have a British archival source reporting to London of an interview that took place between Mustafa Kemal, as the president of the republic, and Maxwell Macartney, the İstanbul correspondent of *The Times* of London. This interview, which took place on November 21, 1924, is mentioned in a consular report sent to London on November 25, 1924, by Ambassador Ronald Lindsay, the British ambassador of Turkey. The consular report is most revealing with a postscript attached to Macartney's interview. In it, based on Macartney's description of the way the interview was conducted, the British ambassador includes his own assessment of Mustafa Kemal's reaction to the formation of the PRP. The postscript reads,

> If I have been wondering what the President will do next, here is an answer for me in this very remarkable document [the Macartney interview]. The Progressives are insincere in their republicanism, their programme is a fraud, and they are mere reactionaries. Everything reported implies that the President will have nothing to do with the new opposition, and his language to Mr. Macartney, not reported, and the tone of his remarks indicated clearly that *he meant war to the knife* [emphasis added]. The Ghazi worked himself into a perfect frenzy; he turned red in the face as he ticked off each

> member of the opposition in turn, characterizing them as ungrateful to himself, to whom they owed all, and traitors to their country. The deputy who acted at the interview as introducer and half as interpreter interrupted more than once, exclaiming: Be calm "Ghazi Pasha, do not be so indiscreet," but nothing could check the flood of indignation. Mr. Macartney has come away from Angora thinking that pistols will be going off in earnest in a very short time, and that Vassif and Nejati have left the government in order to come down to Constantinople at the head of a more businesslike Tribunal of Independence which will decorate the Galata Bridge with hanging of corpses.[23]

This report has been quoted by two scholars, Erik Jan Zürcher and Mete Tunçay. Both scholars indicate that Macartney complied with Mustafa Kemal's request and waited to publish the interview in *The Times*. Meanwhile, the Turkish newspaper *Hakimiyet-i Milliye* published it on December 11, 1924, albeit in a highly modified form.[24] After this, Tunçay, relying apparently on Zürcher, claims that *The Times* gave up on publishing the interview, for it lost its news value.[25] However, the interview was indeed published in *The Times* on December 18, 1924, without any mention of Mustafa Kemal's "frenzy."[26] Nor did any of the observations exist that were mentioned in Ambassador Lindsay's report. No explanation was offered for the discrepancy.

Even before this interview, Mustafa Kemal did not keep secret his thoughts about an opposition party in general. In a speech he delivered on September 20, 1924, in Samsun, Mustafa Kemal made his position very clear:

> Today we stand at the head of a clear-cut road. The distance covered is as yet too small to influence our plans. All positions must first acquire the necessary clarity and precision. Until that has happened, the thought of having more than one party is common partisanship and, ladies and gentlemen, from a point of view of order and safety of our country and nation the conditions to open the way for the establishment of more than one party have not been met yet.[27]

Although his close associates tried to soften Mustafa Kemal's position in relation to political opposition in their memoirs, there is sufficient evidence for us to believe that Mustafa Kemal did not approve of the formation of the PRP as a political opposition the leaders of which had the potential to replace his leadership.

One More Amendment

As the political realities in the new era changed, the TGNA felt the need to amend the very same article one more time with law number 556, which passed on February 26, 1925. The date coincides with the immediate aftermath of the Sheikh Said Revolt, the religious and Kurdish nationalist aspects of which are still being debated. However, one thing is hardly questioned, namely, that the Naqhsbandi facade and participation in the rebellion enabled the Kemalists to further pressure and silence the ulama, which, for centuries, established itself inside and outside the Ottoman state machinery.[28]

However, it was not only the religious establishment that was targeted. Law number 556 availed itself of any interpretation of political action that made direct or indirect references to religion. In other words, the law aimed at those who used religion as a platform for their discontent, those whose discontent centered around religion, and those who made any reference to religion for political gain. The amended article 1 included the following: "Formation of societies by using religion for political purposes is forbidden. Those who establish and become members of such organizations are considered traitors."[29]

This amendment afforded the Kemalists better opportunities to restrict their opponents' political moves. Since the majority of them came from "conservative" backgrounds and since religion was an integral part of their identity and of their political platform, the opposition lost its main justification to campaign for votes and to establish sustainable opposition in parliament. It is noteworthy to point out that when this amendment passed, the PRP was in parliament and overwhelmingly voted for the amendment. The amendment passed the TGNA immediately after the inauguration of the Sheikh Said Revolt without any objection. This rebellion, thus, served as a catalyst in the political process in which the opposition was silenced and the PRP closed down. Therefore, it is mandatory that we examine certain aspects of the rebellion.

SOME OBSERVATIONS ON THE SHEIKH SAID REVOLT AND ITS AFTERMATH

The Sheikh Said Revolt commenced on February 13, 1925, in Piran (later Dicle, administratively tied to Diyarbakır). The rebels quickly captured many towns in the region and came as far as Diyarbakır.

Initially, the rebels were successful in defeating several local military units; however, when the government mobilized and dispatched larger units, the rebellion was contained in two months. Sheikh Said and his 47 followers were tried and hanged on June 29, 1925.

This revolt has been regarded in republican history as one of the greatest internal challenges to the new Turkish state. However, at the same time, it is often postulated that the Sheikh Said Revolt provided Mustafa Kemal with the appropriate milieu in which to complete his radical reforms without any political opposition. According to Metin Toker, son-in-law of İsmet Pasha (İnönü), who became the prime minister at the time of the revolt, the new reforms were incompatible with the freedom that the Kemalists pledged. Hence, in order to eliminate the opposition and to introduce the reforms, the Kemalists postponed implementing democracy, and this revolt was instrumental in that regard.[30] We examine this proposition in greater detail, for it had significant ramifications for the future of the new Turkish state. But now, let us begin by making several observations about the revolt.

Since many publications have dealt with the narrative and nature of this rebellion,[31] I limit myself here by introducing some unexplored archival documents and making some observations regarding the revolt. Following these observations, I examine the timetable of the government's response to the rebellion, which is directly related to the subject under examination.

The first observation concerns the cost of the rebellion, which reveals clues about the financial impact of the revolt on the new regime. If the Turkish government fomented the rebellion in order to conspire against the newly formed political opposition, it would be reasonable to expect that a sufficient budget had been allocated to organize the rebellion. On this aspect, much conflicting information exists.[32] According to U.S. consular reports, which so far have not been utilized to study this revolt, the TGNA approved a budget of 10 million Turkish lira (US$5 million) for the arms purchases from Poland.[33] On March 27, 1925, the U.S. military attaché in Turkey stated in his report that "the Turkish Minister of National Defense told a foreign military attaché that the expenses of his department [for] the suppression of the Kurdish revolt would be 7.000.000 Turkish pounds [or lira, approximately US$3.5 million] up to the 1st of April."[34] Another U.S. report confirms this number, indicating the Turkish Joint Chief of Staff as its source.[35] The same figure of 7 million Turkish pounds was given, this time to the Italian military attaché. The U.S. observers seemed to be surprised about such a high expense for the suppression of the rebellion, for it seemed that the revolt was not a very successful one. However, the U.S. diplomats concluded that the Turkish minister or joint chief of staff had no reason to exaggerate.[36]

Another U.S. document informs us of the total figure of the cost. On August 27, 1925, Sheldon L. Crosby, the U.S. chargé d'affaires, relayed a valuable report by an unnamed U.S. military attaché to Washington. This report details the Turkish budget for 1925 and the estimated cost of the Sheikh Said Revolt.[37] According to this report, the budget for the fiscal year from March 1, 1925, to February 28, 1926, was 153,046,854 Turkish pounds (US$84,175,770), and the expenditure was 183,932,777 Turkish pounds (US$101,163,030), which created a deficit of 30,885,923 Turkish pounds (US$15,987,250).[38]Another report, titled "Cost of Suppression of Kurdish Rebellion," indicates that

> the [Turkish] government officially published ten million Turkish pounds as the cost of the suppression of the uprising. However, government officials now admit that the cost is twenty million pounds, and information comes from a reliable source that the cost is thirty million pounds. The latter estimate is believed to be nearer correct. The amount does include the pay and upkeep of the forces mobilized.[39]

These figures indicate that 16.3 percent of the total budget of the fiscal year 1925–1926 went to the suppression of the rebellion.

If the U.S. estimates on the cost of the rebellion were correct, then this figure nearly matched the budget deficit. By all accounts, the cost of 60,000,000 liras given by Süreyya Bedirhan seems to be an exaggeration, as was the estimation by Hamid Bozarslan, who claims that 35 percent of the total budget went to the suppression of this revolt.[40] In any case, the cost of the rebellion was an additional burden on the Turkish government. Accordingly, we can safely assume that the rebellion was a major reason for the budget deficit and that the government was unprepared for the revolt, at least financially. In other words, even if the Turkish government planted the rebellion, financially it was not prepared for it. However, this certainly does not mean that Ankara did not exaggerate and manipulate the rebellion in terms of its danger to the emerging state and its potential for a counterrevolution supported by the political opposition.

Another observation can be made regarding the British involvement in the rebellion. Here also, we can look at the U.S. consular reports, which include accounts regarding this issue. For example, reports in two files, numbers 867.00/1853 and 1855, inform us that the general belief in Turkey was that Sheikh Said had been on the British payroll from 1918 to 1922. This report hardly goes beyond informing Washington of the rumors circulating in Turkey; no conclusive evidence is available for this claim.[41] The Turkish side long maintained that the British incited the rebellion in order to get concessions on the Mosul issue.

On the other side, rather interestingly, some British archival sources make the opposite claim. One particular claim speculates that it was probably the Turks who planted the rebellion. Coming from a British intelligence analyst, this is an extraordinary allegation. If properly documented, this claim could certainly present the conclusive evidence that we have been seeking regarding the Kemalists' incitement of the revolt. However, the report does not go beyond speculation. We encounter this British report in FO 371/10867, in which James Morgan, a British intelligence analyst, speculates on the reasons why Turkey would support and benefit from the Sheikh Said Revolt:

> It is known that His Majesty's Government at *one time or another have interested themselves in a Kurdish State* [emphasis added], and a good portion of the inhabitants of the Mosul Vilayet are Kurds. The Turks seek to regain possession of the Mosul Vilayet partly because they do not wish the Kurds of that Vilayet to remain under British control, and in time to become the nucleus of an independent Kurdistan under British influence which would attract to itself Kurdish territories now under Turkish rule, or at least from a focus of dissatisfaction against Turkey to the Kurds inhabiting Turkey.
>
> If the present rising has been engineered by Angora and exists, attracting to itself, numerous "deserters" from the Turkish regular forces. We may hear that the successful rebels have determined to free their brothers in the Mosul Vilayet, and for that purpose have crossed the present frontier, aided by the deserting Turkish troops, in order to take possession of Mosul. If this were so, they would, on obtaining possession of the Mosul Vilayet, probably surrender to Turkey, leaving Turkey in possession of the conquered territory.
>
> Another possibility is that a successful rising in Turkey (countenanced by Angora) might be taken as a pretext for a rising of Kurds in Irak (also engineered by Angora) to throw off the Irak yoke and proclaim union with the Turkish Kurds, all ultimately submitting to Angora.

> A further possibility is that the rising may afford a pretext for a concentration of Turkish troops on the Irak frontier, who might ultimately find it their duty to pursue flying Turkish rebels across the Irak border.
>
> The [Turkish][42] government pretended to take the view that the movement is reactionary and due to certain influences playing on the religious instincts of the rebels. The attempt to use religion as a cloak for treason is strongly condemned. At the same time reactionary and religious movement afford the Government the opportunity of seeking out under cover of martial law of its opponents of whatever colour and of dealing with them. While martial law has not been declared in Constantinople, the idea has been mooted, and it may be that "Independence Tribunals" will again be set up there.[43]

First, it must be noted that this view was not uniformly accepted by British intelligence analysts.[44] Nevertheless, what is interesting about this report is that it reverses the Turkish claim that the Mosul issue was the primary motive for the belief that Great Britain incited or supported the Sheikh Said Revolt. This report suggests that the very same issue could be interpreted to support the opposite claim—that is, the Turks fomented the revolt for the control of Mosul. Incidentally, this report is also one of the rare ones by a British officer to solidly confirm the interest of the British government in establishing a Kurdish state.

However, James Morgan's "Memorandum" is particularly insightful, as it suspected that another reason for the Turks planting the revolt would be the elimination of the religious opposition. Here we should remember that this report was dated March 4, 1925, which was the same date as the passing of the Takrir-i Sükun in parliament. It is likely that the report was sent before the British had full knowledge of the content of the Takrir-i Sükun; this would certainly further validate the British suspicion that the rebellion could be used as a pretext to deal with the religious opposition. Furthermore, British analysts also entertained the possibility that the same revolt could be manipulated to silence the entire political and intellectual opposition in Turkey, not just the religious one. It must be repeated that there exists no conclusive evidence to substantiate the Kemalist instigation of the revolt. We have the court reports and eyewitness accounts regarding the trial of Sheikh Said.[45] We know that Sheikh Said did not make any such claim even after he was sentenced to death by hanging and not even during his execution. Therefore, for this claim, we have only circumstantial evidence and the fact that the revolt helped the Kemalists more than it did the Kurds. Nevertheless, I should make my position clearer on this subject. I do not claim that such a governmental plot did not exit; instead, I do point out that we lack "conclusive evidence" to prove it. Therefore, one should regard this conspiracy theory as plausible but a theory nonetheless.

D. A. Osborne, another British officer in the Foreign Office, informs us that even French authorities in Syria entertained the possibility that the revolt was "fictitious" or exaggerated. Osborne states, "We have seen in a telegram from Aleppo that the French authorities in Syria are inclined to regard the [Sheikh Said] rising as fictitious or largely exaggerated, which implies some ulterior purpose."[46] Foreign observers seem to agree that the government in Ankara was trying to exaggerate the rebellion; however, the question lingering in their minds was, for what purpose?

In order to look further into the circumstantial evidence in the exploitation of the rebellion for political gain, we should turn our attention to political developments in Ankara. For example, a close examination of the timetable of the revolt can shed some valuable light on the issue under examination, that is, the silencing of the opposition, which was embodied by the PRP under the leadership of Kazım Karabekir, Rauf (Orbay), and Ali Fuat (Cebesoy), all one-time close associates of Mustafa Kemal.

When the rebellion broke out on February 13, as was mentioned, the government was headed by the moderate Fethi Bey (Okyar). After assessing the urgency of the rebellion based on telegrams he irregularly received (due to the rebels cutting off the telegram lines), on February 23 the government declared a state of emergency for one month in the "rebellion territories" (*isyan bölgesi*).[47] Fethi Bey was able to collect somewhat sufficient information to prepare his first report to the General Assembly of the TGNA 11 days after the breakout of the rebellion.[48] In his speech, Fethi Bey described the rebellion as local and explained his government's policy in dealing with the rebels.[49] Ahmet Süreyya Bey (Örgeeveren), then a member of the TGNA and later a prosecutor of the Eastern Independence Tribunals that tried the Sheikh Said and his followers, is one of the most informative primary sources that deals with Ankara's response to this rebellion. In his memoir, Süreyya Bey remembers that prior to Fethi Bey's speech, Mustafa Kemal in private meetings showed a grave concern that the rebellion would spread nationwide (*memleketşumül bir durum ihdasına müsaid*).[50] Mustafa Kemal's concern was also documented in another source.

Kazım (Özalp) Pasha, the president of the TGNA, informs us of a meeting that took place in his office. We do not know the exact date of this meeting, but it must have taken place before March 3, 1925, when Fethi Bey resigned as the prime minister. Present at this meeting were Fethi Bey, Mustafa Kemal Pasha, and Kazım Pasha, who, in his memoir, remembered this meeting as follows: "Mustafa Kemal asked Fethi Bey in my room what kind of preparations the government has been undertaking [regarding the rebellion]. Fethi Bey responded, 'Rebels and inciters will be sent to military courts (*Divan-ı Harb*).' Mustafa Kemal was not satisfied and stated that '*the real inciters are hiding in different parts of the country. Do you not think that the government needs to expand its area of investigation*' [emphasis added]. Fethi responded, 'If you like, I can resign.'"[51]

Offering his resignation rather than complying with Mustafa Kemal's inquiry certainly suggests that Fethi Bey was not convinced of the president's argument. Then a striking question arises: Did Mustafa Kemal have better intelligence than that of the government on the rebellion, did he not share it with the government, or was he simply exaggerating? How is it possible that looking at the same data, Mustafa Kemal Pasha and Fethi Bey arrived at conclusions that were strikingly contradictory to each other? The Kemalist historiography tends to question the statesmanship of Fethi Bey in failing to immediately recognize the severity of the rebellion.[52] It seems highly unlikely that Mustafa Kemal would be able to collect better intelligence in such a short time (less than 10 days) to warrant his caution.

It is possible that Mustafa Kemal regarded this rebellion as the commencement of a nationwide counterrevolution and was extremely suspicious about it. Yet it is equally possible that he wanted to benefit from this "timely" rebellion to silence his critics and needed to exaggerate it. Rıza Nur, a former minister of health and a one-time close associate and later opponent of Mustafa Kemal, echoed a view to which many of Mustafa Kemal's opponents subscribed when he described the rebellion as "God-sent" to eradicate the opposition.[53] Here it should be mentioned that we lack conclusive evidence to subscribe to either possibility. However, we may have again circumstantial evidence that suggests that the Kemalists intentionally overestimated the strength of the revolt. For example, the known scale and strength of the rebellion in the first weeks did not justify the vigilance that Mustafa Kemal demonstrated. Fethi Bey's report to the TGNA clearly indicated that the Ankara government was convinced of the locality of the revolt and confirmed the ability of the military to crush it.[54] The U.S. consular reports also indicate that the Sheikh Said Revolt was not spreading.[55] In another report dated as late as April 8, 1925, the U.S. military attaché observes that "from a strictly military point of view, the revolt was never sufficiently widespread as to cause alarm, and the steady advance of the regulars [Turkish military], since the inception of their offensive, gives good reason to believe that order and tranquility will be restored in the near future except in certain mountainous regions."[56] The statement that "the revolt was *never* sufficiently widespread as to cause alarm" is also consistent with the position adopted by Fethi Bey and contradicts the hard-line position of the İsmet Pasha government, which came to power on March 4, 1925. As mentioned above, the exaggeration of the rebellion was also an alternate view of some British military analysts. D. A. Osborne at the Foreign Office, for example, suggested that "once the revolt broke out its seriousness may have been exaggerated to enable [Mustafa] Kemal to reinstate İsmet [İnönü] as Prime Minister and to institute a variety of repressive measures against the rising tide of criticism and oppression."[57] Osborne's assessment seems to be a valid one. Indeed, İsmet Pasha became the prime minister one more time as a result of this revolt.

Regarding the reliability of foreign sources concerning the rebellion, I must state that both British and U.S. intelligence were watching the rebellion closely and sharing information. Although some of their information came from Turkish sources, they had their own intelligence as well. Confidential reports to London or Washington were intended for internal use, not for propagating a view. Nevertheless, I found the U.S. consular reports to Washington particularly reliable for two reasons. First, the United States, unlike Britain, was not a party to any ongoing conflict, such as the Mosul issue. Second, U.S. reports took the pain of grading the information they gathered on the basis of its reliability. In many instances, the U.S. high commissioner in Turkey relayed the information with a warning that reliability of the information could not be confirmed. For that reason, the U.S. consular reports, in some instances, are more reliable than those of British and Turkish sources. Nevertheless, the historian must consider the possibility that these sources contained unintentional misinformation.

In any event, on March 2, 1925, the RPP, the party in power, met in a closed meeting to reconsider its position on the government's response to the rebellion. It was an extraordinary move since only several days before in a parliamentary session, Fethi Bey's program in suppressing the rebellion was overwhelmingly endorsed.[58] In the party meeting, Recep Bey (Peker), the spokesperson for the radical wing of the RPP, suggested that the government's response to the rebellion was inadequate and that harsh measures were necessary (*şiddet şarttır*).[59] Fethi Bey could not hide his astonishment at this move but responded,

> I am surprised by Recep Bey's objection [to the government's handling of the revolt]. Because, we inherited this last rebellion, which was the continuation of the previous Nasturi rebellion . . . , from Recep Bey. He was then the Minister of the Interior. At that time, he did not take any [concerned] measure. Now what is the reason for him subscribing to violence and anger (*tehevvür*)?[60]

To demonstrate the position of the PRP regarding the radicals' new move, an interesting newspaper article is noteworthy. Published on April 1, 1925, by the daily *Hakimiyet-i Milliye*, an RPP organ, the article mentions a speech by Kazım Karabekir, the leader of the opposition party: "Kazım Karabekir Pasha's speech astonished us. According to the respectful General, the government knew that a rebellion was in the making. Yet it did not do anything to prevent it in order to use it possibly as a pretext to crush the opposition party."[61]

The article does not specify where and when Kazım Karabekir made such statements; however, there is no reason to doubt that such an accusation was leveled against the government. What is significant here is that Kazım Karabekir's accusation matches that of Fethi Bey. Clearly, Kazım Karabekir, like Fethi Bey, was implying that the previous İsmet Pasha government ignored the warnings. Kazım Karabekir went further to boldly suggest that the government's aim was to silence the opposition.

Based on Fethi Bey's and Kazım Karabekir's statements, can one suggest that the Sheikh Said Revolt was purposefully allowed to happen? It is very tempting to respond to this question positively. After all, the same accusation came from the members of two opposing parties. However, we cannot go any further than to point out that the accusations come from different credible sources, yet they fall short of providing any hard evidence. What we can safely state is the following: the radicals in the RPP wanted to topple Fethi Bey's government, and they were encouraged by Mustafa Kemal to increase their criticism of this moderate government.

At this point, it is important to note that there were attempts by Mustafa Kemal and İsmet Pasha to tame the İstanbul press and the newly formed PRP with the accusation that the latter had intentionally incited reactionaries. Avni Doğan, a member of the TGNA, remembers a secret meeting requested by Mustafa Kemal in an RPP meeting. Doğan does not give us any specific date for this meeting but mentions that the next day the İsmet Pasha government resigned and that Fethi Bey formed the new government. He must have been referring to the date of October 21, 1924, for we know that İsmet Pasha resigned from his premiership on October 21 and that the next day Fethi Bey became the new prime minister. In this meeting, Mustafa Kemal shared his concern regarding the İstanbul press and the PRP—established *only three days* before this meeting on October 17, 1924. Mustafa Kemal began by stating,

> I invited you here to decide on a significant issue. Negative incitements (*menfi tahrikat*) in the country have reached dangerous levels. Propagation by the İstanbul Press and the PRP encourages reactionaries who have been hiding here and there. . . . Available laws are far from protecting our reforms and new Republic. . . . Even in the most progressive democracies harsh measures were taken. We also need preventive measures to protect [our] reforms. Therefore, the prime Minister and I examined the situation. İsmet Pasha is of the opinion that we need some legislative measurements to support the executive branch and the police. What do you think?[62]

Avni Doğan informs us that the majority in the meeting did not share Mustafa Kemal's pessimism and the proposed harsh legislative adjustments. On hearing this, Mustafa Kemal smiled and said,

> I smell blood and gunpowder. I hope I am wrong. Fethi Bey thinks he can govern the country without such precaution. Today Prime Minister İsmet Pasha will resign and the new government will be formed by Fethi Bey. Keep our meeting a secret.[63]

Considering that this meeting took place before the Sheikh Said Revolt, it is not difficult to suggest that Mustafa Kemal and İsmet Pasha were exploring the possibilities of silencing the opposition in the name of protecting the infant regime. This discussion provides us valuable evidence that the Sheikh Said Revolt was open to exploitation and manipulation and that motives did certainly exist.

Fethi Bey remained in power only two and a half months. On March 3, 1925, Fethi Bey gave his resignation to Mustafa Kemal, and consequently İsmet Pasha again was appointed as the new prime minister. The very next day, the Takrir-i Sükun passed the TGNA. Before looking at the İsmet Pasha government's dealing with the revolt in the region and with the political opposition nationwide, a very significant but often overlooked detail needs to be examined. This examination will give us further clues about the intentions of Mustafa Kemal and his close associates to dominate the political landscape by muting the opposition.

We know that only one day before the voting took place in the TGNA for the previously mentioned law number 556, the prime minister, Fethi (Okyar) Bey, invited Kazım Karabekir (the chairman of the PRP), Rauf Bey, and Ali Fuat Pasha to a private meeting. During the meeting, Fethi Bey said, "I was charged with a duty to ask you to close down your party on your own. Otherwise, I see the future very dark. Much blood will be shed."[64] To this open threat, Kazım Karabekir replied, "On a legal ground we can form a political party; but closing it down is beyond our ability. You are in the government. You possess the power and the means [to close down our party]. If this is your wish, you can certainly accomplish it by yourself."[65] After hearing that Kazım Karabekir had no intentions of surrendering, Fethi Bey apologized, stating, "I am deeply sorry to come to you with such a demand. As you well know, I oppose all forced action (*örfi muamele*). [But] I am afraid that I will be in the minority."[66] Who did charge Fethi Bey, the prime minister, with such an improper mission? Ergün Aybars, a specialist on the Independence Tribunals, and Metin Toker, the son-in-law of İsmet Pasha, suggest that no one but Mustafa Kemal had the means to order Fethi Bey to carry the message.[67] On this subject, Aybars and Toker cannot be challenged. Fethi Bey was probably carrying Mustafa Kemal Pasha's note, which clearly indicated that the political opposition would not be tolerated. In any case, Ali Fuat Pasha, in his memoir, states that before the meeting concluded, Kazım Karabekir Pasha confirmed his party's support for the government in dealing with the rebellion.[68]

Kazım Karabekir Pasha's refusal to comply with the "suggestion" of dissolving his party indicates that he must have been keenly aware of the intentions of the radical group in the RPP to take every measure to eliminate the political opposition. Yet the following events proved that neither Kazım Karabekir nor the other members of the PRP had any idea of the extremes the radicals were willing to go to establish their rule unchallenged. Aware that the radical faction in the RPP was undermining the moderate Fethi Bey government, the PRP decided to do all it could to keep Fethi Bey in power. Therefore, it should not be a surprise that the very next day, the PRP joined in the

RPP to pass law number 556, which banned the use of religion for political gains.[69] Ironically, although it was not this law that was utilized for the closing of the PRP several months later but rather the infamous Takrir-i Sükun, the use of religion for political gain was one of the major accusations leveled against the members of the PRP. We can now turn our attention to the Takrir-i Sükun, the law that was responsible for the silencing of the opposition.

TAKRİR-İ SÜKUN DISCUSSIONS IN PARLIAMENT[70]

When Fethi Bey resigned as the prime minister, İsmet Pasha became the new premier and immediately introduced a new bill to the TGNA in its meeting on March 4, 1925, a bill that caused much controversy. This bill, number 1/638 and named as Takrir-i Sükun, played a decisive role in the future of the new republic. With its draconian content, the bill (later law number 589) became the most significant instrument that the radical Kemalists would use to silence the internal opposition by legitimizing its suppression.

In the session held on March 4, 1925, the new prime minister, İsmet Pasha, introduced this new bill to parliament as the following:

> To the exalted Presidium and the Grand National Assembly of Turkey. Because of the necessity demonstrated by the recent extraordinary circumstances and events, in order to strengthen the power of the Turkish Republic and to safeguard the foundations of the revolution and in order to persecute and subject quickly the foolhardy ones who are harming and humiliating the innocent masses, through the adoption of the necessary measures against the reactionary and subversive actions and initiatives which may threaten the safety, law and order and social structures in the country, I request you to agree that this bill, which has been approved in the cabinet meeting of March the 4th, 1925, be submitted to the exalted Assembly for the approval and adoption.

The bill contained three articles:

Article 1

> The government is empowered to prohibit on its own initiative and by administrative measure (subject to approval of the President) all organizations, provocations, exhortations, initiatives and publications which cause disturbance of the social

structures, law and order and safety and incite to reaction and subversion. The government can hand over the perpetrators of these acts to an Independence Tribunal.

Article 2

This law will be in force for a period of two years from the date of its promulgation.

Article 3

The cabinet is entrusted with the implementation of this law.[71]

Naturally, when it was discussed in parliament, the bill encountered staunch objection by the opposition members embodied by the PRP. After the Takrir-i Sükun was introduced in the TGNA, Gümüşhane representative Zeki Bey, a member of the opposition, objected to the bill on the grounds that it contradicted the Constitution (*Teşkilat-ı Esasiye*). Since the perpetrators could be sent to the Independence Tribunals, which could impose capital punishment without parliamentary approval, the opposition members were uneasy. "This bill violates the Constitution," suggested Zeki Bey. "The article 26 of the Constitution is quite clear. [It stipulates that] the TGNA is responsible for [the confirmation of] capital punishment. First, Article 26 of the Constitution needs to be amended, and then we should be able to deliberate on the [Takrir-i Sükun]." In response, Karesi representative Ahmet Süreyya Bey, who later became a prosecutor in the Independence Tribunals that were formed to enforce the Takrir-i Sükun, stated that this bill was already discussed in the Judicial Committee of the TGNA, which decided that it did not violate the constitution.

The opposition of Dersim representative Feridun Fikri Bey was more to the content of the bill. In his speech, Feridun Fikri objected to the bill on another ground, namely, that it would give extraordinary power to the government, which could potentially abuse this power by labeling people's ordinary political activities (*faaliyet-i beşeriye*) a danger for the security of the regime. "It is possible," maintained Feridun Fikri, "to provide security (*emniyet*), happiness (*huzur*) and order (*sükun*) which the motherland needs without [the Takrir-i Sükun]."

Drawing on this foundation, Kazım Karabekir, the chairperson of the opposition party, the PRP, presented his objection to the bill as the following:

Dear friends, as I indicated earlier from this very lectern, we [the PRP] have supported all the legal business of the government in

> the region where this [Sheikh Said] incident occurred, and I repeat the pledge of our support. However, we do not support the process that put pressure on the natural [inalienable] rights of people in this particular incident. The bill that is now before you is not clear (*gayri vazıh*) and elastic. If this bill becomes a law and if it attempts to limit the political structuring (*siyasi taazzuv*) to which our Constitution has given birth, and efforts to pressure the newspapers are intended, that would mean that the people's sovereignty will be abandoned. Because, this would mean that the voices of people's representatives will not [be heard]. Passing this bill is not an honor for the history of the Republic.
>
> As for the Independence Tribunals, as its name suggests, these courts were established during our War of Independence. . . . If İsmet Pasha thinks that he can use these tribunals as a tool to tame [the opposition], he is gravely mistaken.

The fear of Kazım Karabekir was entirely justified, and in fact it was exactly what the government intended to do. This law would severely limit the PRP's political activities and hence its ability to constitute any opposition in parliament. However, they lacked the necessary political strength to stop the radicals, who constituted the majority. The Sheikh Said Revolt provided Mustafa Kemal and his supporters, namely, many members of the RPP, with an exceptional opportunity to silence the political opposition. To this end, not only the opposition in the TGNA but also the İstanbul press, which openly demonstrated distaste for Mustafa Kemal and the İsmet Pasha government, were the subject for the attention of the Takrir-i Sükun. It is not a misjudgment to suggest that the law's primary aim was not the handling of the Sheikh Said Revolt but rather the opposition. The law contributed very little to the success of the military action taken by the government against the revolt. Fethi Bey's statements in parliament on March 3, 1925, concerning his resignation from the office of the prime minister are noteworthy:

> I understand that my colleagues do not consider the actions taken by my government concerning the rebellion adequate, and advocate for broader and stronger measures. I am of the opinion that all necessary measures required by the rebellion are in place and these measures are sufficient to suppress the rebellion. I do not want the responsibility for shedding much

> blood by promoting stronger measurements. Therefore, I resign from my post.[72]

Until the Sheikh Said Revolt, the radicals felt threatened by the publications of İstanbul newspapers and saw them as a major obstacle in the process of implementing the pending reforms. Although this fear certainly had merits, it should not escape scrutiny. We know, for example, that some journalists' opposition centered not around the reforms that Mustafa Kemal intended to implement but around Mustafa Kemal himself. Hüseyin Cahit (Yalçın) and to some degree Ahmet Emin (Yalman), for example, were implying in their columns that Mustafa Kemal was becoming increasingly despotic. These Western-educated intellectuals did not share the aspirations of the Islamic segments of society and their leaders. They shared the vision of westernization as Mustafa Kemal did. However, bold disregard of the fundamentals of a democratic regime was the core of their opposition to Mustafa Kemal. We return to the issue of the journalists later.

At this point, we should turn our attention back to the discussions in parliament to see how the government also targeted the İstanbul press. Fearing the potential that the İstanbul press possessed to create or perhaps solidify the reaction to the Kemalist administration, Mustafa Kemal had a meeting with the journalists in İzmit (January 16–17, 1923).[73] However, this meeting did not prove to be very productive in terms of controlling the pens of the İstanbul journalists. While debating on the Takrir-i Sükun bill on March 4, 1925, minister of defense Recep Bey accused the İstanbul press of challenging the authority of the TGNA, a charge that was punishable even under the Law on the High Treason:

> The most significant point that needs to be addressed [here] is the İstanbul Press, which is the main reason for the present day weakness [of our state]. . . . Of course, there are exceptions. . . . [The İstanbul press] has attacked the TGNA, all of its political institutions, and members with vicious lies and manipulations. . . . Every morning, [it] manipulated the people with [innuendo] that the [Ankara] government . . . does not deserve credibility and trust (*itibar*). . . . In order to provide security for the general public (*emniyet-i umumiye*), for the law (*emniyet-i hukukiye*) and for the nation (*emniyet-i milliye*), and in order to establish a government powerful enough to destroy these poison centers (*zehir yuvaları*), it is the duty of this parliament to pass this law.

With these statements, Recep Bey presented the position of the İsmet (İnönü) government in reference to the İstanbul press. The revolt was a great chance for the hard-core radicals to settle old scores with the İstanbul newspapers that were not very friendly—to say the least—to some in the Kemalist circles.

Although memoirs describing the Sheikh Said Revolt deemed it a significant one and criticized Fethi Bey for not being vigorous enough to undertake the necessary measures, during the Takrir-i Sükun deliberations in the TGNA, speakers in favor of the bill did not make any case for the severity of the rebellion.[74] The radicals framed their argument for the necessity of the Takrir-i Sükun, suggesting that this revolt was the tip of the iceberg. The real problem, as they suggested, was the unknown inciters of the rebellion, as they hid in many segments of society. İsmet Pasha, responding to Kazım Karabekir's accusations of abusing the authority of the Independence Tribunals, stated that the tribunals were only tools to provide the nation with security and order. However, in response to Rauf Bey's assertion that stated, "I do not see the Republic in danger. Therefore, such a [drastic] law is not necessary," İsmet Pasha was polemical. After confirming that the regime was safe, İsmet Pasha rhetorically asked, "Can a Republic [like ours], which recognizes the dangers and takes necessary measures, be in danger?" This answer did not really respond to the question posed by Rauf, whose question intended to ask whether the government considered the revolt an imminent threat to the state. In the parliamentary discussions, İsmet Pasha did not speak to the specific danger that the Sheikh Said Revolt posed but instead chose to present the issue as a general security concern that was instigated by unnamed individuals and groups hiding outside the rebellion area. However, there was little doubt in parliament that the real target was the political opposition. For that reason, the discussions on the sixty-ninth parliamentary session, dated March 4, 1925, focused on how this law would affect the general individual liberties in the country, not on how this law would help suppress the rebellion.

In fact, almost exactly two years later, İsmet Pasha clearly stated that the real danger was not the Sheikh Said Revolt; it was the general confusion and degenerate intellectuals (*mütereddi münevverler*).[75] These people were hiding within the general population as journalists and politicians who needed to be weeded out. Thus, while in appearance this law was serving a noble cause, in reality the Takrir-i Sükun conferred an extraordinary power on the government to monopolize the definition of these "degenerate intellectuals" and the newspapers and political parties in which they hid themselves. As is shown below, in general it was the oppositional press (mainly in İstanbul) and the PRP as the main opposition in parliament that were targeted.

In any case, the bill became law number 589 on March 4, 1925, with 122 "yes" and 22 "nay" votes, which were cast by all PRP members present at the voting. The PRP did not muster enough votes to block the Takrir-i Sükun. After this vote, in the same session, İsmet Pasha requested the formation of two Independence Tribunals, one in Ankara and one in the region where the military operations were taking place (*harekat-ı askeriye mıntıkası*). What is most consequential about this development is that while the Ankara tribunal still needed parliament's approval to carry out capital punishment, the other tribunal—based mainly in Diyarbakır—did not need such an approval.[76] Judgments of the latter would be final and carried out immediately.[77] This tribunal was going to judge cases that were related to the rebellion and that took place within the defined region where the rebellion took place. The Ankara tribunal was assigned to deal with cases that were outside the jurisdiction of the Eastern Independence Tribunal. As will be seen below, in practice, the Eastern Tribunal was involved in cases that were technically beyond its jurisdiction.[78]

Another significant development that sealed the fortune of the PRP was the election of the members of the Independence Tribunals. The election took place on March 7, 1925. Expectedly, the members elected for these tribunals were close associates of Mustafa Kemal, and many belonged to the most radical wing of the RPP.[79]

THE TAKRİR-İ SÜKUN AND THE CASE OF THE JOURNALISTS

On March 6, 1925, only two days after the passing of the Takrir-i Sükun, the government closed down the following newspapers: *Tevhid-i Efkar, İstiklal, Son Telgraf, Orak Çekiç,* and *Sebilürreşat*. A month later, *Tanin*, whose editor in chief was Hüseyin Cahit Bey, joined the list.[80] Hüseyin Cahit (Yalçın) was a well-known CUP member and an ardent critic of the Ankara government. On August 11, 1925, *Vatan*, whose editor in chief was Ahmet Emin (Yalman), also joined the list. Some other newspapers that were closed down during the period of the Takrir-i Sükun also included *Yoldaş, Presse du Soir, Resimli Ay, Millet, Sada-yı Hak, Doğru Söz, Kahkaha, Tok Söz, İstikbal,* and *Sayha*.[81] Only *Hakimiyet-i Milliye* (Ankara) and *Cumhuriyet* (İstanbul), both organs of the government, circulated freely as major newspapers.

It is interesting that *Tanin*, the CUP organ, was closed down not immediately but rather a month after the first round of paper closings. This may indicate that the radicals were still not sure how to deal with the CUP members. Many CUP members were already in the RPP,[82] so it is possible that the delay was intended to measure the reaction of CUP members within as well as outside the RPP. The government must have become more confident in controlling the possible reaction that on April 15, 1925, *Tanin* was also closed down. The pretext for this decision was a frivolous one: that the paper used the word "raid" (*baskın*) to describe the closing of the PRP's İstanbul headquarter and branches.[83] The İsmet Pasha government, based on Takrir-i Sükun, charged that this word could be considered inflammatory and hence could endanger public safety. In the end, no substantial protest materialized to the targeting of the CUP organ. Nevertheless, the radicals were still uneasy in dealing with the other CUP members and suspicious of their political activities at least until 1926, when the major CUP leaders were executed in their alleged connection to the İzmir assassination attempt of Mustafa Kemal.[84]

Not all closed newspapers were published in İstanbul and hence were members of the so-called İstanbul press. In fact, this roster was highly eclectic and included not only Islamist and other oppositional newspapers that were critical of the government and hence the main target of the law but also the communist newspapers. Ironically, the communist newspapers were highly critical of the Sheikh Said Revolt from the beginning, considering it a manifestation of backwardness in the East. They supported the government's harsh standing against these revolts. The *Orak Çekiç* particularly was very complimentary to the government.[85] Erik Jan Zürcher correctly observes that "the first to be prosecuted by the new Ankara Independence Tribunal were not the PRP members, but the leftists." Thirty-eight socialists and communists were arrested and sent to Ankara with the charge of "propagating for communist organizations and hence endangering the public safety and attempting to change the regime."[86] This is a clear signal that any political and intellectual movement that was not in line with that of the radicals would be branded as dangerous to public safety.

For example, on May 27, 1925, Hüseyin Cahit (Yalçın), the editor of *Tanin*, was sentenced to a life-term banishment in Çorum, a small town in Anatolia, for the word "raid" that the newspaper used in his article.[87] It was during this trial that Hüseyin Cahit uttered his famous line describing the Independence Tribunals: "I would much prefer to be a defendant in such a court than a member of it."[88] In addition, Cevat Şakir (Kabaağaçlı—later known as "Halikarnas Balıkçısı") and Zekeriya (Sertel) were sentenced to three years in exile in Bodrum. The cause for this sentencing was an article by Cevat Şakir in *Resimli Ay* on April 23, 1923, titled "Hapishanede İdama Mahkum Olanlar Bile Bile Asılmaya Nasıl Giderler?" (How do those condemned to death go to their execution knowingly?). In this article, the author[89] claimed that the deserters in the military were executed without due process. The article angered the government, and the Ankara tribunal handed out the previously mentioned verdict to Cevat Şakir, the author, as well as Zekeriya Bey, the editor of the journal *Resimli Ay*.[90] The Ankara Independence Tribunal also condemned Ata Çelebi, the editor of *Doğru Söz* in Mersin, to one year in prison.

The issue of the journalists who were sent to the Eastern Independence Tribunal (Şark İstiklal Mahkemesi) is in fact more telling. Available information concerning their trial in Diyarbakır and later in Elazığ shows that the government wished to silence the opposition press and by doing so to set an example for the newspapers, which were not entirely controlled by the government. On June 7, 1925, Süreyya Bey, the prosecutor, requested the arrest of some journalists and stated the reason for the prosecution of these journalists as the following:

> There are several reasons for [the Sheikh Said] rebellion. Among these is the attitude of the journalists whose publications, knowingly or not, influenced the rebellion and who manipulated "the freedom of the press" for political and personal gains. For this reason, the issues of the [related] newspapers should be brought to [the court for examination] and the journalists whose essays are believed to influence the rebellion must be brought to justice.[91]

Süreyya Bey's request for the arrest of the journalists was based on Sheikh Said's interrogation in which the sheikh stated that "the articles in the newspaper *Sebilürreşat* would increase our anger for the government and encourage us [for such a rebellion]."[92] We will see below that these accusations leveled against the journalists may have been a result of false promises to Sheikh Said.

Nevertheless, on June 22, 1925, Velit Ebuziya of *Tevhid-i Efkar*; Sadri Ethem (Ertem), Fevzi Lütfi (Karaosmanoğlu), and İlhami Safa of *Son Telgraf*; Abdülkadir Kemali (Öğütçü) of *Toksöz*; and Eşref Edip of *Sebilürreşat* were arrested and sent to Ankara and later Diyarbakır. Other journalists who were named as defendants in this case included Gündüz Nadir, Ahmet Şükrü (Esmer), Suphi Nuri (İleri), İsmail Müştak (Mayakon), and Ahmet Emin (Yalman).

Ahmet Emin, in his memoir, states that his paper *Vatan* was the only newspaper in İstanbul that was not closed down until August 1925 thanks to the support of Mustafa Kemal and İsmet Pasha. However, when the government asked Ahmet Emin to publish an essay to defend the government's decision of the closing of the PRP, he refused to comply.[93] Consequently, *Vatan* was shut down, and Ahmet Emin was sent to Diyarbakır with an obscure charge that "the newspaper caused the rebellion by undermining the authority of the government."[94]

The memoir of Avni Doğan, the acting prosecutor for this case since Süreyya Bey was in Ankara, is revealing. He claims that the journalists were tried over the objections of the prosecutor Süreyya Bey (Örgeeveren), who stated that there is no legal ground for such prosecution.[95] Furthermore, it is in his memoir that Avni Doğan discloses an impressively honest observation regarding the case for the journalists. This information is especially significant, for it comes from the very prosecutor of the trial:

> In our private meetings [as the members of the tribunal], the conversations always ended up with the necessity of punishing the journalists. The other members repeatedly pressured me with the questions as to how I would construct the case for the prosecution and what I think about how to proceed to prosecute the journalists. I was hesitant to reveal my real thoughts on this matter, because after thoroughly investigating the matter, I learned the reason why Sheikh Said mentioned the names of these journalists in his interrogation. Sheikh Said's accusations [that he was encouraged by the articles of some of these journalists] were not his own. These names were given to him and he was pressured to accuse these journalists in exchange for a lighter sentence. [Furthermore,] every day I received coded messages from Ankara, from the second tier officials. In these messages, I was encouraged to prosecute them to the fullest extent, for they took position against the government since the proclamation of the Republic. [These messages also suggested that] their punishment would gain me credibility and influence.[96]

Therefore, we are informed by one of the most authoritative sources concerning this case that the journalists' prosecution was a set up by the government. This information was corroborated by another memoir by

Eşref Edip, one of the prosecuted journalists, who recorded that when he was en route to Diyarbakır, he spent a night in a prison in Urfa. There he met several Kurds who were exiled to Western Anatolia by the same tribunal. These Kurds, who were probably jailed with Sheikh Said or at least had contact with him in jail, informed Eşref Edip that Ali Saip, a member of the court, gave Sheikh Said the impression that if he involved the journalists in this rebellion, his life would be spared. Therefore, "until the last moment, Sheikh Said was under the impression that he would be exiled to Edirne."[97] This was also evident by Sheikh Said's statements just before his execution: "Ali Saip Bey, you were going to save me if I told the truth (?)"[98] It is quite possible that Sheikh Said was referring to such a secret agreement.

Similar abnormalities regarding the function of the tribunal can also be found in the memoir of the main prosecutor, Süreyya Bey. In his *Şeyh Said İsyanı ve Şark İstiklal Mahkemesi*, Süreyya Bey remembers Ali Saip Bey's reaction to his position that the tribunal should not be involved in crimes that were not specified in the law for the formation of the Independence Tribunals. Upset, Ali Saip Bey asked,

> Süreyya Bey! You are of the opinion that our court cannot get involved in any crimes that were not specified in the law for the Independence Tribunals. Look at the newspapers. The Ankara Independence Tribunal also deals with all other crimes that relate to military or other laws. How can you explain this?[99]

It was obvious that Ali Saip Bey and the other members of the court wanted to have greater jurisdiction in choosing what cases to prosecute and that Süreyya Bey was hesitant to prosecute them. At one point, Ali Saip Bey bluntly asked, "If the court decides to prosecute [some other crimes], would you object to it?" Süreyya Bey's response was equally blunt: "Of course, I would."[100] In a countermove, Ali Saip and Lütfi Fikri threatened Süreyya in a thinly veiled fashion that the court should inform Ankara of Süreyya Bey's lack of cooperation. "Please listen to me," Süreyya retorted. "Let me repeat briefly. The jurisdiction of our court is clearly determined by the law. We cannot disregard it. But if you [the other members of the court] wish to do so, I will not interfere or try to stop you. I will simply use my right to object as the prosecutor."[101] This time, the chief judge, Mazhar Müfit Bey, got involved and reminded him, "But sir, there is also a law called the Takrir-i Sükun." It was clear to Süreyya Bey that he was isolated in the court. The next day, when Süreyya Bey tried to reason with Lütfi Müfit Bey, a member of the court, he heard a statement that summed up the mind-set of those who promoted the idea of the Independence Tribunals: "We have a certain objective" stated Lütfi Müfit Bey, "*in order to achieve it, we sometimes rise above the law*" [emphasis added]. This was an extraordinary admission that also confirmed Avni Doğan's previously mentioned experience concerning Ankara's pressure. The memoirs of Avni Doğan and Süreyya Örgeeveren certainly confirm that the tribunals were the tools of the government in its attempt to silence the opposition. The telegrams that Süreyya Bey received from Recep Bey and İsmet Pasha, the minister of defense and the prime minister, respectively, pressured Süreyya to cooperate with the other members of the court.[102] Süreyya Bey indicates that as a result of these pressures by Ankara, he gave in, and the Eastern Independence Tribunal prosecuted any crimes it wished.

There should be no doubt that the Independence Tribunals were guided by the radicals in Ankara. Eşrep Edip, the editor of the Islamist daily *Sebilürreşat*, goes further to claim that Ali Saip Bey was the point man for the secret directives the court received from Ankara. Eşref Edip informs us that the accused journalists followed Ali Saip's position very closely, for he received special coded messages from Ankara. Therefore, his opinion was basically Ankara's opinion, and that was what counted. In his memoir, Eşref Edip states,

> Other than the official Tribunal account for messages from Ankara, there was a personal account for Ali Saip. The secret directives were sent to this account. . . . We would learn about the content the official correspondence between the court and Ankara through the clerks. But it was impossible to know what the secret directives to Ali Saip Bey contained. Therefore, we would watch him closely, for his opinions were basically those of Ankara.[103]

The event that is known in Turkish republican history as the "*Gazeteciler Davası*," or "the Trial of the Journalists," was only the first step in the elimination of any opposition to the radicals. After many fearful and agonizing months, a coded message from Ankara signaled that they would be released. The message asked the court to encourage the journalists to write a letter of forgiveness to Mustafa Kemal, and they would be forgiven by the president.[104] The journalists wrote the following letter:

> To President Ghazi Mustafa Kemal Pasha in Ankara
>
> In these days that our case is being tried in the Eastern Independence Tribunal, we regard bringing ourselves to your exalted attention a divine blessing. With the hope that we have proven

ourselves as loyal followers of the Republic and sincere servants of the reforms, we with a sense of endless pride, once again confirm to your highness that although our conviction of innocence calms our hearts, at this moment we trust even more the gracious forgiveness of your noble heart. Henceforth, in order to continue our mission with a sincere spiritual tie, to advance towards our high goal by making the spiritual connection that we feel [for you] as the guide to our future actions, we [beg] that you do not spare the favor of your trust in us.

We submit to you, the Great Savior, our deepest respect with the hope that our innocence that has been already demonstrated in the presence of the court will be supported by the good news of your forgiveness and leniency, which are very valuable for us, and which we hope to hear from the exalted conscience of you.[105]

In replying to this request, Mustafa Kemal sent a short telegram:

To the Prosecution of Eastern Independence Tribunal:

I have previously submitted to the attention of the court telegrams of the journalists, admitting mistakes in their [crimes] that have been observed (*meşhudat*) in Anatolia and in the rebellion territories and showing their remorse. This time, again, they apply with the abovementioned telegram. It is appropriate to take this telegram also to merciful consideration, sir.[106]

As a result, on September 13, 1925, the acting prosecutor Avni Doğan requested from the court that the case be dismissed on the grounds that articles published in their respected newspapers, although it was "proven" that these articles facilitated the rebellion, did not have intent. As such, the journalists could be tried not for high treason but rather for the crimes under the Press Law. Since Article 32 of the Press Law does not allow courts to try a case more than three months old, the journalists needed to be dismissed.[107] In other words, the court did not clear them from the accusations that they incited the rebellion but released them based on technicality.

Moreover, the telegrams to and from Ankara clearly demostrate Ankara's influence on the tribunal and in the end its willingness to set them free. However, they raise several significant questions as well. For example, based on Eşref Edip's memoir, we do know under which circumstances this telegram was prepared. The request of writing such a telegram came not from the journalists but from Ankara.[108] Why did the radicals in Ankara find it necessary to request such a letter? One possible explaination comes from Velid Ebüzziya, who originally objected signing a telegram requesting forgiveness. Velid Ebüzziya was the editor of *Tevhid-i Efkar* and was upset by the request that such a telegram would mean admitting the guilt for a crime he did not commit. His explanation for Ankara's request for such a telegram was the following. By receiving such a request from the accused, the court wished to justify the unlawful imprisonment of the journalists and protect itself from the outcome of such tyranny.

One may justifiably suggest that such a fear was the last thing the radicals had, for, as revolutionaries, their lives were on the line regardless. However, it should be remembered that in 1925, the radicals were not entirely in control of the political process, and, however weak, there was still a political opposition in parliament. Such a telegram would silence their criticism and would justify, at least on paper, the action of the tribunal. The existence of such a written apology would discredit the journalists, who were hostile to the government, and would ensure their silence. Yet their execution would do more harm to the credibility of the government.

Another possible but more cynical explanation can be that, short of executing the journalists, the radicals and Mustafa Kemal wanted to humiliate them in the eyes of the public for their anti-Kemalist standing. Without a doubt, the journalists could have been given the same verdict without a pleading telegram to Ankara since the primary goal of intimidating them about their future political actions was clearly and completely achieved. However, some radicals, such as Recep Peker and Ali Saip, may have wanted to settle personal scores with the journalists.

The text of the telegram contains more of a begging tone than that of an apology or an admittance of guilt. This indicates that the journalists were very careful in crafting the text and in convincing Velid Ebuzziya. Thus, the trial of the journalists ended. From that point on, the acquitted journalists sought ways to build bridges with the Kemalists and did not publish any oppositional articles.

THE CLOSING OF THE PRP

Mustafa Kemal was not favorably disposed to the formation of the new party, fearing mainly that such a division would encourage the opponents of the emerging and fragile regime. There were also some radicals in the government who did not like any criticism and were threatened by the high prestige and outstanding reputation of some members of the PRP leadership (such as Rauf Orbay, General Ali Fuat Cebesoy, and General Kazım Karabekir) among the populace. A U.S. consular report sent by Admiral Mark L. Bristol, the U.S. high commissioner, to the U.S. secretary of state evinces this point. In this particular dispatch, Mark Bristol included his "War Diary," which informed Washington about his trip to Ankara to meet Turkish ministers and also Prime Minister İsmet Pasha. The entry dated April 25, 1925, gives a transcript of the conversation that took place between İsmet Pasha and Admiral Bristol as interpreted by Howland Shaw, a member of the U.S. consulate. This meeting took place at İsmet Pasha's residence in Ankara and lasted one hour, during which time Bristol brought up the issue of political opposition. Following is the translation of this conversation by Shaw:

> The conversation then drifted to the difficulties of political life, especially the difficulty of handling a parliament. The Admiral asked İsmet Pasha point blank what he thought of a two-party system. İsmet Pasha replied that two parties were clearly desirable. He made this statement; however, it seemed to me, with very little conviction. The Admiral pointed out that the advantage of having two parties was that the various questions brought up in parliament were looked at and discussed from several points of view. İsmet Pasha admitted the truth of this. He asked how many members of Congress we had in America. The Admiral replied that we had some 420. İsmet Pasha expressed the greatest horror at this and was inclined to sympathize with the United States Government, even more when learned that besides 420 Congressmen we had a number of Senators. Apparently İsmet Pasha felt that 288 Deputies was more than sufficient as a source of trouble. He said that an opposition in a parliament was quite all right, but not an opposition which was opposed to the Constitution and to the foundation of the society.[109]

Bristol and his translator Shaw described the meeting as cordial and frank but seem to have been surprised at İsmet Pasha's remark about deputies in the Turkish Assembly being a source of trouble. It was in this meeting that Bristol received firsthand information regarding the government's unfavorable attitude toward the opposition party in Turkey. It is noteworthy that the conversation took place two months before the closing of the PRP offices nationwide.

The legal political opposition was no doubt a source of anxiety for the RPP, for the PRP recruited very prestigious leaders into its ranks. Hence, it is fair to say that without the charisma of Mustafa Kemal, the RPP in all likelihood would not have been able to enjoy any popular majority in parliament. The possibility was not too remote that had the PRP continued to attract former CUP members in particular, it could have been a major contender for power. However, among the rank-and-file members of the two parties, personal enmities were very visible, as demonstrated by the number of accusations leveled by RPP members against PRP members. According to Ahmet Yeşil, the author of a comprehensive study on the PRP, there were three commonalities in the accusations leveled against the PRP. The first is the fact that all accusations included complaints that the new party was manipulating religion for the purpose of gaining political power and registering members based on the claim that their party respected religion while the government party did not; second, that all accusers came from the ranks of the RPP; and, third, that accusers had preexisting enmities against the accused inside or outside the political arena.[110]

By the same token, we do know that some leaders of the PRP harbored envy against Mustafa Kemal and his close associates. The U.S. archives house documents that demonstrate this point. For example, the "War Diary" of Bristol has an entry dated October 25, 1923, dealing with the status of the caliph in relation to the president. As is known, the sultanate was separated from the caliphate in 1922, and the former was abolished. The Ankara government elected Abdülmecid Efendi as the new caliph. However, between 1922 and 1924, the legal and political status of the new caliph in relation to the president of the republic was a source of confusion, particularly for the diplomats in İstanbul. On this subject, Bristol recorded in his diary a conversation between a certain Mr. Scotten, a member of the U.S. diplomatic mission under Bristol, and Refet Pasha, who was the representative of the Ankara government in İstanbul but later became a member of the opposition:

> I [Mr. Scotten] tried to ascertain Refet's view as to the relative rank of the Calif and the "head of the State." I stated that it was conceivable, for instance, that a ship of war might be in Constantinople when the head of the State arrived and it would be necessary to fire a salute both to him and to the Calif, and I asked him what he conceived to be the proper salute to be rendered to each one. He laughed uproariously, and stated, "Fire as many guns as you wish for that spiritual gentleman up there in the palace at

> Dolma Baghche. Give him all the honors you choose, but don't salute the head of the State at all. Leave that poor fellow alone." He said, "He is simply a man who is unhappy enough to have fallen into a disagreeable job and who in a few years may have to be riding on a tram car again."[111]

This conversation demonstrates that a certain level of confusion about the relative rank of the caliph existed. It is also possible that the question was geared toward understanding Ankara's attitude toward the caliph. However, this piece of information is even more significant for scholars whose research concerns the personal rivalries among the ruling elite in Turkey. We know that Refet Pasha, one of the leaders of the Turkish War of Independence, joined the ranks of the opposition party (PRP) in 1924. This information clearly demonstrates that even before the formation of the PRP, there was a certain level of jealousy. In fact, Mr. Scotten and Admiral Bristol specifically noted in the same entry that Refet Pasha came across in the interview as very envious of Mustafa Kemal.

This level of personal rivalry and struggle for power may be understandable during a period in which the power vacuum was not entirely filled. However, with Mustafa Kemal's solid support of the RPP, the playing ground was certainly not even, and the PRP was very vulnerable to government sanctions. Moreover, the closing of the opposition party did clearly contradict Mustafa Kemal's expressed desire for democracy. Although there were earlier indications that the government wanted to silence the political opposition by intimidation, such as the previously mentioned request of Prime Minister Fethi Bey from Kazım Karabekir for the PRP to dissolve itself on February 25, 1925, it was, as mentioned repeatedly, the Sheikh Said Revolt that provided the government with a pretext for silencing the political and intellectual opposition.

Complaints about the PRP members and their political activities were finding their way into the TGNA soon after it was formed. A complaint mentioned in a document dated February 1, 1925, claimed that the PRP recruiters signed up new members by asking the question, "Do you prefer the sultan or Mustafa Kemal?"[112] The rivals of the PRP soon realized that the most effective complaint was the use of religion in the political arena, as the party program of the PRP included an article (Article 6) confirming its respect for religion. Accordingly, a great many complaints came after the Takrir-i Sükun Law was passed on March 4, 1925. In the TGNA archives, as Ahmet Yeşil informs us, there exist 68 different documents and one notebook of court proceedings against several PRP members.[113] The court proceedings include 14 sessions about complaints against the PRP. As a result of the investigation of these complaints, the Ankara Independence Tribunal, which was formed on March 7, 1925,[114] decided to confiscate all documents in possession of the PRP's İstanbul headquarters and other İstanbul branches on April 11, 1925. The tribunal was also interested in examining the documents related to the accounting of the PRP and ordered that all branches and headquarters be entered simultaneously.[115] Two large sacks of documents were confiscated by the police and sent to Ankara on April 13, 1925. Ahmet Yeşil has mentioned that the PRP's former Beykoz branch director, Hüseyin Bey; the branch secretary, Hayri Bey; and Nuri Bey were taken into custody and sent to Ankara for questioning on the same day.[116] There were other members of the PRP—such as Salih Paşo and Kamil Efendi—who were accused of using religious propaganda for political gain.

The verdict of the Ankara tribunal—after examining the documents and questioning the accused—was that the crime of religious propaganda in politics did take place. Accordingly, the court sentenced the accused to imprisonment, ranging from life sentences to one-year terms. One accused, Resul Hoca, was exiled to Ayaş, a small town in Anatolia.[117] It is important to note, however, that the tribunal did not limit itself to individuals committing the crime. It decided to "warn" the government about the PRP's activities. In other words, the PRP became entirely responsible for the actions of every single registered member. This was certainly a heavy burden for the PRP, as it was impossible to control every member of the party.

The major blow to the PRP did not come from the Ankara tribunal but the Eastern (Diyarbakır) Independence Tribunal. While the proceedings of the Ankara tribunal continued, a similar case was brought before the Eastern Independence Tribunal. Mehmet Fethi Bey, the Urfa-Siverek representative of the PRP, was accused of manipulating religion for political gain. The case was significant, for it resulted in the closing down of the PRP branches in Eastern Anatolia on May 25, 1925. Correspondingly, eight days later, on June 3, 1925, the government, based on the Takrir-i Sükun, ordered the closing down (*sedd*) of all branches of the PRP. It is noteworthy that technically the party was not dissolved, but all its offices were closed. The PRP members continued to vote as a bloc in parliament. Nevertheless, for all practical purposes, this was the beginning of the single-party era, which lasted until 1946. The PRP was not allowed to reopen.

Was the closure of the PRP justified? A quick glance at Fethi Bey's case before the Eastern Independence Tribunal may raise doubts about the impartiality of the verdict. For that reason, let us first look more closely at the case. The most useful primary source in this context consists of the proceedings that can be found in the TGNA archives.[118] The official records of the case indicate that those who accused Fethi Bey came from the ranks of the opposition party, the RPP.[119] Ahmet Yeşil has drawn attention to the fact that the accusers used the exact same sentences and failed to bring any witnesses to the stand but each other. The accusers' identical sentences, claimed to be uttered by Fethi Bey, were the following: "They [the government] shut the madrasas down. They did away with the Shari'a. We [the PRP] want the Shari'a of the Prophet (*Şeriat-ı Muhammediye*). Our party will advance the religion [Islam]. Let's work together."[120]

These statements certainly fell into the category of treason and were punishable under the High Treason Law and the Takrir-i Sükun. Based on the previously mentioned accusation, Fethi Bey appeared before the tribunal on April 30, 1925. His trial was rather swift and lasted only three sessions (on April 30, May 12, and May 18, 1925). Fethi Bey denied all accusations of having manipulated religion and instead accused Mehmet Emin Bey, the director of the Urfa/Siverek branch of the RPP and the mayor of the town, of manufacturing such baseless rumors to harm the PRP.[121] Next, the prosecutor, Süreyya Bey, asked questions about Article 6 of the PRP's party program, which stated that "the party respects religion." The prosecutor wanted to know whether Fethi Bey ever considered this article being the culprit for the public's thinking of the PRP as a religious party. The implication was simple: the PRP had included this article about religion in its program in the hope that it would attract more conservative-minded people. This may be the case; however, Article 6 itself did not constitute a crime. In fact, the party had been formed with this program in November 1924 with the permission of the government. The only crime would have been the abuse of the article for political gains. Aware of this, Fethi Bey's response was more political: "It is the responsibility of the TGNA to judge the legality of our 6th article. For this reason, I never referred to this article in my political activities."[122] In other words, Fethi Bey denied the charge that he had manipulated religion.

Other than the accounts of the accusers belonging to the rival party, as mentioned above, the prosecutor also utilized the statements of Sheikh Eyüp, the director of the Siverek branch of Fethi Bey's own party. In his accounts, Sheikh Eyüp stated that Fethi Bey stayed in his house for 15 days when they were trying to form the Siverek branch. Sheikh Eyüp added that Fethi Bey "was trying to establish the PRP branch here and was recruiting members. He was indicating that Mustafa Kemal gave permission for this, and their party has respect for religion. The other party [RPP] does not comply with religion that much. He said this openly."[123]

Ahmet Yeşil has speculated that such an accusation could be the result of possible false promises made to him.[124] However, we do not have any record of such a deal, except that such a possibility did exist. Fethi Bey categorically denied the charge but was not able to escape the verdict that found him guilty as charged. He was sentenced to five years in prison in Sinop. Because of his previous good standing as a citizen and his service to the nation, the sentence was reduced to three years.

The verdicts of the Ankara Independence Tribunal on May 3, 1925,[125] as well as of the Eastern (Diyarbakır) Independence Tribunal on May 19, 1925,[126] resulted in a government (cabinet) decree on June 3, 1925, to close down all offices of the PRP nationwide.[127] The decree was signed by Mustafa Kemal Pasha (the president), İsmet Pasha (the prime minister), and six other ministers of the government.[128] According to the decree,

> During the [prosecutions] and trials concerning a number of provocations taking place before the Independence Tribunal of Ankara, it has been established that a number of persons holding official functions within the Progressive Republican Party in the İstanbul area have used the principle of respect for religious opinions and beliefs, included in the party's program, as a means to deceive public opinion and to stimulate religious incitement, and the decision of the tribunal, to the effect that it has been decided to draw the government's attention to the current attitude of the party, has been laid before the government by the public prosecutor's office.
>
> During the [prosecutions] and trials of the Independence Tribunal of Diyarbakır it has been established that official representatives of the Progressive Republican Party have used the principle of respect for religious ideas and beliefs, included in the party program, as a means to gain support for the propaganda of reactionaries who pretend to save the country from atheists and that this has led to many serious incidents during the manifestations of the

> latest [Sheikh Said] insurrection. . . . Under these circumstances, it is impossible to allow a movement aimed at the use of religion for political purposes to exist.[129]

CONCLUSION

In this study, I have tried to examine several questions. The first and most consequential question concerned the relationship between the Sheikh Said Revolt and the radical Kemalists. Although foreign observers—American, French, and British—entertained the possibility and even suggested that the Ankara government fomented the rebellion, this view was not uniformly accepted. These sources base their claim on circumstantial evidence that the Sheikh Said Revolt benefited the Kemalists more than the Kurds or the British. Circumstantial evidence by its very nature is not conclusive; however, it is not necessarily false.

We have more convincing evidence to support the claim that the Sheikh Said Revolt was manipulated by way of exaggerating its possible overall effects in the country. It is well documented that even before the Sheikh Said Revolt, Mustafa Kemal, İsmet İnönü, and the radical wing of the RPP were highly insecure about and sensitive toward any criticism, let alone political opposition. Therefore, they were highly suspicious of the formation of the new political party, the PRP, in opposition. It was almost a natural reflex to force the opposition to dissolve, for it was obvious that what the radical Kemalists hoped to accomplish and the methods to achieve them would be hindered by any political opposition. They were aware that use of religion would be a great weapon for the opposition in elections and that the new radical reforms required total silence.

In many primary sources, even those by members of Mustafa Kemal's inner circle, methods of accomplishing new reforms were regarded as despotic.[130] However, it should be noted that the political landscape of the early republic presented a dilemma for Mustafa Kemal. He would either deal with the opposition within democratic means at the expense of risking his reforms and position in power or entirely damage the opposition in a way that it could not recover in a meaningful way. Such a dilemma did not exist in the minds of Mustafa Kemal's radical followers, such as Recep (Peker), Mazhar Fuat, Kılıç Ali, Ali Saip, and so on. To them, the end justified the means, and the new regime (or their hold on power) had to be protected by any means. The radical wing of the Kemalist faction—which controlled the means of power—opted for the latter; by doing so, however, it laid the very foundation of the political culture of republican Turkey. In the following decades, the successive governments' main goal was to tame, if not to eliminate, the opposition as much as possible and monopolize the government. Such a lack of respect for a healthy political opposition is also one of the problems modern Turkey faces even in the twenty-first century.

At this point, one may pose another significant question. If Mustafa Kemal and the radicals did not have much respect for political opposition, why did they insist on creating the new regime as a republic based on democratic principles? In my judgment, republicanism was the only viable regime for Mustafa Kemal and his friends after the dissolution of the Ottoman Empire. Mustafa Kemal's assuming the title of caliph was not realistic and contradicted his own political orientation. However, as a soldier and a statesman who was influenced by the political ideals of the West, Mustafa Kemal's commitment to "republicanism" came only in the practical sense. The power struggle and the political realities of the country made it impossible for Mustafa Kemal to fully commit himself to practice true democracy. Therefore, lip service was always paid to this ideal, yet in reality, as the Takrir-i Sükun and the Independence Tribunal experience teach us, there was no obligation to practice it. Nor was there any remorse within the ranks of the RPP radicals that the regime was not a republic in which there existed room for political opposition.

When we look at more specific conclusions in this study, the first question becomes this: did the PRP and the İstanbul Press incite the Sheikh Said Revolt? All evidence suggests that this is not the case. Most participants of the Kurdish rebellion did not speak Turkish and were illiterate. There was little in common between the leaders of the rebellion and members of the press and of the PRP. Such a link was invented only to deal with the opposition. Avni (Doğan) Bey's memoirs also testify to the fact that the so-called established link between the journalists and the revolt was based on the false promises made to Sheikh Said if he accused the journalists in his testimony.

The closure of the PRP, the only legal opposition in Turkey, was also the direct result of the Sheikh Said Revolt. Although the government suggested a link between the revolt and PRP activities, it was not proven. It was the use of religion for political gain that was utilized as the pretext for the decision. Article 6 of the PRP program—the party respects religious opinions and beliefs—created an environment to connect the individual's activities to the party in general. This article gave the government an opportunity to blame the entire party apparatus for the actions of individuals. It must be mentioned that the prosecutors clearly failed to prove without reasonable doubt that even the individuals who were accused of manipulating religion for political purposes were guilty as charged. Verdicts were handed down based on suspicious accounts by eyewitnesses, most of whom were active members of the rival party.

Foreign observers were following the developments in Ankara with great interest and making accurate evaluations. Let us end this study with one of those. After the passing of the Takrir-i Sükun Law and reactivation of the Independence Tribunals, Admiral Bristol, the U.S. high commissioner in İstanbul, sent his assessments to the secretary of state in Washington on May 8, 1925. It reads as follows:

> Angora is rapidly modeling itself on the Tcheka. Its aim is seemingly to remove all political opposition; its methods are to convict on the basis of a settled policy and not on the evidence presented; its victims, in addition to nonconsequential citizens, are men of influence and standing. It has tried editors not only for the offensive use of a word, but for a state of mind. It has succeeded in so terrorizing the press, that its most flagrant lapses from equity have not even been criticized; it has so terrorized the opposition that protests are no longer being made against its unconstitutionality.
>
> This diatribe may seem strong to the [State] Department, but I do not think it stronger than the circumstances justify. The atmosphere of suspicion and distrust which the activities of the Tribunal have engendered recalls the atmosphere of Hamidian days, and there is a distinct danger, if the appetite of the Tribunal grows with the eating, personal liberty may well be entirely suppressed in Turkey. . . .
>
> [The trials of the journalists] may be regarded as yet further manifestations of the Government's decision to stamp out by strong measures all open opposition. Thus policy was perhaps never stated more forcibly and clearly than by Redjeb Bey, Minister of National Defense, who gave out the following interview to the "Hur-Fikir" (Free Thought) of Ismid: "All individuals or associations, whomsoever they may be, whose actions on Turkish soil are to the detriment of the Turk or Turkism, have no right to life, and are condemned to destruction. We will amputate all gangrenous limbs."[131]

4

Opposition at Large: The İzmir Assassination Plot and the Conspiracy Trials

Another cornerstone in the process of silencing the political opposition in early republican Turkey is the 1926 plot to assassinate Mustafa Kemal in İzmir. Like the Sheikh Said Revolt in 1925, this attempt provided the Republican People's Party (RPP) government with another pretext to complete the process in which there remained to be no political opposition to the new regime and to the government in power. In the end, the process was so complete that there was not a single dissent for any bill brought to parliament until the new elections in 1927. Those deputies who remained in the Turkish Grand National Assembly (TGNA) voiced their dissent by not showing up for the vote. For example, when a vote of confidence for the government was requested on November 6, 1926, only half the deputies cast their votes. Mahmut Goloğlu correctly points out the fact that none of the bills had sufficient votes because of lack of participation in the first rounds. Only in subsequent rounds, which required bills to receive a majority of available votes, did the bills become laws.[1] It was in this political environment that many radical westernizing reforms (such as the alphabet reform of 1928) passed the TGNA with unimaginable ease and speed.

The İzmir plot and the following conspiracy trials can readily be seen as the continuation of a process that commenced with the Takrir-i Sükun of 1925. This was the final stage of the purging of the existing and potential opposition. At the end of the İzmir and Ankara trials in 1926, the opposition in parliament (the members of the closed

Progressive Republican Party [PRP]) and the potential opposition outside it (some former high-ranking members of the Committee of Union and Progress [CUP]) were purged.

The İzmir assassination plot of 1926 has been studied by a number of nonprofessional historians.[2] Therefore, in many cases, scholarship on this rather significant portion of early Turkish republican history lacks authority. However, these sources, overwhelmingly in Turkish, contain significant leads to primary sources. Among the available primary sources on the subject, memoirs are the most numerous. However, the reader must be careful about the reliability of these memoirs, for most of them are colored by the political ambitions of their authors at that time. Official documents, such as statements by government officials and Mustafa Kemal himself, are also limiting since all were party to this incident. There are, however, primary accounts by foreign sources, such as U.S. consular reports and also court proceedings (on the İzmir trials), that recently became available in print to researchers.[3] All these sources allow us to expand our knowledge of the subject under examination.

This chapter reexamines the İzmir plot in the context of the elimination of political opposition. Many studies on the issue correctly conclude that the İzmir assassination plot served the government's interest in purging the opposition.[4] However, exactly how this was done was not satisfactorily documented and critically examined.[5] In addition to using the available primary and secondary sources, I introduce U.S. diplomatic archival sources into my examination. These sources are significant, for they give us information about how an outside power viewed the unfolding events. Needless to say, their perception was not free of error; however, the mistakes were unintentional and their biases inconsequential. These accounts also enable us to compare the information already utilized in secondary sources. Therefore, in addition to bringing in fresh data from the U.S. consular reports in the entire text, this chapter also includes a subsection that deals specifically with the U.S. archival sources and examines the implications of the information presented in them.

Much has been written about the following questions concerning the plot. Was there really a plot against Mustafa Kemal's life? In other words, did the Kemalists foment such a conspiracy to silence the opposition as claimed for the Sheikh Said Revolt earlier? What was the role of the PRP and the CUP in this plot? Were the executions of those who were accused of the involvement in the conspiracy justified? I address these questions only briefly since my aim is to demonstrate how this plot was manipulated to silence the current and potential opposition to the government.

We know that the internal power struggle in Turkey was of great interest to the international community, especially for Great Britain but also for the United States. In the post–Takrir-i Sükun environment, foreign observers were almost expecting a move by Mustafa Kemal to complete the job he started after the Sheikh Said Revolt. Therefore, it was not a surprise that the İzmir plot would provide him with a second chance. After the uncovering of the plot, Sir R. Lindsay, British representative in İstanbul, informed Sir Austen Chamberlain, secretary of state in London, about the plot. In reference to rumors that the plot was fomented by Mustafa Kemal himself to silence the opposition, on June 23, 1926, Sir R. Lindsay judged that there was indeed an attempt on Mustafa Kemal's life but continued, "The [Turkish] Government is naturally not going to miss such a chance of enquiring into the activities of all possible opponents."[6] The U.S. consular reports also agree with this assessment as Mark L. Bristol, the U.S. high commissioner in İstanbul, reported to the secretary of state on July 7, 1926, that "the conspiracy was real and that the plot itself had extensive ramifications."[7] As will become clear in this chapter, Turkish sources also corroborate this assessment. Indeed, there was a failed attempt to kill Mustafa Kemal. Yet this attempt made Mustafa Kemal and the RPP government much stronger than ever before. It was surely "the second chance" to complete the unfinished business of silencing the opposition. Let us first start with a brief summary of what happened in İzmir in 1926.

THE UNCOVERING OF THE PLOT[8]

On May 7, 1926, Mustafa Kemal left Ankara for an inspection tour of the southern and western provinces of the nation. After Eskişehir and Afyon, he arrived at Konya on the next day. Following the route of Tarsus and Mersin, he spent some time in Silifke on his farm. After visiting Adana, back to Konya, and Bozüyük (in Bilecik), Mustafa Kemal spent 24 days (from May 20 to June 13) in Bursa, a historic town in the Marmara region. On June 14, Mustafa Kemal was in Bandırma. According to the itinerary, he was expected to arrive at İzmir on June 15, 1926. However, Mustafa Kemal unexpectedly delayed his departure for one day. It was in Bandırma that he received a telegram from Kazım Pasha, the governor of İzmir, informing him of a plot to assassinate him on June 15. It is interesting to note that Kazım Pasha waited one more day to inform the prime minister, İsmet Pasha, in Ankara. We know from İsmet Pasha's memoir that he received the telegram from Kazım Pasha on June 16.[9] We do not know the reason for the delay.

At this point, the reader should be informed that most of our information regarding the plot comes from the prosecutor's plea and court proceedings. It is clear from the testimonies of the accused in their trials that there was indeed a plan to assassinate Mustafa Kemal in İzmir. The prosecutor of the Independence Tribunal claimed that the plot to assassinate Mustafa Kemal was planned for a long time by the members of the opposition party, the PRP.[10] Although there were several other previous attempts—none of which moved beyond the planning stage—the İzmir plot came closest to being executed.[11] Those who were primarily responsible for carrying out the plot were Ziya Hurşit (former representative from Lazistan), Laz İsmail, Gürcü Yusuf, and Çopur Hilmi, all of whom were captured in their separate hotels with guns, ammunition, and hand grenades. At least one of them, Ziya Hurşit, readily admitted that he was planning to kill Mustafa Kemal. During his interrogation, he informed the İzmir police that the former Ankara governor, Abdülkadir Bey; Sarı Edip Efe; and the İzmit representative for the opposition party PRP, Şükrü Bey, were closely involved in the organization process of the plot.

The plot was discovered based on information provided by Giritli Şevki, who was involved in the conspiracy. He, with the aid of his boat, was the person responsible for helping the killers flee to the Greek island of Chios (Sakız). According to the plan, Ziya Hurşit, Laz İsmail, Gürcü Yusuf, and Çopur Hilmi were going to wait at the corner of a street in İzmir for Mustafa Kemal's car to slow down to negotiate the sharp turn. They would then throw hand grenades into the crowd for confusion. Using the mayhem as a cover, they would shoot Mustafa Kemal and flee to Giritli Şevki's boat, which was docked at the harbor, and escape to the Greek island. However, a one-day delay in Mustafa Kemal's arrival in İzmir and the disappearance of Sarı Edip Efe (one of the plotters) changed everything. Afraid that the plot was about to be exposed, Giritli Şevki went to the İzmir police station and informed the authorities about the plot.

THE GOVERNMENT'S ACTIONS FOLLOWING THE PLOT[12]

At this point, we need to start with the most reliable sources to reconstruct the communication between Mustafa Kemal and the government.

We have a collection of telegrams published in full that were exchanged by Mustafa Kemal and various government and military personnel.[13] What do these telegrams between Mustafa Kemal and İsmet Pasha (and some other sources) reveal about the nature of the İzmir conspiracy? The earliest available information regarding the conspiracy in these telegram collections was dated June 16, 1926, two days after the attempt was foiled. Mustafa Kemal's telegram to İsmet Pasha in Ankara acknowledges that an assassination attempt was avoided and warns that since the conspiracy was planned for June 16, there still might be co-conspirators in Ankara to take over the government on this date.[14] Clearly, Mustafa Kemal was convinced that there were many unsatisfied elements in İstanbul—and perhaps in Ankara—waiting to overthrow the government. An alleged underground organization that resembled (if not manned by) the former CUP members, now active in the PRP, was the first suspect behind the plot.

Mustafa Kemal's other telegram was sent to İstanbul Police Chief Ekrem Bey, in which he singled out Sarı Edip Efe as one of the conspirators and requested his speedy arrest. Furthermore, Mustafa Kemal predicted that, based on the news from İzmir, there might be a meeting of co-conspirators (associates of Sarı Edip Efe). He urged the İstanbul Police to be diligent and prepared.[15] This telegram shows Mustafa Kemal's sensitivity toward a possible government takeover or perhaps a counterrevolution. We saw a similar sensitivity by Mustafa Kemal in the case of the Sheikh Said Revolt and its aftermath.

Interestingly, İsmet Pasha's reply the next day to Mustafa Kemal was calmer: "we do not judge that the conspiracy is supported by a wider organization."[16] This reply exhibits a stark contrast to his response to the Sheikh Said Revolt a year earlier. İsmet Pasha seemed to be convinced that the plot did not pose any danger to the regime; however, he was mindful of the opportunities it would provide to garner much-needed support from the public for the regime. In another telegram on the same date, İsmet Pasha registers his astonishment at foiling the conspiracy only a day before it was executed and only because of a regretful informant. However, İsmet Pasha's second point in the telegram was more revealing. "The incident is totally under control," suggested the prime minister. "There is no doubt that we should inform the public of it with grandeur (*azamet*) and display (*debdebe*). This indeed benefits us greatly."[17] In other words, from its earliest stage, dealing with the plot destined to involve a public display. On June 18, 1926, Mustafa Kemal issued a press release claiming that the conspiracy was not against him in person but against the republic and the principles on which it was based.[18] It is in this context that Mustafa Kemal made his well-known statement, "Surely, my humble body will one day become dust, but the Turkish Republic will endure forever."[19]

Mustafa Kemal seems to be genuinely suspicious of the counter-revolutionary potential of the assassination plot. On June 18, 1926, in another telegram to Şükrü Naili Pasha, commander of the Third Army Corps in İstanbul, Mustafa Kemal requested that the army also had to be on high alert for the arrests in İstanbul and that suspicious officers needed to be paid careful attention to.[20] It is likely that he wanted to be sure of the loyalty of the lower-ranking officers in the military since it had been proven that no counterrevolution could be successful in Turkey without the support of the army.[21]

On June 18, 1926, four days after the foiled plot, Mustafa Kemal sent a telegram to Prime Minister İsmet Pasha and stated,

> Based upon the confessions made by the arrested, I am of the following opinion: we are dealing with an organization operating clandestinely (*gizli çalışan bir komite*) under the control of the Progressive Republican Party whose sole aim is to capture the [political] power. The former Second Group members [the opposition in the First Assembly] are also included in this plot. . . .
>
> This political organization also maintains an armed (*fedai*) section, the same way the CUP had. . . . The decision for the assassination was made collectively by all the members of [the PRP's] general committee. . . . It is telling that Rauf Bey left earlier for Europe, Kazım Karabekir met secretly with Ziya Hurşit in Ankara, . . . and Adnan Bey [Adıvar] extended his stay in London. . . . Therefore, it is necessary to arrest and punish all leaders and some members of the PRP.[22]

First of all, why was there a rush to accuse the PRP without obtaining all available information? For example, Giritli Şevki, who informed the authorities of the conspiracy, implicated the entire party in power, the RPP, and especially Kazım (Özalp) Pasha, then Speaker of the Assembly.[23] Furthermore, Ziya Hurşit, the assassin in charge, denied in no uncertain terms that Kazım Karabekir, Refet (Bele) Pashas, and Rauf (Orbay) Bey were involved in the plot.[24] Here, one can clearly see Mustafa Kemal's attempt to involve his political rivals in this plot (based mostly on suspicion).

In another telegram to İsmet Pasha on June 19, 1926, Mustafa Kemal insisted that Gürcü Yusuf and Laz İsmail, two other assassins, confirm that there were talks of Kazım Karabekir's presidency after the assassination. Ziya Hurşit had commendations and letters (contents of which were not made public) from Rauf Bey and Ali Fuat Pasha, leaders of the PRP. Mustafa Kemal urged İsmet Pasha to arrest Kazım Karabekir.[25] We know that İsmet Pasha was not entirely sold on a blanket arrest of all PRP leadership, especially Kazım Karabekir and Ali Fuat Pashas.[26] However, with the insistence of Mustafa Kemal, İsmet Pasha caved in. The following example demonstrates how İsmet Pasha became convinced of the PRP involvement in the plot.

İsmet Pasha, on hearing of the arrest of Kazım Karabekir by order of the Independence Tribunal, then in İzmir, issued a direct order to Dilaver Bey, Ankara police chief, to release the pasha from custody.[27] However, when the news of the release reached İzmir, the Independence Tribunal threatened Prime Minister İsmet Pasha with arrest for interfering with a judicial process.[28] Secondary sources suggest that Mustafa Kemal stepped in just in time as an arbiter and invited the prime minister to İzmir for consultation.[29] On June 20, 1926, İsmet Pasha arrived at İzmir, and after several private meetings with Mustafa Kemal and the members of the court, he declared that, based on the information he had received in İzmir, he was convinced that the court was acting within its authority.[30] It is fair to state that İsmet Pasha was strongly urged by Mustafa Kemal not to interfere; therefore, the prime minister remained "neutral." However, we do not know why he abandoned his hawkish attitude toward the opposition, an attitude that was evident during the Sheikh Said Revolt a year earlier. One can speculate that he was not comfortable with the growing tension among the people and especially the military. In any case, from this point forward, the government and especially İsmet Pasha stayed out of the trials in İzmir and also later in Ankara.

THE İZMİR TRIALS

Based on information collected from the accused, the Independence Tribunal began the trial on June 26, 1926.[31] According to a statement released by the court, more than 50 people were arrested in different parts of Turkey and sent to İzmir for trial.[32] Only a U.S. consular report gives us the full list of those arrested.[33] The PRP's Kastamonu representative, Halit Bey, escaped the arrest because of a mistake of the court, confusing him with an independent deputy.[34] Among the arrested, there were several active members of the TGNA for the PRP. Since, as such, they enjoyed legislative immunity, they could have been arrested only if they had been caught in the act of committing a crime (*en flagrant delit*) or with the sanction of parliament. We do know that this constitutional right was plainly violated, evident from the verdict that some of the deputies were found "not guilty." By definition, however, if they were caught "red-handed," their acquittal could have been impossible. This point was forcefully made by Rauf Bey (Orbay), one of the accused, in his memoirs.[35]

The trial began with the prosecutor's indictment on June 26. The prosecution's main point was that this was not a simple act of a failed assassination attempt against President Mustafa Kemal. On the contrary, it was an attempt committed against the new regime and hence was punishable by death. The prosecutor demanded that the following individuals should be tried for having conspired to take the life of the president and that they should be convicted under Turkish Penal Codes 55 and 57.[36] The prosecutor's job to prove that there was a plot against the life of President Mustafa Kemal was easy, as some of the conspirators, such as Ziya Hurşit, readily confessed to the plot.[37] The harder part, at least for the observers of the trial, was to prove beyond any reasonable doubt that the plot in fact aimed at toppling the government and that many PRP and former CUP leaders were directly involved in it. In order to establish such a connection, the prosecutor relied on the testimonies of some of the accused. For example, Ziya Hurşit admitted that he went to İzmir on July 12, 1926, in the company of Laz İsmail and Gürcü Yusuf to assassinate Mustafa Kemal on the latter's arrival in the city. When asked by the president (chief judge) of the court, Ali Bey, whether any other people were involved in the plot (since such a tremendous undertaking could not be accomplished by four or five people), Ziya Hurşit replied that Şükrü Bey and Abdülkadir Bey were the only other two who were aware of the plot. In fact, the assassination was originally planned in Ankara first by killing the members of the cabinet as well as Mustafa Kemal. However, Şükrü Bey later objected to this scheme, saying that this was too risky and prone to failure. Ziya Hurşit admitted that he planned to accomplish this by bombing the Grand National Assembly when the president and ministers were present.[38] Ziya Hurşit further informed authorities that Şükrü Bey had earlier given him 400 Turkish lira and several revolvers to execute the plan. When Ziya Hurşit's brother, Faik Bey, deputy from Ordu, heard of the plan, he rebuked his brother severely.

The Ankara assassination plot also came to the attention of Rauf Bey, who threatened Ziya Hurşit that he would turn him in if he did not give up on such a plan. It is important to note that Rauf Bey, a one-time close associate of Mustafa Kemal and a major figure in the opposition, was later sentenced to 10 years in prison because of his failure to report the incident to authorities. In any case, when the Ankara plot failed, it was finally decided that İzmir was the safest place to execute the plan and escape abroad.[39]

Desiring to establish a link between the opposition and the plot, the prosecutor and president of the Independence Tribunal asked Ziya Hurşit of the PRP's and Kazım Karabekir's involvement in the plot. Ziya Hurşit flatly denied any such involvement. The prosecutor had the depositions of Laz İsmail and Çopur Hilmi Bey, reporting that Ziya Hurşit had told them that the PRP had supported the plot. However, Ziya Hurşit himself denied the accuracy of this information; therefore, the prosecution was deprived of a firsthand accusation.[40]

The prosecution's evidence came from the testimony of Sarı Edip Efe, who stated that "the assassination of [Mustafa Kemal] had been secretly decided at a meeting of the Progressive Republican Party; and that Kiazim Pasha, President of the Grand National Assembly, and Fevzi Pasha, Field Marshall were aware of the conspiracy."[41] Sarı Edip Efe added that the ultimate plan was to elect Fevzi (Çakmak) Pasha as the president of the republic. The testimony of Sarı Edip Efe is significant for several reasons. He provided the prosecution with the rationale, however unsubstantiated it may have been, to accuse the PRP members. Based on this statement, significant members of the PRP, such as Kazım Karabekir, Ali Fuat (Cebesoy), Rauf (Orbay), and Refet (Bele), all of whom were worthy opponents of the government, were accused of a crime against the state, which carried the penalty of capital punishment. However, the greatest hole in the accusation was the following. Sarı Edip Efe based these accusations on the information he received from Ziya Hurşit also.[42] However, Ziya Hurşit, supposedly the source of this information, repeatedly denied any involvement of the PRP leaders.[43]

One of the accused, Faik Bey, who was the brother of Ziya Hurşit, stated in court that even if the RPP leaders were uninformed of the İzmir plot, they surely did know of the earlier plot in Ankara.[44] Thirty years after the incident, Faik Bey published his reflections on the plot, stating that "many years after my retirement from parliament [in 1927], I learned that the PRP had a higher [secret] committee in İstanbul than that of its known board of administration. The secret committee must have been the CUP in İstanbul. . . . Apparently, actions were taken based upon the decision and instructions of this committee."[45]

In retaliation, on September 21, 1956, the weekly *Dün ve Bugün* magazine[46] published a response to Faik (Günday) Bey's claims in which it questioned the motives of revealing such information decades later.

In any case, Kazım Karabekir, in his statement to the court, denied any involvement in the plot. Furthermore, he openly criticized the government for its attempt to silence the opposition once and for all. His defense was similar to that in the Sheikh Said Revolt in that he refused to accept responsibility for a few misguided PRP members. As to the accusation for the toppling of the government (*taklib-i hükumet*), Kazım Karabekir stated that with not more than 15 members of the PRP in parliament, how could a political party topple a government of the RPP's strength? Without the assistance of the military, he continued, no government could be overthrown in this country.[47] When Ali Bey, the president of the court, said to Kazım Karabekir, "You established an opposition party in a period when the country could not tolerate any opposition," Kazım Karabekir simply responded by saying, "I disagree. Our nation is mature enough."[48] Ali Bey's line of questioning strengthens the belief that the court aimed also at punishing the political opposition simply because it existed.

On June 30, 1926, the prosecutor introduced an addendum to his original plea in which he extended the scope of the trial to fine-tune his accusations of the PRP and the CUP leaders. In the original indictment on June 26, 1926, the prosecutor signaled that the PRP members were currently being interrogated and that the official charges were pending. In the addendum, the prosecutor mentioned by name the following PRP leaders: Cafer Tayyar, Ali Fuat, Refet, Kazım Karabekir, Rüştü Pashas, Sabit, Halis Turgut, İhsan, İsmail Canbulat, and Münir Hüsrev Beys. Furthermore, the prosecution claimed that the PRP allied itself with a secret committee, consisting of former CUP members, to capture the government by force. The addendum concluded with a request from the court to prosecute the following CUP members: Faik (Ziya Hurşit's brother), Cavit (former minister of finance in the CUP governments), Necati (ex-deputy from Erzurum), Hilmi (ex-deputy from Ardalan), and Kara Kemal (in absentia) Beys. The charge carried the death penalty.[49]

The significant issues are the following. The prosecution claimed that it included these names based on the alleged statements made in court by Ziya Hurşit. However, available court proceedings failed to establish that Ziya Hurşit made any such accusations against these CUP leaders.[50] Furthermore, we have a copy of the original addendum and another copy of the addendum that was provided to Kazım

Karabekir by the court. When compared, the two are not identical. In fact, Kazım Karabekir has a note on the corner of the "official," longer version that he received during the trial. Kazım Karabekir marked a certain paragraph and scribbled that "this section is quite different in the copy we received."[51] It seems that the section about the accusations against the PRP members were omitted in the copy provided to the pasha. We do not know the reason for this discrepancy.

In any case, in July 1926,[52] the second addendum by the prosecutor added several other people from the opposition to the list of accused. The list now included Rauf, Adnan, Rahmi Beys (in absentia), Bekir Sami, Feridun Fikri, Kamil, Zeki, Necati (Bursa), Besim, Necati (Erzurum), Selahattin, Ahmet Nafız, Kara Vasıf and Hüseyin Avni Beys, and Cemal Pasha (Mersin). In addition, Hafız Mehmet (who was mentioned at the beginning of this chapter as an ardent opponent of Mustafa Kemal) Vahab, and Keleş Mehmet were accused of conspiring against the government.[53] All these names belonged to the political opposition inside or outside parliament and, in the opinion of Mustafa Kemal, would always pose a danger to his vision and leadership for the new Turkey. Invariably, they came from the ranks of the Second Group (the opposition in the first TGNA), the PRP, and the former CUP.[54]

Perhaps one of the most memorable aspects of these trials was the sessions in which the generals (pashas) who had been significant actors in the nationalist movement were on trial. These were the people who served the nationalist cause at the highest levels and were once the close associates of Mustafa Kemal himself. These generals included Cemal (Mersinli), Rüştü, Kazım Karabekir, Ali Fuat, Cafer Tayyar, and Refet Pashas, all of whom were members of the PRP in opposition. Some of these generals were still well respected in the military. In the end, all accused generals were found "not guilty" with the exception of Rüştü Pasha, who was executed. Claims have been made that the government was not unsure of the military's reaction to execute or jail the pashas, and hence the court was lenient toward them. For example, Faruk Özerengin, a son-in-law of Kazım Karabekir, claimed that there were several armed military officers in the court ready to kill the members of the court if they issued death sentences for the accused generals and to trigger an uprising. Because of such fears, the pashas were spared.[55]

Fahrettin (Altay) Pasha, one of Mustafa Kemal's close associates, remembers the reason for the generals' acquittal differently. In a meeting with Fahrettin Pasha and İsmet Pasha, Mustafa Kemal asked the former, "Ali Bey [the president of the Independence Tribunal] will hang the generals, what do you make of it?" Fahrettin Pasha chose to be silent on this question, but İsmet Pasha demonstrated a level of apprehension. In response, Mustafa Kemal pressed, "How can we be sure of the future if we do not hang them?" According to Fahrettin Altay, who witnessed this exchange, İsmet Pasha convinced Mustafa Kemal of the dangers that such a move could pose. Finally, Mustafa Kemal was convinced and stated, "Alright then; let me talk to Ali Bey [the president of the court] one more time."[56] Fahrettin Altay's memoir hints at the authority of Mustafa Kemal over the court, contradicting the claim made by one member of the court, Kılıç Ali Bey, when he stated that "we received orders from no one."[57]

In the İzmir trials, at least 36 people appeared before the court.[58] The ruling of the tribunal condemned the following 15 people to death sentences: Şükrü Bey (deputy from İzmit), İsmail Canbulat Bey (deputy from İstanbul), Arif Bey (deputy from Eskişehir), Abidin Bey (deputy from Saruhan), Halis Turgut Bey (deputy from Sivas), Rüştü Pasha (deputy from Erzurum), Ziya Hurşit (ex-deputy from Lazistan), Hafız Mehmet Bey (ex-deputy from Trabzon), Laz İsmail, Gürcü Yusuf, Çopur Hilmi, Sarı Edip Efe Bey, Albay Rasim, Kara Kemal Bey (former CUP leader), and Abdulkadir Bey (ex-governor of Ankara). The last two received their sentences in absentia since they were not captured by then. Kara Kemal killed himself on July 27, 1926, when surrounded by the police in İstanbul.[59] Abdulkadir Bey was arrested close to the border around Edirne while attempting to cross into Bulgaria on August 19, 1926, and was hanged on September 1, 1926.[60]

Vahap Bey, nephew of Hafız Mehmet, was sentenced to 10 years of exile in Konya. Other accused people were released, including the generals Kazım Karabekir, Refet, Cafer Tayyar, and Ali Fuat. They must have been informed of the court's decision beforehand, for they declined to defend themselves in court after their initial statements. Only Rüştü Pasha begged for leniency, but, as mentioned, he was sentenced to death. We do not know why he was singled out.[61] After their release, the generals were put under police surveillance for years to come.[62]

Most important, the court decided that in order to shed light on the CUP involvement in the plot, there would be another trial in Ankara, where high-level CUP members would be tried for their involvement in the overthrow of the current regime and in the assassination plot. Seven people, who were transferred from İzmir to Ankara, were the following: Rauf Bey (deputy from İstanbul and former prime minister), Adnan Bey (former deputy from İstanbul and former minister of health), Rahmi Bey (former governor of Smyrna), Hilmi Bey (former deputy from Ardahan), İhsan Bey (deputy from Ergani), Cavit Bey (former minister of finance), and Selahattin Bey (former deputy from Sivas).[63] Rauf and Adnan Bey were already in Europe and refused to return; therefore, their trials were in absentia. All these names were potential rivals to the leadership in Ankara with significant international and national clout.

Therefore, the Ankara trials promised to be more interesting than that of İzmir and were purely political in nature. Closer examination of these trials reveals not only the government's insistence on silencing this group—whose loyalty to the new regime would not be trusted—but also how defenseless these once-all-powerful people were.

THE ANKARA TRIALS[64]

The İzmir trials clearly went farther than dealing with those who were directly involved in the conspiracy. It marked the final blow to the ill-fated PRP, which constituted the legal opposition in parliament. However, there was still potential political opposition outside parliament (namely, the former CUP elite) that could enter it in the next election in 1927. Accordingly, the Ankara Independence Tribunal seems to have had two objectives in separating the İzmir phase from that of Ankara. The first one undoubtedly was to eliminate these CUP elite who refused to submit to the government's will and who were, as such, deemed potentially dangerous. By doing so, the court aimed at establishing a point of reference to deter other lower-level CUP members who might entertain the idea of challenging the authority of the government (not necessarily the regime). The second objective was that the court, which ironically included some lower-level former CUP members, wished to collect information on the inner workings of the CUP, the secret knowledge to which they were not privy in the earlier periods. For example, Falih Rıfkı Atay, a member of Mustafa Kemal's inner circle, later qualified the hostile attitude of Ali Bey, the president of the court, toward Cavit Bey, former minister of finance, as the enmity and jealousy of a former lower-level CUP member of the CUP elite.[65] The questioning of Cavit Bey was of great interest to foreign observers, as it dealt mainly with the Ottoman entry to World War I and the secret negotiations of the CUP members with European diplomats.[66]

The Ankara trials commenced on August 2, 1926. The prosecutor claimed that the İzmir trials clearly demonstrated the existence of a secret committee to overthrow the current government and that the PRP became the new face of the former CUP. The prosecutor, Necip Ali, mentioned that although the ideas in the political program that were penned by the former CUP elite in the house of Cavit Bey were protected by the freedom of ideas and consciousness (*fikir ve vicdan hürriyeti*), plans to realize them, which involved the assassination of the president, certainly constituted crimes against the state.[67] Accordingly, Necip Ali requested the punishment of 39 people. The following 16 people were to be tried based on Articles 57 and 58 of the Criminal Code (death sentence or exile for life): Dr. Nazım (member of the Central Committee of the CUP), Cavit Bey (former minister of finance and member of the CUP), Kör Ali İhsan Bey (responsible secretary of the CUP), Hilmi Bey (former deputy from Ardahan), Küçük Talat Bey (member of the Central Committee of the CUP), Azmi Bey (former chief of police of İstanbul), Kara Vasıf Bey (former deputy from Sivas and a member of CUP and the Second Group), Hüseyin Avni Bey (former deputy from Erzurum and a member of the Second Group), Selahattin Bey (former deputy from Mersin and a member of the Second Group), Nail Bey (former deputy from Kütahya and member of the CUP), İhsan Bey (deputy from Ergani and a member of the CUP), Mithat Şükrü Bey (secretary-general of the CUP), Hüseyin Cahit Bey (editor of *Tanin* and former deputy from İstanbul), Hüseyin Rauf Bey (deputy from İstanbul and former prime minister), Dr. Adnan Bey (former deputy from İstanbul), and Rahmi Bey (former governor of İzmir).

The prosecutor asked for the exile and imprisonment of the following 30 people based on Articles 55 and 58[68] of the Criminal Code: Hüseyinzade Ali Bey (professor at the Medical School), Hamdi Bey (member of the CUP), Hilmi Bey (former director of the posts and telegrams), Vehbi Bey (responsible secretary of the CUP), İbrahim Ethem Bey (resident secretary of the CUP from Bakırköy), Cemal Ferit Bey (secretary of the Union of Porters), Eyüp Sabri (member of the Central Committee of the CUP), Dr. Rusuhi (member of the Central Committee of the CUP), Ahmet Nesimi Bey (former minister of foreign affairs and member of the CUP), Salah Cimcoz Bey (former deputy from İstanbul and member of the CUP), Rıza Bey (retired major), Hüsnü Bey (responsible secretary of the CUP), Naim Cevat Bey (retired major and president of the Batum Congress), Tırnakçı Salim (member of the CUP), Said Bey (brother of Yakup Cemil of the CUP), Ali Osman Kahya (chief of boatmen), Salih Reis, Cavit Bey (police sergeant), Nazım Bey (former inspector of Public Debt), Çerkes Bey (retired colonel), İzzet Bey (director of the Bakers Company), Rıfat Bey (former prefector of Üsküdar), Hasip (servant of Kara Kemal), Ahmet Muhtar Bey (responsible secretary of the CUP, Bakırköy), Neşet Bey (major of Bakırköy), Gözlüklü Mithat Bey (director of the National Products Company), Mehmet Ali Bey (director of the Bank of Economy), Rıza Bey (chief cashier of the Bank of Economy), İhsan Bey (representative of the National Trading Company, İzmit), and Hasan Fehmi Bey (representative of the National Product Company).[69]

As can be seen, a great majority of the accused were affiliated with the CUP. A small number came from the Second Group. Names that are not associated directly with the CUP were those who the court thought would provide valuable information about CUP members. At the İzmir phase, almost all PRP members were already silenced; only Rauf Bey and Dr. Adnan Bey were included in the Ankara phase of the trials, simply because they were overseas and the government was not sure how to deal with them as yet. Erik Jan Zürcher in his *The Unionist Factor* correctly states that the Unionists were targeted, for Mustafa Kemal judged them as worthy competitors for power and some of them came from the *komitadji* (political assassin) background.[70]

During the Ankara trials, the court gave more attention to the following issues than the plot itself: (1) the political activities of the CUP leaders in exile, (2) the nature of communication among the CUP leaders inside and outside the country, (3) the nature of the secret political maneuverings of the Unionists in the First and the Second TGNA, (4) the nature of the meetings of former CUP leaders at the house of Cavit Bey and at the office of Kara Kemal Bey, (5) the partially successful CUP agitations during the elections of the Second TGNA, and (6) the role of the CUP members in the formation of the opposition in the TGNA through the creation of the PRP.[71]

Most independent observers of the trials agreed that the prosecutor's accusations were not properly documented and that the court adhered to "the famous principle of the Napoleonic code that the accused is guilty until he can prove himself innocent."[72] A British report judged the Ankara trials a farce: "The evidence of complicity in the conspiracy was negligible. The court had plainly made up its mind to secure the Ghazi's position by removing Javid, the best brain, and Nazım, the arch-conspirator, of the Committee of Union and Progress. . . . The country was thoroughly cowed and opposition was eliminated, or, at any rate, driven further underground."[73] A U.S.

observer noted that the court was not worried by the possibility that the political charges leveled against the CUP members violated the spirit, if not the letter, of the Lausanne Treaty.[74]

In the end, death sentences in conformity with Articles 55 and 57 of the penal code were handed out to Cavit Bey (former minister of finance), Dr. Nazım Bey (member of the Central Committee of the CUP), Hilmi Bey (former deputy from Ardahan), and Nail Bey (responsible secretary of the CUP). Ten years of banishment, consistent with Articles 55 and 58, were accorded to Vehbi Bey (responsible secretary of the CUP), Hüsnü Bey (responsible secretary of the CUP), İbrahim Ethem Bey (responsible secretary of the CUP), Hüseyin Rauf Bey (former prime minister and deputy from İstanbul), and Rahmi Bey (former governor of Smyrna). In accordance with Article 64 of the Penal Code, Ali Osman Kahya (chief of the Corporation of Boatmen) and Salih Reis (chief of the Corporation of Porters) were sentenced to 10 years of banishment to their native city. The remaining 37 CUP members were acquitted. It is noteworthy that although Rauf Bey was named as the mastermind of the conspiracy, he did not receive the death penalty.[75] Understandably, there was a level of apprehension in court to condemn Rauf Bey, a significant member of the nationalist movement, to death.

To date, the İzmir assassination plot against the life of Mustafa Kemal remains one of the most controversial aspects of Turkish republican history. At this point, we need to examine the suspicions surrounding the plot more closely.

SUSPICIONS SURROUNDING THE PLOT

As mentioned previously, there have been many conspiracy theories that encircle the İzmir plot. They were raised by many in the opposition, including, Kazım Karabekir, Ali Fuat Cebesoy, and Rauf Orbay.[76] It must be noted that there is sufficient reason to be suspicious about the government's connection with the plot; however, there is no concrete or even convincing evidence that Mustafa Kemal or the government premeditated and fomented it. Like the Sheikh Said Revolt, the government utilized the plot to the maximum for political benefit.

Let us look at some of the suspicious facts surrounding the incident. For example, one can be justifiably suspicious of the date of the letter confessing the plot. We know that Giritli Şevki, one of the designated participants in the plot, came to the İzmir Police on June 14, 1926, with the intention of turning in his co-conspirators. However, the letter that Şevki wrote to Mustafa Kemal bears the date June 15, 1926. If he surrendered to the authorities in İzmir on June 14, that would mean that he was not turning in a prewritten letter for Mustafa Kemal and that the letter was written the next day. The first suspicion is that he may have been instructed to manufacture such an allegation at the police station. However, this claim would be weak when we consider that perhaps he verbally informed the authorities and then was asked to document it in a letter. It would mean, however, that Mustafa Kemal's delay of visit was not the cause for Giritli Şevki's panic since he already knew that Mustafa Kemal was informed by the police and asked to delay his visit.[77] We do not know for sure what the reason was for Giritli Şevki's change of heart. Some sources suggest that it was possibly the hazy departure of Sarı Edip Efe from İzmir that struck fear in Giritli Şevki.[78]

Another speculation about the plot was that Sarı Edip Efe was the agent of the government, charged to inform the authorities of the activities of the conspirators.[79] Hence, according to this view, the government (or Mustafa Kemal) was fully aware of the hatching of the plot. Kazım Karabekir, in his defense, was quite forceful in claiming that there was a good chance that this plot was allowed to happen, like the Sheikh Said Revolt, for the purpose of crushing what was left of the opposition in parliament. After all, Sarı Edip Efe's close association with Kazım (Özalp) Pasha, the president of the TGNA and member of the RPP, was common knowledge in Ankara. According to Kazım Karabekir, Sarı Edip Efe, who accused the PRP of being involved in the plot, needed to be questioned in court about his current association with the government.[80] What strengthens this assumption is that Sarı Edip Efe was not questioned on this subject and that during his trial he was silenced quickly by the president of the court when he stated, "My service to the government is being overlooked."[81] We do not know what the nature of this service was. Samuel W. Honaker states,

> The trial of Edib Bey had been eagerly awaited by the people of Smyrna, for there were various rumors in circulation with respect to his former connection with the Government as an individual who had possibly given money from the secret funds. The visitors to the courtroom were disappointed in the latter respect; no opportunity was given by the President of the Tribunal of Independence for the disclosure of details of that character.[82]

The court seems to be unconcerned by the allegations, but we do know that this rumor created another suspicion about the plot.

In connection with Kazım Karabekir's allegations that the government was aware of such a plot, we also know that Mustafa Kemal was upset that the court allowed Kazım Karabekir to openly raise these questions. On July 5, 1926, when at a ball in Çeşme, a suburb of İzmir, an angry Mustafa Kemal invited members of the Independence Tribunal to the ball and clearly showed them his displeasure in allowing Kazım Karabekir to make such allegations in public.[83]

To further corroborate this allegation, one can point out the interview given by Atıf Bey, the governor of Ankara, on June 29, 1926. According to this interview, the government was aware of the preparation of an imminent assassination attempt on Mustafa Kemal's life since the winter of 1926. Governor Atıf Bey clearly stated, "We knew of the plot and Ziya Hurşit was under our surveillance for a long time. We collected many documents and turned them in to the Independence Tribunal."[84] There does not seem to be any reason to question the accuracy of this information. Therefore, a suspicion certainly exists that Mustafa Kemal was monitoring the situation and was looking for an opportune moment to exploit it for his political benefit. However, the reader should not take this as proof of the government's involvement in the plot. It can, at best, be seen as evidence that Mustafa Kemal would have sufficient time, if he wished, to devise a counterplan to enhance his political standing.[85]

There should be no doubt that the political environment of 1926 allowed plenty of room for suspicion regarding the government's involvement in the plot. However, one should not accept the circumstantial evidence as fact and form a solid judgment based on this. On the other hand, ignoring the possibility of Mustafa Kemal's prior awareness of such a plot and his desire to benefit from it would be equally irresponsible. We know that Mustafa Kemal manipulated the plot for political gain and eliminated the opposition entirely. At which point he devised such a plan to accomplish this goal does not change this fact. We also know that Mustafa Kemal was regarding the opposition as a hindrance to progress and a challenge to his leadership and, hence, was hoping to eliminate it. It is the judgment of this study that he acted pragmatically with a desire to silence the opposition. The legal and political moves were executed not idealistically but practically. It is, therefore, fair to state that Mustafa Kemal's political success was based more on his pragmatism than on his idealism. The following section brings in primary sources that were not previously examined to further demonstrate this point.

THE İZMİR CONSPIRACY IN THE U.S. CONSULAR REPORTS

As stated before, we lack independent primary sources on the subject of the İzmir conspiracy. One of the most neutral primary sources comes from U.S. consular reports about the incident. These documents are significant and relatively more reliable than the rest, for they lack motive for manipulation. In other words, these sources were reporting their findings to Washington without any hidden agenda.

The first report about the İzmir conspiracy was sent on June 18, 1926, the same day the plot was made public by the U.S. high commissioner in Turkey, Rear Admiral Mark Lambert Bristol.[86] This was simply a short telegram informing the State Department of the plot. Bristol waited over a month to send a rather comprehensive report about the incident. However, on June 22, 1926, Bristol reported the information he collected from newspapers. He also reported a rumor that was circulating in Turkey during the trials in İzmir:

> [The rumor has it] that the Government has either manufactured the entire conspiracy or else is utilizing an actual plot of a non-political nature as a pretext for discrediting the leaders of the Progressive Party, whose parliamentary and general political opposition it has been unable to silence despite its autocratic administration of national affairs. It is reported that this opposition has considerably increased since the conclusion of the Mosul treaty, which the Progressives denounce as an unjustified surrender of Turkish rights.[87]

The reader may remember that such a rumor was also present during the Sheikh Said Revolt and the previously mentioned closure of the PRP in 1925. These rumors were indications that beneath the surface there existed suspicion and mistrust for the Ankara government, particularly in İstanbul and İzmir. We do not know how widespread this mistrust was. We do know that Ankara was fully aware of such feelings.[88]

In another report on July 7, 1926, High Commissioner Bristol seems to be convinced that "the conspiracy was real and that the plot itself had extensive ramifications."[89] The report goes on to claim that "the government appears to be making a special effort to fix maximum responsibility for the attempt on Progressive leaders. On the other hand, the depositions which have been taken to date tend to minimize their guilt and to make the government's case against them appear rather weak."[90] We know that since the Sheikh Said Revolt, critics of the government were suspicious of the government's secret plots to completely eliminate the opposition. This report clearly confirms that the Independence Tribunal did not make an effort to erase such an assumption.

A 13-page report written on August 3, 1926, reveals the judgment of the U.S. high commissioner about the İzmir trials by the Independence Tribunal. The general feeling of Bristol was that the trials were a show for the Turkish public and that the legal rights of the accused were not respected. A strong implication in the report was that the fates of the accused were predetermined. For example, Bristol pointed out that, contradicting the recommendation of the prosecution that Rüştü Pasha and İsmail Canbolat Bey deserved imprisonment, the court handed both of them death sentences. Bristol stated that one of the outstanding features of the court had always been the unity of action between the prosecution and the judges. Why, then, Bristol asked, did there seem to be a disagreement on the fate of these two people? He subscribed to the already circulating theory that the court wished to give the impression that the prosecution and the judge did not always see eye to eye—one of the most significant characteristics of a "real court." Hence, this was for "imagery" purposes.

According to Bristol, when the İzmir proceedings were examined in totality, they became unusually interesting from two points of view: the legal and the political. Legally, Turkish jurisprudence "did not distinguish itself for neither was the evidence as it appeared in court convincing nor were the trials conducted in a spirit of refined justice. The most flagrant departure from established principles being that the accused was allowed neither counsels for defense, nor appeal."[91] Politically, the İzmir trials further discredited the PRP to the point that it would take a very long time for them to regain the prestige it formerly enjoyed. In this sense, the main goal of the İzmir trials was accomplished.

Referring to the Ankara stage of the proceedings, Bristol pointed out that one of the main differences between the İzmir and Ankara trials was that the former dealt with the issue of the plot, whereas the latter sought to "clear up political differences of long standing and dispose of, once and for all, the question as to what lines the Turkish Revolution shall henceforth follow."[92] The expulsion of the PRP members from the TGNA and the elimination of notable leaders of the CUP from the political scene were goals they wished to accomplish. In other words, the İzmir trials already discredited the PRP leaders in the eye of the public and ended their political careers as an opposition bloc in parliament.

However, there was another, more dangerous group that was preparing for the upcoming elections in 1927. The Ankara trials were specifically aimed at silencing the potential opposition that would come from these CUP members, some of whom were already serving in the ranks of the Ankara government. On this subject, Bristol reports that in order not to alienate those former CUP members in the RPP, the general tendency was to point out the distinction between former Unionists who served the Kemalist government and Unionists as adherents to a new national political party. This was the view of the daily *Cumhuriyet* of Yunus Nadi and also the view of Ali Bey (Çetinkaya), chief judge of the Independence Tribunal. Another daily, *Milliyet*, under the editorship of Falih Rıfkı (Atay), suggested that these trials should liquidate once and for all the Unionist problem. Yunus Nadi, a former Unionist himself, claimed that the Independence Tribunal was dealing not with the CUP per se but with the secret machinery of a certain group.

Bristol reported the position of another daily newspaper, *Vakit*, which suggested that the Independence Tribunal was competent only to try those implicated in the İzmir plot. Because of the stipulations of the Treaty of Lausanne, the court did not possess the legal jurisdiction to try the former CUP leaders for their political activities. This position is significant in that none of the Allied Powers further investigated the issue. This report clearly indicates that at least the U.S. diplomats were aware of the question.[93]

On the contrary, another report by Charles E. Allen, the U.S. consul in charge, advised the U.S. secretary of state that "it would be extremely unwise to attempt, either directly or indirectly, to make any excuse for the executions ordered by the Tribunal of Independence in connection with efforts to secure the ratification of the Treaty of Lausanne."[94] The author suggests that since no U.S. interest or the interests of the minorities were violated, the United States should refrain from agitating the Ankara government so that those in the U.S. parliament would not have another reason to oppose the ratification of the Treaty of Lausanne despite the fact that "these executions are inexcusable for the reason that the tribunal . . . disregarded totally the elementary rights of the accused."[95]

Another report from Charles E. Allen, the U.S. consul in charge in İstanbul, to the secretary of state gives brief biographical information and compares the backgrounds of those executed in İzmir on July 14, 1926. He suggests that aside from three vagabonds (Laz İsmail, Gürcü Yusuf, and Çopur Hilmi), all others had education that could be rated from fair to excellent. These were people "whose accomplishments compare favorably with those of any member of the present government."[96] More important, notes Charles Allen,

> with a few exceptions, these persons were active members of a wing of the Union and Progress Party to which Mustapha Kemal Pasha, even when he was a member of that party, opposed, the reason being, it is alleged, his own ambition and jealousy of others. There would, therefore, seem to be an excellent reason for suspecting that the execution of these persons was due as much to Mustapha Kemal Pasha's fear and hatred of them as to their guilt.[97]

Another significant report, prepared by Samuel W. Honaker from the U.S. consulate in İzmir, relayed the summaries of the court proceedings in İzmir and Ankara.[98] The report, prepared on August 12, 1926, seems to be one of the most comprehensive accounts of the İzmir trials (68 pages long). It informed Washington of events preceding the assassination plot, of the trials and of the Independence Tribunals, and of their previous activities in İzmir. The report does not include the complete account of the court proceedings; however, it is significant in that it contained information that was not previously reported. For example, the testy interaction between chief judge of the tribunal, Ali (Çetinkaya), and the accused Abidin Bey did not take place in the official minutes of the İzmir trials.[99] We learn that Abidin Bey reacted to a comment by the chief judge, Ali Bey, accusing him of not telling the truth. Abidin Bey responded that "he was a Deputy, and not a murderer like the chief judge of the Tribunal of Independence." The report continued, "[Abidin Bey] was evidently referring to the incident between Ali Bey and Halit Bey [Pasha] during which the former shot and killed the latter in the building of the Grand National Assembly. The chief judge immediately ordered Abeddin Bey to maintain silence, but the latter refused and continued saying that 'two years ago Moustafa Kemal Pasha had been loved and trusted by the nation but the hypocrites like the presiding officer had spoiled him, the President of the Republic and lowered him in the eyes of the people.' "[100] This incident took place on the third day of the trial but was not published in the newspapers or in the court proceedings of that date. Clearly, the court blocked the publication of the exchange. We do know that the rumors of the killing of Halit Pasha by Ali Bey were circulating before. Why, then, was this interaction removed from the official proceedings? It raises the suspicion that perhaps there were other omitted incidents in the proceedings.

Another piece of information that is not available in Turkish sources is the intelligence that Sheldon Leavitt Crosby received regarding the desire of some deputies to dissolve the TGNA. Crosby reported,

> An interesting possibility arising from the Smyrna and Angora proceedings is the dissolution of the Assembly. It has come to this Mission from confidential sources that a number of deputies have approached the President of the Republic on the subject of the desirability of dissolving the present Assembly because of the general atmosphere of suspicion which has been created by the recent hearings and which has even extended as far as at least to one cabinet officer. It is understood that informal conferences are even now being held between Moustapha Kemal, İsmet Pasha and a few of the more trusted deputies with a view to deciding upon the desirability of such action. Should the decision be in the affirmative, it will probably be seen that the Government is yet strong enough to obtain the Assembly's concurrence as required by the Constitution and also to maneuver the new elections entirely to its taste.[101]

Understandably, the government did not take the risk of dissolving parliament at the time since there were still many unknowns that would embarrass the government in the immediate elections. However, we do know that the next elections were a year away, affording the government sufficient time to control almost all seats of the TGNA (only six out of 288 deputies were "independent," the rest belonging to the party in power, the RPP).

One other observation by Crosby is also insightful. It seems that death sentences were handed out arbitrarily. For example, one of the questions that still remains today after the Ankara trial is why Cavit was executed but Hüseyin Cahit acquitted. The latter was equally despised by the government and potent enough to cause alarm. Crosby speculated that "the Government was responding to a popular agitation which for some time has prevailed in his favor and has elected this as a form of palliative to offset the effect of the executions of the other prominent Unionists."[102] The U.S. chargé d'affaires points out a possibility, but we will never know the reason.

By now, the reader should be convinced that there was an attempt on Mustafa Kemal's life and that this plot was skillfully used by Mustafa Kemal to eliminate the opposition. However, not much has been said regarding the availability of a secret organization that aimed to overthrow the government and even change the regime. By all accounts, the Independence Tribunal performed poorly in proving that such a conspiracy did exist. However, should the court's lack of ability to pin down the accused with irrefutable evidence of a conspiracy to change the regime be interpreted in a way that no such conspiracy ever existed? In other words, was there a conspiracy against the regime prior to 1926?

We have documents suggesting that such a conspiracy may have existed. Before presenting these documents, the reader should be warned that there is no corroborating evidence or other independent confirmation for these claims. Therefore, they should not be taken as facts. Nevertheless, several U.S. diplomatic reports prepared by Mark L. Bristol, the U.S. high commissioner in İstanbul, may shed some light on this question.

On June 17, 1924, Bristol sent a report to the secretary of state in Washington detailing the information he collected from Osman Fahreldine (Fahrettin) Bey, private secretary to Seyyid Mahdi Ahmet al Sanussi (also known as Ahmet Şerif El Sanussi and Sheikh Ahmed Cherif El Senoussi in the original text).[103] According to this information, there existed a secret organization "which has as its avowed objects the return of Abdul Medjid to Constantinople and his restoration as Caliph."[104] Seyyid Sanussi was known for his closeness to the nationalist movement in Turkey and to Mustafa Kemal himself and originally supported the abolition of the sultanate and the establishment of a caliphate with purely spiritual powers. However, he seemed to be agitated by Mustafa Kemal's decision to abolish the caliphate altogether. Osman Fahrettin Bey informed the U.S. high commissioner that Seyyid Sanussi was now in sympathy with this secret organization. It is in this context that one finds information about an active secret organization aiming at a regime change in Turkey as late as 1924 and perhaps afterward. According to the informant, Prince Ömer Tosun of Egypt was collecting funds for the return of Abdülmecit to İstanbul as caliph, and he would give financial support to this secret organization. There is no name mentioned for the group, but the names of some members were recorded: İzzet Pasha (former grand vizier), Refet Pasha, Ali Rıza Pasha (former grand vizier), Kemal Bey (minister of supply in the CUP government), Yusuf Kemali Bey (former deputy from Mersin), Selahattin Adil Pasha (military commandant of İstanbul in 1923), Velid Bey (editor in chief of *Tevhid-i Efkar*), Zeki Bey (deputy from Gümüşhane), Hoca Sabri Efendi (former deputy from Afyonkarahisar), Hulusi Efendi (former deputy from Konya), Ahmet Bey (notable of Diyarbakır), İsmail Nadi Bey (notable of Diyarbakır), Vehbi Bey (notable of Diyarbakır), Abdulfettah Efendi (notable of Van), Halil Efendi (notable of Van), and Abdulvatap Efendi (notable of Van).

When this list is compared to the list of the accused in connection with the İzmir assassination plot of 1926 and with the accused after the Sheikh Said Revolt of 1925, some of the names overlap. For example, (Kara) Kemal Bey, who was condemned to death by the Independence Tribunal in Ankara, committed suicide in 1926. Refet (Bele) Pasha later became a member of the PRP, and his name was associated with the İzmir conspiracy. He was later acquitted in İzmir in 1926. After the Sheikh Said Revolt, Velid Bey, along with some other oppositional journalists, was arrested and later released.

Furthermore, another U.S. document (867.00/1812) continues on the information gathered from the same Osman Fahrettin Bey. The quotation is lengthy. However, it makes significant claims; therefore, it is necessary to cite it in full:

> The political leaders of the [secret organization] favor a much more active and immediate program. *Their ultimate objective is the overthrow of the present* [Kemalist] *Government and the establishment of a constitutional monarchy* [emphasis added]. . . . The future constitutional monarch of Turkey, in the opinion of these leaders, would be either Abdul Medjid Effendi or Selim Effendi, the eldest son of Sultan Abdul Hamid II. A meeting of the political leaders of the movement was held a short time ago at Erenkeuy. Some twenty-five persons, including Raouf Bey and Refet Pasha, were present. Raouf Bey spoke at length in favor of a constitutional monarchy for Turkey along English lines and declared that the republican form of government was not suited to Turkey. Refet Pasha said they had been willing to follow Moustapha Kemal Pasha as a military leader in the war against the Greeks, but they did not propose to follow him and his "gang" in a political dictatorship. He said the National Assembly should rule the country and not Moustapha Kemal Pasha. The tactics of these leaders are characterized by great caution. They have taken little or no action heretofore desiring to await the coming into effect of the

> Lausanne Treaty in order to avoid the danger of placing Turkey in a disadvantageous position towards the Powers. They are now very discreetly spreading propaganda by means of agents who are working in various parts of Anatolia. Abdul Kader Bey [former governor of Ankara who was executed in 1926] . . . is working for the movement. The first definite move will be to force the dissolution of the Assembly and the holding of new elections which will doubtless return an even larger number of unruly Deputies than there are at present. Then will be the time for bringing out the idea of a constitutional monarch. It is interesting to note that it is proposed to bring back but one member of the House of Othman—the one selected as constitutional monarch. The others will not be allowed to return, but will be pensioned.[105]

It is worth repeating that there is no independent confirmation for this intelligence. However, if accurate, this report is extremely valuable. At present, we do not have any reason to doubt the authenticity of the source. However, it is possible that for an unknown reason, Fahrettin Bey was feeding the U.S. embassy with false information. Nevertheless, it is equally possible that this information was correct. As such, the report brings Rauf Bey (one of the main leaders of the opposition) into the center of the conspiracy against the regime and confirms the fear of Mustafa Kemal of the existence of a secret organization for a regime change if not a counterrevolution.

In order to examine the accuracy of these documents, let us first place them in proper context. They were dated June 17 and July 26, 1924, just over three months after the abolition of the caliphate. We know that Rauf Bey and Refet Pasha, along with some other significant figures in the War of Independence (1919–1922), were increasingly upset with Mustafa Kemal and his new inner circle. We also know that four months after these reports, the first opposition party, the PRP, was established (November 17, 1924) and that Seyyid Sanussi was in Turkey with his small entourage. As it is known, he actively supported the nationalist movement in Turkey by issuing fatwas for the legitimacy of the Kemalist movement early on. After the abolition of the caliphate, he was involved in negotiations with Mustafa Kemal regarding the next caliph.[106] Therefore, it is historically possible that Osman Fahrettin Bey was in Turkey, where he was collecting intelligence.

Who was Osman Fahrettin Bey? Unfortunately, we do not have sufficient information as to his background and motivations. Mark L.

Bristol, the U.S. high commissioner in İstanbul, informs us that Osman Fahrettin Bey was an associate of people representing Bolsheviks and other Near Eastern countries to propagate Bolshevism.[107] With this background, it is possible that Osman Fahrettin Bey collected this information from foreign intelligence sources in Turkey. Perhaps he received such intelligence from the Bolshevik agents active in Turkey.

We know that the RPP was suspicious of Rauf Bey's loyalty to the regime in 1923 and accused him of not favoring republicanism. Rauf Bey refuted the accusation and maintained that he was in favor of people's sovereignty.[108] This document claims that in a meeting unknown to the government, Rauf Bey made speeches in favor of constitutional monarchy and that a secret organization was spreading antigovernment/pro-monarchist propaganda. We do know that both Rauf Bey and Refet Pasha held the view that Mustafa Kemal's regime was a "political dictatorship."[109] However, the RPP's accusations that Rauf Bey and Refet Pasha preferred constitutional monarchy over republic had never been independently confirmed until this document. The government must not have been privy to the information that was available to Osman Fahrettin Bey, for it would give the Independence Tribunals a more solid base for claims that opposition was in favor of a regime change by any means.

Another significant piece of information revealed in this document is the attitude of this mysterious organization toward the exiled Ottoman dynasty. Although these oppositional figures favored constitutional monarchy, they were willing to go only as far as allowing one member of the dynasty, the newly selected constitutional monarch, to return to Turkey. The other members would be compensated monetarily but would remain in exile. This attitude clearly demonstrates that even the opposition, which favored a form of monarchy, had limited tolerance of the dynasty, as they too regarded the Ottoman dynasty a worthy competitor for power.

Nevertheless, this information does not substantiate any claim that former CUP and PRP members were plotting to kill Mustafa Kemal; rather, they intended to pacify and replace him. In fact, İsmet Pasha later in his memoir hesitates to connect many of the accused with the İzmir assassination plot. Commenting on the guilt of the condemned, İsmet Pasha, years later, reflected, "I can only accept that Rauf Bey had an intuition for such a plot. I have never been convinced that he was involved in such a conspiracy."[110] As to the CUP's involvement in the plot, İsmet Pasha is rather vague. The CUP members of the accused, according to İsmet Pasha, were "very dangerous people in terms of their nature and temperament."[111] However, for Cavit Bey, one of the notables of the CUP, İsmet Pasha is more remorseful: "I have never entertained the possibility that Cavit Bey had any connection with the plot. What happened to him is the worst that could happen to a leader of a [political] organization."[112] In other words, İsmet Pasha admitted that Cavit Bey was sacrificed because of his leadership position in the CUP. İsmet Pasha's memoir registers a degree of hesitancy, wrapped in a surprise, to connect many of the executed members of the opposition to the plot.

CONCLUSION

There has been much debate about the nature and consequences of the İzmir plot against the life of Mustafa Kemal. Many conclusions in current scholarship are based on secondhand knowledge that cannot be fully sustained. The aim of this chapter was to categorize and scrutinize the available information on the plot and to promote further primary documents that would contribute to the debate. Conclusions that have been presented in this chapter can be put into three categories: those that are supported with conclusive evidence, those that are based on circumstantial or suggestive evidence, and those that are speculative. There should be little doubt that in 1926 there was an assassination plot against Mustafa Kemal in İzmir. Equally certain is that Mustafa Kemal manipulated this attempt to continue on his general policy of silencing the political opposition. As the previous chapter demonstrated, this process of silencing the political and intellectual opposition in the TGNA began a year before with the passing of the Takrir-i Sükun. We also know that the prosecution failed to prove the guilt of some convicted CUP and PRP members (such as Cavit and Rauf Beys) beyond any reasonable doubt. Moreover, we can safely state that there was visible discontent among people whose interests were harmed by the emergence of the new government and who were ideologically opposed to a republican and secular regime. Surely, some opposition members had personal reasons to oppose Mustafa Kemal and his authoritarian style of government.

Conclusions that we can draw based on circumstantial evidence are the following. We have only suggestive evidence that there was a well-organized and well-financed opposition in the country aiming at overthrowing the government and changing the regime. One can readily assume that the ultimate goal of the plot, if carried out, would be to replace the government. It is probable that Ziya Hurşit was hoping to kill Mustafa Kemal and to create a power vacuum in the government, ultimately resulting in the replacement of those in power. We can also state that some members of the opposition (such as Hafız Mehmet) were aware of the plans to assassinate Mustafa Kemal, though they might not have known the specifics.

With reasonable confidence, we can also state that it was during the İzmir trials that Mustafa Kemal realized that he could use the plot as a pretext not only to silence the PRP leaders but also to eliminate the remnants of the CUP that had a great potential to weaken the government in the next elections in 1927. Otherwise, the condemned CUP members (besides Cavit, Şükrü, and Abdülkadir Beys) would be dealt with immediately along with the PRP members in İzmir. Unlike the tribunal's claim, there is no convincing evidence coming out of the İzmir trials that implicated a conspiracy organized by the CUP to overthrow the government. Encouraged by the lack of public outcry after the İzmir trials, the Independence Tribunal must have felt confident in taking on the CUP. However, the fact that a significant oppositional figure, Hüseyin Cahit (Yalçın), was found "not guilty" shows that the court was mindful of pushing their limits too far.[113]

It is interesting to note that İsmet Pasha's attitude toward the conspiracy trials of 1926 radically differed from his stance against the PRP after the Sheikh Said Revolt a year earlier. How can we explain his change of position toward the opposition? It is possible that İsmet Pasha was uneasy about the possibility that the Independence Tribunal would go out of control and destabilize the system. It is also possible that he was weary of the unknown reaction of the CUP's sympathizers.

Conclusions that can be considered "suggestive" include the following. It should be noted that "suggestive" does not mean incorrect; rather, it means based only on deductive reasoning. Therefore, it can only point to logical possibilities. For example, we can only speculate that Mustafa Kemal and a small group of his inner circle were aware of the specific plans for the plot. They decided to allow it to move forward with the preconceived aim that such a failed attempt would boost his waning popularity in the country and provide the government with a pretext to silence its opponents.

There are many other questions that can be answered only speculatively. For example, was there a master plan in the mind of Mustafa Kemal to eliminate the entire opposition? We know that he was unhappy with the PRP in parliament and the counterrevolutionary potential of the CUP network still active in the country. I submit, however, that Mustafa Kemal advanced in his quest to silence the opposition only pragmatically. He surely wanted to push the members of the closed PRP out of the TGNA, where they still voted as an oppositional bloc. Erik Jan Zürcher concluded that Mustafa Kemal was also threatened by the prestige of some of the PRP members in the nationalist movement, a prestige that almost rivaled his own (such as that of Ali Fuat, Refet, Kazım Karabekir Pashas, and Rauf Bey). In addition, the social makeup and the followers of the PRP, which included the military elite, commercial groups, former bureaucrats, and so on, was a concern for him.[114] Therefore, a period commencing with the Sheikh Said Revolt of 1925 was devoted almost entirely to silencing this opposition in parliament. However, he was also alarmed by the potential of the CUP network, especially those who refused to be absorbed by the RPP. The network, as it was proven time and again, was quite capable of carrying out extrajudicial/*komitadji* activities, such as political assassinations.[115]

A significant question needs to be posed here. Why was it that the CUP was not targeted after the Sheikh Said Revolt within the same context of the Takrir-i Sükun? The government had more reason to fear some CUP members than they did the PRP. I submit that one of the main reasons was the following. The RPP enjoyed the support and service of many former rank-and-file members of the CUP, and the government was not confident that the RPP could contain its members' reactions to the purging of their former leaders in 1925. However, their loyalty to the RPP government assured Mustafa Kemal that these former CUP members and their political interests were fully incorporated into the RPP regime. During the İzmir trials, it must have been decided that this problem should be solved once and for all. Such flexible political maneuverings are further evidence of Mustafa Kemal's practicality in establishing the new regime. It is a political pragmatism par excellence that was vital for the success of the establishment of modern Turkey as a Western-oriented secular republic. Mustafa Kemal's "vision" for the new Turkey must have been in constant negotiation with the opportunities that became available to him during his tenure as president of the Turkish Republic.

We know that high-level officers in the military remained loyal to the new regime. However, what was the position of the rank-and-file officers in relation to the Ankara trials and the purging of the CUP? We know that Mustafa Kemal was instrumental in securing a substantial pay raise for the armed forces from the TGNA on October 20, 1923, just nine days before the proclamation of the republic, and also in forcing those military officers whose loyalty to the new regime was in question.[116] We can speculate that the release of Kazım Karabekir, Ali Fuat, Refet Bele, and other generals calmed considerably the existing opposition in the military. The CUP-sympathetic military personnel were already forced out by the Damat Ferit governments prior to the republican regime. Therefore, expectedly, the military remained calm during this period.

Another significant question that requires reasonable speculation to answer is the nature of the CUP-PRP relationship. We know that CUP members were not a monolithic group; some of the members found employment in both the PRP and the RPP. However, was the PRP a front for those CUP members who wished to undermine the government? A British document can shed some light on this question. In a confidential conversation with Mr. Macartney of *The Times*, Hüseyin Cahit Bey of *Tanin* and a leader of the CUP stated on October 8, 1924 (little over a month before the formation of the PRP), that the popularity of Mustafa Kemal was on the wane and that the RPP did not enjoy support in the eastern provinces of the country. Therefore, Hüseyin Cahit suggested, an opposition party would be formed:[117]

> [The new party was not intended] to reconstitute the old Committee of Union and Progress as the new opposition party, though undoubtedly many of the old organization would join it. Nor was it intended to afford cover to any anti-republican or other reactionary elements. The new party was to be an Opposition organized with the definite objection of opposing the Government on Constitutional and republican lines; and towards the President it would initiate no marked hostility, but would reserve its attitude until the President's attitude towards it was more clearly defined.[118]

Hüseyin Cahit Bey, who was spared from being executed in Ankara, seemed to confirm that many CUP members viewed the formation of the PRP with sympathy and intended to take part in it. However, the PRP was not an arm of the old CUP. In fact, many higher-level CUP members (such as Hüseyin Cahit and Cavit Beys) refrained from entering the ranks of the party. We can only speculate that CUP leaders had plans to form another party before the elections in 1927 and did not want to commit to the PRP. Once established, they might have thought, it would not be too difficult to recruit their former members back from the PRP and even perhaps from the RPP.

In any case, the Ankara trials effectively ended the short period of a power struggle in the early Turkish Republic. In the following decades until the switch to the multiparty system in 1945, the country was governed by a single party, the RPP. This period (1925–1926) created a political culture in Turkey in which even the subsequent governments in the multiparty system showed little or no regard for a healthy opposition. One can still see the remnants of this attitude in the present political environment in Turkey almost a century after it was initiated. The main difference is that Mustafa Kemal had a justified fear for a counterrevolution and for his life.

5

Concluding Remarks

It has always been postulated that Mustafa Kemal Atatürk's commitment to republicanism and a parliamentarian regime laid the very foundations of the democratic Turkish state. However, because of the sacred space assigned to the early years of the Turkish Republic, systematic studies on the nature of the formative years—as they relate particularly to the issue of political diversity—are very rare. Only a few available studies have been able to escape the polarizing bias and to remain loyal to the standards of an academic study. This is most visible especially on the subject of the power struggle in the transition period from the Ottoman Empire to the Turkish Republic.

When the War of Independence (1919–1922) was concluded in favor of the nationalists in Ankara, there were many unknowns in regard to the future and nature of Turkey. Although the nationalists were in an advantageous position to dominate the new administration and to dictate their vision on government, there were still very visible and potent internal groups in the remaining land of the Ottoman Empire that would pose a significant challenge to the nationalists in Ankara and to the emerging regime as a republic.

By way of conclusion, let us first remember the identity of the opposition in this period and then highlight the conclusions of each chapter in this study. Who were the most significant internal opponents of the emerging regime in Ankara, a regime that intended to alter the flow of Turkish and, to some extent, Islamic history? To address this question, I would like to draw on a somewhat insightful document from the U.S. diplomatic archives.

This document, dated October 15, 1923, attempts to portray the possible actors of an inevitable power struggle in Turkey. Penned by Maynard B. Barnes, the U.S. consul and the delegate of the U.S. high commissioner in Turkey, this report, titled "Political Situation in Turkey," was prepared in Ankara for the U.S. Secretary of State in Washington.[1] It is important to note that the report was written only two weeks before the proclamation of the new Turkish regime as a republic. It shows us a view of the U.S. diplomatic personnel in Ankara on the internal power structures in Turkey. The report begins with a statement that after the signing the Treaty of Lausanne in 1923, the "nationalists" showed signs of factionalism. Specific names that were mentioned in the report against Mustafa Kemal include Nureddin Pasha, the former commander of the Ottoman army who entered İzmir; Rahmi Bey, former governor-general of İzmir; Refet (Bele) Pasha; Kazım Karabekir Pasha; and Rauf (Orbay) Bey. The report also alleges that a large portion of İzmir's population was out of sympathy with the Kemalist regime. Barnes continues to list other possible oppositional groups:

> Many of the older army officers of the rank of Lieutenant Colonel and of Colonel are disgruntled as a result of having seen during the past three years many younger officers promoted over them to the rank of General. Furthermore, the recent transfer of six thousand officers from the regular army to reserve officer categories in order to cut down the budget has created another center of discontent in military circles.

It is important to note that the report sees certain segments of military as "disgruntled" and a source for opposition to Mustafa Kemal. Since, historically, the Turkish military constitutes the means for political change, if materialized, its opposition to the emerging regime would have altered the Kemalist vision. Barnes also observes the factionalism among Mustafa Kemal's former confidants such as Refet Pasha, Kazım Karabekir Pasha, and Rauf Bey, who a year later established the first opposition party in the Turkish Grand National Assembly (TGNA).

Based on his observations in Ankara and the intelligence he collected in Turkey, the U.S. consul lists several other oppositional groups. Former "monarchists" and the "Hodja Party"[2] are at the top of the list of "serious opposition" to Mustafa Kemal:

> By abolishing the Sultanate, Kemal alienated from his cause the more conservative elements of the educated class and especially the old families of wealth and influence in Constantinople, Smyrna and other large centers, thus creating what may be

> termed for lack of a better phrase the Monarchist group. This act also accentuated the opposition of the Hodja Party which during the past year has become not only apparent but quite effective at times and which will doubtless steadily increase with the inauguration of educational, social and religious reforms which it is expected, in view of the anti-clerical tendency of the Nationalists, that the present regime endeavor to effect.

Two observations are noteworthy in this portion of the report. First, one year after the abolition of the sultanate (October 1, 1922), the "monarchists" (those who were loyal to the Ottoman monarchy) were still regarded as a major threat to the Kemalists. The second is that even before the abolition of the "caliphate," the ulama, aware of Ankara's "anti-clerical" tendencies, constituted a visible opposition to the nationalist regime. In connection with these groups, the report continues, a large number of unemployed civil functionaries of the old regime also existed as a possible oppositional force. The report singles out that the Committee of Union and Progress (CUP) posed the greatest threat to Mustafa Kemal:

> *The most serious opposition comes from the recently resuscitated Union and Progress Party* [emphasis added], which is being ably led by Hussein Djahid Bey, editor of the Tanine which is the most influential newspaper in Turkey, Rahmi Bey of Smyrna, Djavid Bey, who was Minister of Finance during the reign of the Triumvirate, Shukri Bey, who was Minister of Public Instruction in the same cabinet of which Djavid Bey was a member, Kemal Bey, who as Minister of Revictualment was a colleague of Shukri and Djavid, and Midhat Shukri Bey, who was Secretary-General of the Union ad Progress Party from its inception.

The report acknowledges that until the Mudanya Armistice (October 11, 1922) and perhaps even much later, the nationalists and the CUP were thought to be synonymous. However, when the general elections took place, many of the nationalist followers came to realize that certain well-known unionists were not within the ranks of the Republican People's Party (RPP). This was the first indication that the CUP was not entirely absorbed by the RPP and stands apart from the Kemalists. The report continues,

> The fact that the Union and Progress Party does exist apart from the Peoples Party has become more apparent. The Peoples Party leaders still persists in their contention that the Unionism has

> evoluted [evolved?] in to Nationalism and the old Union and Progress Party does not exist. However, despite the fact that the old [CUP] leaders have not yet seen fit to formally register the party, there is no doubt that it exists in fact. Indeed, it has even inherited nearly intact the old party machine which the present leaders have been diligently renovating during the past few months. *In truth it is the Peoples Party, which does not actually exist. It is a purely fictitious organization built upon the popularity of Moustapha Kemal Pasha* [emphasis added]. The rank and file of the Party are still Unionist who will revert to their original party as the popularity of Kemal wanes and when strong Unionist leaders openly enter the political arena.

This section of the report is extraordinary for several reasons. First, it informs us that the RPP's leaders were portraying the CUP as an organization, dissolved into the RPP, and hence it did not exist anymore. This is significant because during the trials of the CUP members in 1926, the major accusation leveled against them was that they were planning to revive the CUP against the RPP. Based on the information in this report, one can conclude, the nationalists wished to use the influence of the CUP originally and resorted to the elimination of the CUP leaders in Turkey only when it became clear that the CUP would reenter the republican political scene as a separate party.

Another significant observation of the report is the assertion that the CUP was a major force to replace the existing political elite when Mustafa Kemal's popularity waned. The implication is present that his popularity would wane sooner rather than later. We should entertain the possibility that the endurance of Mustafa Kemal's popularity depended, at least partly, on the removal of CUP leaders from the political scene. Mustafa Kemal must have been aware of the fact that RPP's existence depended heavily on the disappearance of the CUP, whose leadership could not be trusted.

In 1923, the U.S. consul was convinced that Mustafa Kemal and the RPP would be replaced by the CUP in the near future and that it was indeed the RPP, which was a "fictitious" organization, with many former lower-level CUP members at its ranks, waiting to switch their loyalties to the CUP at any given moment. If this was visible to a foreign diplomat, it was visible to the local population and certainly to the Kemalists.

Barnes sees the outstanding political issue between the Kemalists and the CUP as nationalism versus pan-Islamism. Kemalists were nationalists and insisted on a state whose boundaries were stipulated by the National Pact.[3] They wished to Turkify everything within these boundaries. The CUP, on the other hand, believed that Turkey could again become a great power through the agency of pan-Islamism. The other clash between the two was on the form of government. Kemalists hoped to have a government evolving around the wishes of Mustafa Kemal and free from any interference from the caliph. The CUP, on the other hand, desired a government based on the European parliamentary system but definitely linked to the caliphate.

The U.S. observer does not believe that the Turkish military would stage a successful coup against Mustafa Kemal, who was conscious of the power of the military in politics. Aware that a popular revolution against the regime in power was an unknown phenomenon in Turkey and that only the military could stage successful coups, Mustafa Kemal carefully watched dissatisfied higher-ranking officers and either retired them or appointed them to positions where they did not command soldier—a practice that was commonly utilized by the CUP earlier. As for the lower-ranked officers, Barnes suggests, "Mustafa Kemal was continually endeavoring to better their lives. Recently, the Assembly raised the officers' pay approximately fifty per cent."

The report claims that CUP members were a lot more experienced as political candidates, and they would be elected with an overwhelming majority in the next elections in 1927. Therefore, they would not adhere to forceful removal of the Kemalists from power. In fact, once the CUP decided to enter the political arena, Barnes maintains, many of the RPP members, who were actually former CUP associates or sympathizers, would switch sides and join the CUP:

> That the downfall of Kemal would be the natural correlation to a Unionist victory is a mistaken idea. The Unionists realize that the present political situation demands that the Turkish state have as its head a strong dominant figure. Furthermore, they recognize Kemal's popularity both in Turkey and in other Moslem countries and in addition are aware of his honesty of purpose. But as the leader of the People's Party, the Unionists could never accept him.

Therefore, the CUP leaders advised him to step down as the leader of the RPP and be aloof from politics. This would have provided the CUP leaders with a strong head of state but would return the government back to the CUP once again. Barnes, as an acute foreign observer, seems to have read the political picture of Turkey quite accurately.

However, his predictions, as history shows, are off the mark, as Mustafa Kemal's vision for the new Turkey and his role in it clashed with that of the CUP. Mustafa Kemal, realizing the threat the CUP posed to his power, opted for taking them on and finally destroying them as a result of several shrewd political maneuverings. As chapter 4 of this book demonstrated, the last influential CUP members were executed a year before the upcoming elections in 1927.

Barnes's report identified the opponents of the emerging regime as rank-and-file members of the military, monarchists, the ulama, civil servants, and the CUP; some of these categories necessarily overlapped. Mustafa Kemal must have been keenly aware of the oppositional attitude of these groups. The oppositional figures in the military at the rank of "general," such as Kazım Karabekir, Ali Fuat, Nurettin, and Cafer Tayyar Pashas, were forced into retirement from the military. Lower-ranked military officers were readily incorporated into the new regime. These groups were targeted by the new regime as possible opponents of the establishment and were silenced.

Examining the report with the information we have in the twenty-first century has clear advantages. We know how history unfolded and how some of the predictions in the report turned out to be wrong. The main reason for the lack of accuracy of forecasting the future is the earlier tendency in foreign reports to underestimate Mustafa Kemal's unmatched political ability to challenge his political opponents. However, the report's description of oppositional forces to Mustafa Kemal gives us a chance to highlight this perceptive man's foresight to recognize these forces and his political maneuverings to eliminate them.

This book selectively focused on three sources of opposition: (1) opposition to Ankara, (2) opposition in Ankara, and (3) opposition at large. Opposition to Ankara included some of the groups that were identified in a U.S. report as monarchists (such as the members of the Liberal Entente, a political party that replaced the CUP government and was in power when unfavorable peace treaties, such as the Treaty of Sevres, were negotiated and signed). This eclectic group was determined after the signing of the Treaty of Lausanne to set an example for those who questioned the authority of the TGNA in Ankara. To represent this group, I selected "the Incident of the 150ers" (*Yüzellilikler Olayı*).

Our analysis began with this group of 150 who were labeled as traitors to their own people by the Ankara regime. After examining the national and international circumstances that gave way to the Incident of the 150ers in early Turkish republican history, the chapter examined the backgrounds of these selected 150 people. The main aim was to establish a meaningful pattern in their backgrounds to justify their inclusion on the list. However, close analysis of the list revealed that this group was highly eclectic. The list was haphazardly prepared, and its members were arbitrarily selected. We know that Ankara's main target was its former counterpart in İstanbul and the nationalists' determination to demonstrate to the nation that Ankara was in control. This was in a sense the declaration of adulthood for Ankara for internal politics. Therefore, several Liberal Entente politicians and statesmen were symbolically selected. The 150ers also included different segments of anti-CUP coalition, such as some high-ranking members of the ulama, the Ottoman civil service, politicians, and the oppositional press, which favored İstanbul over Ankara. They can be loosely categorized as monarchists. Their disdain for the Ankara Circle (the nationalists) came originally from the belief that the nationalists were in fact a front for the CUP that, when in power, pressured its opponents greatly.

Although these former anti-CUP monarchists were the main target for elimination as a potential threat to Ankara, the list was dominated by supporters of Ethem the Circassian, a rebel who originally served and was honored by the nationalist movement. When Ethem found himself at odds with Ankara (especially with İsmet Pasha), he took a position against them with his rebel army. If the monarchists were chosen to constitute a deterrent for the rest of the supporters of the imperial government, Ethem and his Circassian supporters might have been chosen to set an example for other armed unknown rebel groups in Anatolia. In addition, Ethem could surely be a valuable source for the enemy Greek army to create problems for the nationalists. However, despite the claims to the contrary, Ethem's military assistance to the Greeks against the nationalists was not clearly established.

In any case, all the individuals selected for the list of 150 were perceived as enemies of Ankara and hence traitors to the nation. Clearly, there were more than 150 people in the country who carried with them hostile feelings toward Ankara and who constituted potential threats; however, because of the stipulation of amnesty in the Treaty of Lausanne, only 150 names of Muslim origin could have been included on the list for exile. Reducing the list from 600 to 300 and then to 150 was a challenge for the TGNA. Chapter 2 showed that in the process of selecting 150 names, personal rivalries played a role and that the list was finalized only subjectively. Nevertheless, the general purpose of sending a message to opponents of the new regime was achieved.

The incident of the 150ers proved that the Ankara government clearly established its authority over the monarchists in the country. We know from police reports that Ankara even employed some of these people as informants.

Chapter 3 focused on the opposition in Ankara and examined the power struggle within the nationalist movement. This period commenced with the Sheikh Said Revolt of 1925, a Kurdish/Islamist uprising that provided Mustafa Kemal and his inner circle with a pretext in which the only political opposition in parliament was forced to submission. This chapter demonstrated how this rebellion paved the way for the introduction of the Takrir-i Sükun, an extraordinary law that enabled the government to discredit, jail, and effectively silence some members of the only opposition party, the PRP. As a result of the trials by the Independence Tribunal following the uprising, the PRP was shut down, yet its members still remained in the TGNA as an oppositional bloc without a political party until 1926. It is worth emphasizing that the government was experimenting with the limits of its power within the Takrir-i Sükun; it did not know how far it could go in eliminating the entire opposition. It stopped when the PRP was discredited with the accusation that the only opposition party inspired, if not directly aided, the Kurdish rebellion. The main target of the Takrir-i Sükun seems to be the opposition in the TGNA and some intellectuals despite the fact that most Kurds suffered the consequences of this rebellion, regardless of their participation in it, as much as if not more than the opposition. In order to justify the pending silencing policies, the government needed to exaggerate the danger of this rebellion.

Since the public did not have any access to information, such an exaggeration was not difficult; after all, information was disseminated to the public through a government-controlled press. However, what was difficult was connecting the opposition to the rebellion. The PRP was newly formed but led by able statesmen and well-liked soldiers, many of whom were raised to heroic levels in the eyes of the public during the War of Independence. Chapter 3 demonstrated how this task was accomplished and how these oppositional leaders were isolated with political and judicial maneuverings. Surely, the opposition was not a match for the ambition of the RPP to rule, as the PRP miscalculated the extremes to which the RPP was willing to go.

In this process, not only was the opposition in the TGNA isolated, but all oppositional strains of thought were targeted as well, including the leftist and Islamist presses. With the Islamic nature of the Sheikh

Said Revolt, the Islamic press was an easy target, as it published articles that carried a critical tone against the Ankara government. Many potential Islamist leaders were arrested and tried in the Independence Tribunals, which emphasized the government's commitment to pacifying the hostile ulama, whom it regarded as a major obstacle for progress and modernization. However, the government also targeted the leftists with the same accusation that their intellectual orientation and political commitments would endanger the well-being of the new regime.

Clearly, the Sheikh Said Revolt benefited the Kemalist government more than it served the cause of Kurdish nationalism and Islamism at that time. We know that in the following period, the Sheikh Said Revolt became the symbol for the Kurdish nationalist struggle in the Turkish Republic, yet in 1925, it demonstrated only how divided and vulnerable the Kurdish political movements were. Therefore, a sensible question was asked in chapter 3: was the Sheikh Said Revolt fomented by the Ankara government to eliminate political opposition in Turkey? Based on available information, the chapter concluded that we are on more steady grounds to suggest that the revolt was manipulated, not fomented, by the government.

This brings us to the next chapter, which demonstrated the final stage of the silencing process. In 1926, a year before the next general elections, members of the closed PRP were still in parliament. Although tamed considerably in their opposition to the government, they could have broken the silence necessary to pass some more radical reforms (such as the alphabet reform). By this time, personal rivalries between the members of the opposition and the radicals in the RPP were already heightened because of the government's action against the PRP after the Sheikh Said Revolt. Another fear of the government—and especially of Mustafa Kemal—was the unknown nature of the PRP and the former CUP collaboration. The Kemalists were keenly aware of the political challenge that the CUP network would pose to the RPP. Furthermore, the CUP's underground activities and political assassinations were well known to many Kemalists, some of whom had firsthand experience in these activities. Therefore, it is fair to state that in 1926, the government considered the remnants of the CUP as the greatest threat to its power—a threat that needed to be swiftly dealt with before the 1927 general elections. We do not know much about the organizational structure and strength of the remnants of the CUP network in 1926; however, we do know that it worried the RPP and Mustafa Kemal.

The İzmir assassination plot was discovered in this political environment; therefore, it immediately raised questions about the role of the government in it. It was common knowledge that the government was looking for a pretext to complete the silencing process of the political opposition. This plot seemed rather too convenient for the government, so much so that foreign observers and the members of the opposition entertained the possibility of the government's hand in this plot. Chapter 4 examined this plot and concluded that there is no sufficient information to doubt the authenticity of the plot. Nevertheless, from the moment it was discovered, the government manipulated it to enlist support for the regime and to pressure the opposition.

Tamed, if not entirely silenced, opposition was clearly the target of the government; however, it should be noted that the RPP radicals also regarded any opposition as a direct threat to their personal security. In that regard, the 1926 İzmir assassination plot was as timely as the Sheikh Said Revolt of 1925. However, there was a difference in the government's response to these two incidents. Unlike the Sheikh Said Revolt, those in power were not in complete agreement on how to utilize this plot for political gain. We know, for example, that İsmet Pasha wished to use it solely to increase the government's popularity. Mustafa Kemal and his radical followers, however, opted to use it to get rid of any opposition once and for all, be it PRP leaders or the CUP. İsmet Pasha was speedily convinced by Mustafa Kemal of the great opportunity this plot presented to completely weed out any opposition to the leadership. Needless to say, Mustafa Kemal was in complete control of the situation.

It was inevitable that opposition leaders would be linked to the plot. The İzmir trials were geared toward dealing mainly with the PRP leaders. Following the minutes of the court and the prosecutor's plea, one can get the sense that the well-respected generals in the PRP (such as Kazım Karabekir, Refet, and Ali Fuat) would be spared from jail or worse and that the main motivation for their arrest was to taint their reputation. We know this because although the Independence Tribunal adamantly requested their arrest (even to the degree that the court was at odds with İsmet Pasha) during their trials, the prosecutor did not even attempt to make any accusation regarding the arrested generals' guilt in the plot. Why is it that the court insisted on Kazım Karabekir's arrest despite the prime minister's objection but was not concerned with producing any evidence during the trials? We must entertain the possibility that the arrest of these PRP leaders was aimed solely at discrediting them and forcing them out of the political system—an aim that was fully achieved.

The next question is the following: why was the court not as lenient toward the CUP leadership as it was toward that of the PRP? We know that the Ankara trials for the plot aimed at silencing the CUP leadership. This was decided probably during the İzmir phase. The court wanted to display Cavit Bey and other significant members of the CUP as traitors in a trial in the same way that Kazım Karabekir and his friends were dealt with. Why, then, was the latter group acquitted after the trial but the former group faced the death penalty? After all, the court showed similar indifference to establishing any viable link between, say, Cavit Bey or Kazım Karabekir and the plot. Why is it that the former was executed but the latter was acquitted? We do not know for sure, but the answer could be any combination of the following: personal vendetta, fear of vengeance, or deterrence. The Kemalists had every reason to be fearful of the CUP, as its potential to destabilize the RPP was unknown. The PRP, on the other hand, was already crippled and its power structure severely damaged. Executing the heroes of the nationalist movement also carried with it a degree of risk, as the army and even some RPP members respected them greatly. Mustafa Kemal probably was not as confident about taming this group of CUP leaders; they needed to be removed. This could be a reason for the radical remedy that the government (or the radicals in it) chose. They opted to execute the leaders of the CUP.

With a degree of confidence, we can state that the government in Ankara acted only spontaneously in dealing with the opposition, responding to the opportunities and challenges in the early years of the republic. This conclusion can be generalized for the entire period. After all, one of the goals of this research is to invite readers to rethink the developments in this period not as the fulfillment of a clearly established "vision" but as the success of "pragmatism." The flow of early republican history was not predetermined as a result of a fixed vision. Mustafa Kemal and his friends responded to the realities of their times. In this context, one can and should question the generally accepted postulation that the nationalist movement in Anatolia in 1919 would not be settled until the goal of creating a secular republic was accomplished. As professional historians, we should ask the question, "what if?" What would have happened if Sultan Vahdettin recognized the Ankara government as legitimate in 1920 and had not fled the country? What would have happened if Enver and Talat

Pashas were not assassinated and had returned to Turkey? What would have happened if the last caliph, Abdülmecit II, was more useful to Ankara? What would have happened if the opposition in parliament (the PRP) had stronger muscles?

In this book, I have attempted to demonstrate that the flow of history in the early republic owes some debt to the power struggle that existed after World War I. I do not claim that Mustafa Kemal and his friends did not have a vision for the nature of the new Turkey. What I am claiming is that the power struggle helped shape his vision and created an environment where this continuously altered and adjusted vision could be implemented, and this level of adaptability has been one of the most significant assets of the new regime.

As expected, this power struggle could not have ended with a stalemate; the losing side(s) had to pay the price. As this research shows us, some paid with their lives, others with their hopes. We should be careful in ascribing "villain status" to Mustafa Kemal since he emerged victorious out of this power struggle. If Mustafa Kemal had been on the losing side, his fate may not have been too different from that of the CUP or PRP leaders, as Refet Pasha prophesied in October 1925 when he stated that Mustafa Kemal "is simply a man who is unhappy enough to have fallen into a disagreeable job and who in a few years may have to be riding on a tram car again."[4]

Notes

Chapter 1

1. İstanbul was first occupied 13 days after the Armistice of Mudros on November 12, 1918, by the French forces. The occupation became de jure on March 16, 1920. The occupation ended on September 23, 1923, and the Turkish troops entered the city on October 6, 1923.

2. A British document (L 273/273/405) by W. J. Childs of the Foreign Office, dated December 28, 1928, claims that the occupation of İzmir changed everything in the mind-set of the Turks. Until this event in May 1919, "the Turkish people had accepted defeat as a decree of fate. After the landing at Smyrna they did so no longer" (*British Documents on Foreign Affairs: Reports and Papers from the Foreign Office Confidential Print*. Part II, From the First to the Second World War, Series B, Turkey, Iran and the Middle East, 1918–1939. Vol. 31 [Bethesda, MD: University Publications of America, 1997], 235).

3. For a deeper analysis of the İstanbul and Ankara Circles, see Chapter 2.

4. The CUP was the political opponent of the Liberal Entente. The CUP government was responsible for the Ottoman entry into World War I and the disastrous defeat. See Feroz Ahmad, *The Young Turks: The Committee of Union and Progress in Turkish Politics, 1908–1914* (New York: Columbia University Press, 2009); see also Erik Jan Zürcher, *The Unionist Factor: The Role of the Committee of Union and Progress in the Turkish National Movement 1905–1926* (Leiden: E. J. Brill, 1984).

5. He was an Ottoman statesman who held the office of grand vizier (prime minister) during two periods under the reign of the last Ottoman sultan, Mehmet VI, or Vahdettin, the first time between March 4, 1919, and October 2, 1919, and the second time between April 5, 1920, and October 21,

1920. He was asked to form the government five times after the departure of the CUP leadership in 1918.

6. This political party was in fact an umbrella organization that incorporated such diverse groups as the ulama and non-Muslim and non-Turkish elements. It was the political opponent of the CUP after 1911. See Rıza Nur, *Hürriyet ve İtilaf Fırkası Nasıl Doğdu, Nasıl Öldü* (İstanbul: Kitapevi, 1996). For the first period of the Liberal Entente, see Ali Birinci, *Hürriyet ve İtilaf Fırkası: II. Meşrutiyet Devrinde İttihat ve Terakki'ye Karşı Çıkanlar* (İstanbul: Dergah, 1990).

7. See, for example, a report in the U.S. archives, 867.00/1737, from Maynard Barnes to Secretary of State, "Political Situation in Turkey," October 15, 1923.

8. Hakan Özoğlu, "Sultan Vahdettin'in ABD Başkanı Coolidge'e Gönderdiği Bir Mektup," *Toplumsal Tarih* 142 (October 2005): 100–106. A British report dated January 11, 1920, is interesting in that it entertains the possibility of expelling the sultan and the Ottoman government from Constantinople years before the departure of Vahdettin; CAB 23/35, Records of the Cabinet Office, October 25, 1920.

9. On November 1, 1922, with a decree (#308), the office of the sultanate was separated from that of the caliphate, and the sultanate was abolished. The only opposing vote came from Ziya Hurşit from Lazistan, who was later executed for his role in the İzmir assassination plot of 1926.

10. We know that before the abolition of the sultanate (possibly on October 20, 1922), Refet (Bele) Pasha, Ankara's representative in İstanbul, submitted a proposal to Ahmet İzzet Pasha, minister of war in the current Tevfik Pasha cabinet. This proposal has six articles that insisted on the sultan's recognition of Ankara's authority to govern. In return, the sultan would remain as such without any political authority to appoint or dismiss governments. For this telling document, see Ahmet İzzet Paşa, *Feryadım*, 2 vols. (İstanbul: Nehir, 1992, 1993), 190; see also Murat Bardakçı, *Şahbaba* (Ankara: İnkilap, 2006), 227–28.

11. This does not mean that there were no anti-Vahdettin statements made in the TGNA prior to his departure.

12. A U.S. report by Admiral Bristol to the Secretary of State (867.00/1786) states Refet Pasha's view on the abolition of the caliphate. Refet Pasha was in the Ankara Circle, working closely with Mustafa Kemal. Although he was later opposed to Mustafa Kemal's political moves, he remained a significant member of the Ankara Circle. Refet claims that abolition of the caliphate should have been done along with the abolition of the sultanate. When the caliphate was abolished on March 3, 1924, and "since a new caliph [Abdülmecit Efendi] had been elected and behaved well, sentiment in the country is favorable to the Caliph and the imperial family."

13. 867.00/1801, from Admiral Mark Bristol to Secretary of State, August 19, 1924; see also 867.00/1812.

14. Ibid., 867.00/1801.

15. In some Turkish sources Mustafa Kemal's offer to Sanussi appears to be for the office of the *Şeyhülislam* (technically the Mufti of İstanbul), not the Caliph, see Timuçin Mert, *Atatürk'ün Yanındaki Mehdi* (İstanbul: Karakutu, 2006), 145.

16. 867.00/1737. From Maynard Barnes to Secretary of State, "Political Situation in Turkey" 15 October 1923.

17. In his memoir, Joseph Grew, the US Ambassador in Ankara, points out a correspondence between Mustafa Kemal and Fethi Bey which indicates that original request to form an opposition party came from Fethi Bey himself; *Turbulent Era: A Diplomatic Record of Forty Years*, vol. 2 (London: Hammond and Co. Ltd, 1953), 860. In a letter to Mustafa Kemal on 11 August 1930, Fethi Bey, then the Turkish Ambassador to France, requests permission to form an opposition party and Mustafa Kemal responds to it positively; see 867.00/2034. The text of the letter was translated into English in this collection. This correspondence is significant in that it challenges the common understanding that it was Mustafa Kemal who came with the idea of an opposition party.

18. Mustafa Kemal himself hand-picked the leader and the members of this party.

19. Sedat Bingöl's thesis was published in 2010; see *Yüzellilikler Meselesi; Bir İhanetin Anatomisi* (İstanbul: Bengi, 2010).

Chapter 2

1. In the text, for stylistic reasons, I will refer to the Ankara Circle alternatively as Kemalists, nationalists, and the Anatolian movement.

2. One should keep in mind that the ulama were not a uniform body. It included conservative and more liberal elements in it. The latter interacted with the Ankara movement, and some of its members occasionally provided support for the modernist vision of Ankara.

3. *Anadolu'da Yeni Gün* and *Hakimiyet-i Milliye* were among them. See Yücel Özkaya, *Milli Mücadele'de Basın 1919–1921* (Ankara: Türk Tarih Kurumu, 1989); Hülya Baykal, *Türk Basın Tarihi 1831–1923: Tanzimat, Meşrutiyet, Milli Mücadele Dönemleri* (İstanbul: Afa, 1990); Bünyamin Ayhan, *Milli Mücadele'de Basın: Olağanüstü Durumlarda Propaganda* (Konya: Tablet, 2007); and *Hakimiyeti Milliye* (İstanbul: Zaman, 1949).

4. Behçet Cemal divides the İstanbul Press into three: the CUP supporters (Hüseyin Cahit Yalçın), the Rauf Bey supporters (Ahmet Emin Yalman), and the pro-caliph/Islamists (Eşref Edib and Velid Ebuziya); see *Şeyh Said ve İsyanı* (İstanbul: Sel, 1955), 12.

5. We know that the many CUP members were in favor of a constitutional monarchy, but for rather pragmatic reasons, I exclude the CUP from the İstanbul Circle.

6. Kamil Erdeha, *Yüzellilikler Yahut Milli Mücadelenin Muhasebesi* (Ankara: Tekin, 1998), 75–76.

7. Rıza Tevfik, *Biraz da Ben Konuşayım* (İstanbul: İletişim, 1993), 52–53.

8. *150'likler Faciası* (İstanbul: Sıralar, 1946), esp. 45–50. In his MA thesis, Sedat Bingöl, showing a degree of hesitancy toward the accuracy of these memoirs, states that he was unable to locate the newspaper that published İhsan Bey's memoirs. Reportedly, these memoirs were published between November 22 and 27, 1946, by the İstanbul daily *Yeni Türkiye*. Because the newspaper was closed on November 27, 1946, the memoirs were not complete. Bingöl informs us that he interviewed the owner of the newspaper, Mehmet Ali Gökberk, who confirmed that the originals of the memoirs were with Cemal Kutay. Bingöl's request from Kutay to examine the memoirs could not make much headway simply because Kutay's house was burned in 1980 along with the memoirs. Nevertheless, there is no reason to doubt the accuracy of the information presented only in Kutay's work. For Bingöl's argument, see "Yüzellilikler Meselesi" (MA thesis, Hacettepe University, 1994), 83–84, fn.

9. This is the view of Mustafa Kemal and his friends. Yet some members of the İstanbul government objected to this claim, suggesting that they were not hostile to the Kemalists. They in fact supported the nationalist movement by releasing the Allied pressure. See, e.g., Ahmet İzzet Paşa, *Feryadım*, vol. 2 (İstanbul: Nehir, 1993), 205–29, and Cemil Topuzlu, *Oparatör Cemil Paşa'nın Hatıraları* (İstanbul: Türkiye Yayınları, 1945), 132.

10. I translated the text liberally to highlight the implication. For the original, see Kutay, *Yüzellikler Faciası* (İstanbul: n.p., 1955), 47, and İlhami Soysal, *150'likler* (İstanbul: Gür, 1985), 13.

11. Soysal, *150'likler*, notes that Adnan Bey did not wish to include people in this list in their absentia (14).

12. Kutay, *Yüzellikler Faciası*, 50–51; Soysal, *150'likler*, 15; Bingöl, "Yüzellilikler Meselesi," 86.

13. Kutay, *Yüzellikler Faciası*, 50–51.

14. Rauf Bey had his signature under the Mudros Armistice. We know that Mustafa Kemal Pasha smiled at the possibility of including names that signed Sevres and Mudros, which would include Rauf Bey. Was this an early indication of a rivalry between the two respected names of the War of Independence? One can only speculate.

15. Soysal, *150'likler*, 16–17.

16. "Demek ki hadiselere his hakim olmaya başladı." Cemal Kutay, *150'likler Faciası* (İstanbul: Sıralar, 1955), 50; Soysal, *150'likler*, 17.

17. Kutay, *150'likler Faciası*, 50; Soysal, *150'likler*, 17.

18. It is important to note that the abolition of the sultanate was realized with a governmental decree, not a law that was voted in parliament. This subtle but extremely significant point is mostly overlooked in Turkish historiography. We do not know if there were sufficient votes in parliament to make it a law at the time.

19. It should be remembered that both İstanbul and Ankara governments sent representation (Bekir Sami Bey) to the earlier London Conference on March 12, 1921.

20. It should be remembered that the Turkish forces did not win any major battle against Great Britain but did against Greece, its proxy. This fact was also in the minds of Great Britain and Turkey throughout the negotiations. There exists an article on the British position by Erik Goldstein, "British Official Mind and the Lausanne Conference, 1922–1923," in *Power and Stability: British Foreign Policy, 1865–1965*, ed. E. Goldstein and B. J. C. McKercher (London: Frank Cass, 2003), 185–206.

21. The Second Group constituted an opposition to Mustafa Kemal's First Group in the first TGNA; see Ahmet Demirel, *Birinci Meclis'te Muhalefet: İkinci Grup* (İstanbul: İletişim, 1994).

22. Joseph C. Grew, the U.S. observer in the conference, points out that Lord Curzon "treated Ismet like an office boy and covered him with ridicule." On top of the disagreements on the issues, Curzon's attitude was instrumental in the Turkish mistrust of the British; see "The Peace Conference of Lausanne, 1922–1923," *Proceedings of the American Philosophical Society* 98-1 (1954): 1–10, esp. 3–4.

23. On June 5, 1926, the border agreement was signed by Turkey and Great Britain. See Quincy Wright, "The Mosul Dispute," *American Journal of International Law* 20, no. 3 (1926): 453–64.

24. Cemil Bilsel, *Lozan*, vol. 2 (İstanbul: Ahmet İhsan Matbaası, 1933), 288–89; see also Şerife Özkan, "Yüzellilikler and Süleyman Şefik Kemali: A Legitimacy and Security Issue" (MA thesis, Bosphorus University, 2004), 6.

25. Veniselos, the Greek representative, was in favor of an amnesty that included even the ordinary crimes as they relate to the war. See Seha L. Meray, trans., *Lozan Barış Konferansı Tutanakları, Belgeler*. 1. Takım, book 2 (Ankara: Ankara Üniversitesi Yayınları, 1969–1973): 153–54. On this specific volume, the information about the date and the publishing house was given as Paris: Devlet Basımevi, 1923. I assume that this is the publication of the original French copy. The Turkish version was published again in 2001 by Yapı Kredi Yayınları. Since I had access to different editions for different volumes, I indicated the publication date of Meray's translation of the minutes accordingly.

26. A memorandum by Forbes Adam to Lord Curzon clearly indicates this point. See British telegram number E 14575/13003/44, dated December 24, 1922, in *Documents on British Foreign Policy 1919–1939*, vol. 18 (London: Her Majesty's Stationery Office, 1972), 411.

27. We know that Rıza Nur mentions the pressure in the Subcommittee on Minorities to accept the linguistic, religious, and ethnic groups in Turkey as minorities and give them special rights. Nur describes this as a clever plan to divide Turkey. See *Dr. Rıza Nur'un Lozan Hatıraları*, 102–8.

28. See particularly the minutes of the session dated December 23, 1923, in Seha Meray, *Lozan Barış Konferansı Tutanaklar, Belgeler*, 30–34.

29. Meray, *Lozan Barış Konferansı Tutanakları, Belgeler*, 34.

30. A memorandum by Forbes Adam to Lord Curzon clearly indicates this point. See British telegram number E 14575/13003/44, dated December 24, 1922, in *Documents on British Foreign Policy 1919–1939*, vol. 18, 406.

31. Meray, *Lozan Barış Konferansı Tutanakları, Belgeler*, 108–9, appendix C, Genel Affa İlişkin Bildiri Tasarısı.

32. This text was printed in *Düstur*. III. Tertib. Vol. 5 (Ankara: n.p., 1939), 224–30. See also Bingöl, "Yüzellilikler Meselesi," appendix, 4, d. For a draft of the law, dated April 9, 1924, excluding 150 people from the amnesty, see Başbakanlık Cumhuriyet Arşivi, 30.10.0.0/31.175.32. It contained five articles.

33. Meray, *Lozan Barış Konferansı Tutanakları, Belgeler*, vol. 2, 160; see also Özkan, "Yüzellilikler and Süleyman Şefik Kemali," 15.

34. It should be noted that there were people in this list who did not reside in İstanbul but still devoted their loyalty to the İstanbul government.

35. Rıza Nur, *Hayat ve Hatıralarım*, vol. 3 (İstanbul: Altındağ, 1968), 1071. The date for the Nur's consent to the General Amnesty with the exclusion of the 150 people was January 11, 1923, in the subcommittee.

36. Rıza Nur, *Dr. Rıza Nur'un Lozan Hatıraları* (İstanbul: Bogaziçi, 1999), 129.

37. Rıza Nur and Joseph Grew, *Lozan Barış Anlaşmasının Perde Arkası* (İstanbul: Örgün, 2003), 425.

38. Bilal Şimşir, ed., *Lozan Telgrafları*, vol. 1 (Ankara: Türk Tarih Kurumu, 1990), 349.

39. Meray, *Lozan Barış Konferansı Tutanakları, Belgeler*, 312, 318–19.

40. Bingöl, "Yüzellilikler Meselesi," 93, fn.

41. We know that the British side registered its objection initially but ultimately agreed to the protocol. See Meray, *Lozan Barış Konferansı Tutanakları, Belgeler* (2001), Second Set, vol. 1, book 1, 125; also Özkan, "Yüzellilikler and Süleyman Şefik Kemali," 36, fn.

42. Şimşir, *Lozan Telgrafları*, vol. 2, 324.

43. Şimşir, *Lozan Telgrafları*, vol. 1, 371–72. This telegram was penned on January 11, 1923, the same day as Rıza Nur's original request for the protocol. However, it was sent on January 12, 1923. There are several other telegrams exchanged between İsmet Pasha and Rauf Bey related to the General Amnesty; see Şimşir, *Lozan Telgrafları*, vol. 1, telegram number 221, 349, and telegram number 315, 356. For example, one telegram, sent by İsmet Pasha, dated June 4, 1923, confirms that the Allied representatives finally consented to the exclusion of 150 Muslims. Yet they were still forcing the Turkish delegates to agree on the return of hundreds of thousands of non-Muslims (mainly Armenians) who left Turkey during the war. The Turkish side, claiming that non-Muslim individuals surely benefit from the amnesty, vehemently opposed the suggestion that these non-Muslim groups would be allowed to return en masse. Şimşir, *Lozan Telgrafları*, vol. 2, 396.

44. This protocol to regulate the population exchange between Greece and Turkey (with the exception of İstanbul and Western Trace) was signed on January 30, 1923; see *Düstur*, III. Tertip, vol. 5, 13.

45. Ibid., 508–9.

46. "Aff-ı Umumi Kanunu," *Düstur*, 842–43; Bingöl, "Yüzellilikler Meselesi," appendix 6 a,b.

47. We know that there were several lists circulating around in 1923; for example, the Başbakanlık Cumhuriyet Arşivi has a document that lists 37 names. The date on the document is March 22, 1923; see number 30.10.0.0/ 106.695.4. Some of these names did not make the final list.

48. These names were never made public. I failed to locate them in my research. There is a slight possibility that this list exists in the Directorate of General Security Archives. I tried to reach these folders; however, they were transferred to the Prime Minister's Republican Archives (Başbakanlık Cumhuriyet Arşivi), which indicated that they were not cataloged yet. No time frame was given as to when they would be available to researchers.

49. *TBMM Gizli Celse Zabıtları*, vol. 4 (İstanbul: İş Bankası Yayınları, 1999), 433–62. The following information comes from this cited source. To avoid redundancy, I will not repeat the same source.

50. Ferit Bey uses the expression "şuna değmiş buna değmemiş," which originates from a Nasreddin Hoca story and can roughly be translated as "arbitrarily."

51. Ferit Bey must have been referring to an Ottoman law called "Tabiyyet-i Osmaniye Kanunnamesi" enacted in 1869. The citizenship laws in the Turkish Republic came after the date when the TGNA debated the 150ers.

52. *TBMM Gizli Celse Zabıtları*, 436.

53. Ibid., 437.

54. Ibid., 453–54.

55. Ibid., 452.

56. The term that Süreyya Bey used was *hilaf-ı vaki*, which could be translated as "contradicting the obvious." However, Fethi Bey recognized this phrase as *yalan*, or "lie," and became quite upset; see *TBMM Gizli Celse Zabıtları*, 453.

57. Ibid., 452–53.

58. Ibid.

59. Although it was signed on this date, it was published in the *Resmi Ceride* number 81 on January 7, 1925. For the discussions on the publication date, see Özkan, "Yüzellilikler and Süleyman Şefik Kemali," 101, fn, and Erdeha, *Yüzellilikler Yahut Milli Mücadelenin Muhasebesi*, 65, fn. This particular meeting of the cabinet was headed by Mustafa Kemal himself.

60. See Ahmet Emin Yalman, *Yakın Tarihte Gördüklerim ve Geçirdiklerim*, vol. 3 (İstanbul: Rey, 1970), 120–22, and Emin Karaca, *150'likler* (İstanbul: Altın, 2007), 63.

61. Yalman, *Yakın Tarihte Gördüklerim ve Geçirdiklerim*, 121.

62. Karaca, *150'likler*, 63.

63. Ahmet Ferit Tek was a known pan-Turkist in parliament and was a founding member of the Turkish Hearths (Türk Ocakları).

64. Kutay makes this point forcefully in *150'likler Faciası*, 6.

65. Many members of parliament made motions for the names that they thought crucial. However, the motions are not included in the minutes and are missing.

66. *TBMM Gizli Celse Zabıtları*, 448.

67. Ibid., 454.

68. Ibid., 451.

69. There is much literature written on Ethem the Circassian. He was once a significant figure in the Ankara Circle and served the nationalist movement admirably with his militia. However, because of disagreements with Ismet Pasha and Mustafa Kemal, he took a position against them. One cannot categorize him as a member of the İstanbul Circle; however, he was an opponent of the Ankara government in his later years. See Cemal Kutay, *Çerkes Ethem Dosyası* (İstanbul: Boğaziçi, 1973).

70. *TBMM Gizli Celse Zabıtları*, 452.

71. Ibid., 453.

72. I was not able to determine the list of people whose citizenship was revoked. We know from Süreyya Bey's statement at parliament that the government had the list of 300 people to be stripped of their citizenship. It is not clear how many of those lost their citizenship; see *TBMM Gizli Celse Zabıtları*, 450.

73. The minutes misspelled the name as "Mavanoğlu"; it should be "Madanoğlu"; ibid., 461.

74. The Mali calendar begins with the month of March, and January is the eleventh month. Therefore, January comes after April. There are two dates on the newspaper: 7 Kanun-u Sani 1340 (the Mali calendar) and 11 Cemaziyelahir 1342 (the Hicri calendar). The day is noted as Wednesday. A discrepancy is that neither date was a Wednesday, nor did the two dates correspond. 11 Cemaziyelahir 1342 corresponds with January 19, 1340, and it was a Saturday. See *Resmi Ceride*, number 81.

75. Başbakanlık Cumhuriyet Arşivi, 30.18.1.1/13.19.2. This document is dated March 22, 1925, and requested funding from the Ministry of Interior to transport 19 members from İzmir to abroad.

76. *Düstur* III. Tertip, vol. 8, 670; see also Soysal, *150'likler*, 139.

77. Erdeha, *Yüzellilikler Yahut Milli Mücadelenin Muhasebesi*, informs us that in the Judicial Committee (Adliye Komisyonu), the word *istimlak* (to purchase property) was replaced by *temellük* (to own property), 132. This is a significant difference in that the former could mean that the 150ers could keep their property, yet the latter does not allow this. However, Başbakanlık Cumhuriyet Arşivi, 30.18.1.1/11.43.16 (dated September 10, 1924), suggests that already in 1924, the 150ers were given nine months to sell their property in Turkey.

78. For the copy of the decree, see Nihat Karaer, *Tam Bir Muhalif: Yüzellilikler Meselesi* (İstanbul: Temel, 1998), 145.

79. Başbakanlık Cumhuriyet Arşivi, 30.18.1.1/15.54.10, dated August 26, 1925.

80. Erdeha, *Yüzellilikler Yahut Milli Mücadelenin Muhasebesi*, 132.

81. Ibid.

82. Mahmut Goloğlu, *Devrimler ve Tepkileri* (İstanbul: Türkiye İş Bankası, 2007), 237–38.

83. The reader should be informed that the amnesty law included people other than the 150ers. This law was published in the *Resmi Gazete* number 3961 on July 16, 1938.

84. Kutay, *Yüzellikler Faciası*, 5–22.

85. Very likely, Mustafa Kemal's conversation with Fethi Okyar and Celal Bayar took place in early May 1938.

86. Kutay, *Yüzellikler Faciası*, 16.

87. Ibid., 14–15.

88. Erdeha, *Yüzellilikler Yahut Milli Mücadelenin Muhasebesi*, 143–44. Erdeha also includes the humanitarian requests for the family members of the 150ers for forgiveness.

89. *TBMM Zabıt Ceridesi*, vol. 2, (Ankara: TBMM Matbaası, n.d.), 309, 477, as cited in ibid., 144–45.

90. For the full text of the law, see Soysal, *150'likler*, 134–35, and Bingöl, "Yüzellilikler Meselesi," appendix 21.

91. Ali Kemal, a former interior minister in the Damat Ferit Pasha government and ardent opponent of the Kemalists, was kidnapped by the nationalists in İstanbul. He was allowed to be lynched by people in 1922 in İzmit. There is much controversy about his murder; see Stanford Shaw, *From Empire to Republic*, vol. 2 (Ankara: Türk Tarih Kurumu, 1890); Osman Özsoy, *Gazetecinin İnfazı* (İstanbul: Timaş, 1997), 276–78.

92. *TBMM Zabıt Ceridesi*, vol. 26, 473, as cited in Erdeha, *Yüzellilikler Yahut Milli Mücadelenin Muhasebesi*, 160.

93. Kutay, *Yüzellikler Faciası*, 20–21; for more comprehensive treatment of the debates in the press, see Erdeha, *Yüzellilikler Yahut Milli Mücadelenin Muhasebesi*, 147–55, and especially Karaca, *150'likler*, 237–69.

94. Soysal, *150'likler*, claims to have seen a list prepared by the Directorate of General Security, according to which in 1938 only 95 members of the 150ers were alive. Soysal, however, indicates that this number should be even lower, for some deceased members were not accurately reported (140). DGSA 12221/B1-2, B6-7, is a list that indicates the names of those who were alive in 1937. According to this list, 79 people were alive (hence 71 dead) in 1937. See also Bingöl, "Yüzellilikler Meselesi," appendix 22. The daily *Cumhuriyet* on May 30, 1938, declared that only 85 of the 150ers could benefit from the amnesty as cited in Erdeha, *Yüzellilikler Yahut Milli Mücadelenin Muhasebesi*, 240, fn. Another police report lists only 39 names who returned; see İçişleri Bakanlığı, *Cumhuriyetin 75.inci Yıldönümünde Polis Arşiv Belgeleriyle Gerçekler* (Ankara: Emniyet Genel Md. Araş. Planlama ve Koordinasyon, n.d.), 6.

95. Unless otherwise indicated, the prosopographical information on the members of the 150ers comes from the following sources: *Yüzellilikler Albümü* (Ankara: Vilayet Matbaası, n.d.); Emin Karaca, *150'likler;* Soysal, *150'likler;* Erdeha, *Yüzellilikler Yahut Milli Mücadelenin Muhasebesi;* Yalçın Toker, *150'liklerden Portreler* (İstanbul: Toker, 2006); Tarık Mümtaz Göztepe, *Osman Oğulları'nın Son Padişahı Sultan Vadideddin Mütareke Gayyasında* (İstanbul: Sebil, 1994); Şaduman Halıcı, "Yüzellilikler" (MA thesis, Anadolu University, 1998); Bingöl, "Yüzellilikler Meselesi"; Şerife Özkan, "Yüzellilikler and Süleyman Şefik Kemali"; T. C. İçişleri Bakanlığı Emniyet Genel Müdürlüğü, Araştırma Planlama ve Koordinasyon Dairesi Başkanlığı, yayın no: 129, *Cumhuriyetin 75. Yıldönümünde Polis Arşiv Belgeleriyle Gerçekler;* and *TBMM Gizli Celse Zabıtları*, 434–62. I am particularly grateful to Mete Tunçay for a document from his private archives. The document titled "1933 Senesi Asayiş ve Emniyet Vaziyetine Bir Bakış" is a police report that includes information about the activities of the 150ers. The document is organized geographically based on the countries where the 150ers resided. At the end, there is a list of countries and the number of the 150ers residing in these countries in 1933.

96. Tarık Mümtaz Göztepe, *Osman Oğulları'nın Son Padişahı Sultan Vahideddin Mütareke Gayyasında*, 213.

97. For a good account of this party until 1913, see Ali Birinci, *Hürriyet ve İtilaf Fırkası: II. Meşrutiyet Devrinde İttihat ve Terakki'ye Karşı Çıkanlar* (İstanbul: Dergah, 1990).

98. Also known as "Tarik-i Salah"; for concise information, see Tarık Zafer Tunaya, *Türkiye'de Siyasi Partiler*, vol. 2 (İstanbul: İletişim, 1999), 557–74.

99. *Osmanoğulları'nın Son Padişahı*, 369. Sedat Bingöl agrees with this claim after examining some documents in the Directorate of General Security Archives; see Bingöl, "Yüzellilikler Meselesi," 126, fn.

100. Especially DGSA 12221-1 Umumi Dosya I/A 12; 1222-1/A 6, A 8, A 9, A 13, A 14. For these files, I rely on Bingöl, who had an access to them (see "Yüzellilikler Meselesi," 127–28 fn.). My collection of DGSA files does not include these documents. See also TITE archives K58G97B4.

101. It is very likely that his service to Ankara began as early as 1923. DGSA, 12222-1/E 9, in Bingöl, "Yüzellilikler Meselesi," 129.

102. The date for the letter is June 3, 1926, DGSA, 12222-2/D 6. A transliteration of the letter was included in Bingöl, "Yüzellilikler Meselesi," appendix 16a.

103. Rıza Nur, *Hayat ve Hatıralarım*, vol. 4 (İstanbul: Altındağ, 1968), 980; see also Bingöl, "Yüzellilikler Meselesi," 130.

104. DGSA 12222-2/E 4, in Bingöl, "Yüzellilikler Meselesi," 131. Erdeha, *Yüzellilikler Yahut Milli Mücadelenin Muhasebesi*, gives the year of his death as 1929, which should be an error.

105. DGSA 12222-4/A 8, in Bingöl, "Yüzellilikler Meselesi," 132.

106. DGSA 1222-4/E 9, in ibid.

107. For Nizamettin Kibar, see "Muhalefetten Sesler ve Nizamettin Kibar," *Birikim* 35 (1992): 87–88.

108. *TBMM Gizli Celse Zabıtları*, 439.

109. Feridun Kandemir published this interview in a journal *Yirminci Asır* (no bibliographic information available), and the same interview was published in a book form under the title *Sultan Vahdettin'in Son Günleri* (İstanbul: Yağmur yayınları, 2008).

110. The DGSA made a list of 150ers in 1937 to indicate their locations. Şaban Ağa's location was registered in this document as Damascus; see DGSA, 12221-2/B 1, 2, 6, 7.

111. I was unable to find the exact reason for this decision. See *TBMM Gizli Celse Zabıtları*, 439.

112. Ibid.

113. DGSA, 12221-1/A 1-13, in Bingöl, "Yüzellilikler Meselesi," appendix 1.g.

114. DGSA, 12221-2/B 1, 2, 6, 7.

115. Halıcı, "Yüzellilikler," 50.

116. DGSA, 12222-1 Umumi Dosya I/E 11, in Bingöl, "Yüzellilikler Meselesi," 135.

117. See Mustafa Kemal Atatürk, *Nutuk*, vol. 2 (Ankara: Başbakanlık Basımevi, 1984), 305–6.

118. This was not a military rank but an administrative one. For more information, see Uluğ İğdemir, *Biga Ayaklanması ve Anzavur Olayları: Günlük Anılar* (Ankara: Türk Tarih Kurumu Basımevi, 1973), and Zühtü Güven, *Anzavur İsyanı; İstiklâl Savaşı Hatıralarından Acı Bir Safha* (Ankara: İş Bankası yay, 1965).

119. Göztepe, *Osman Oğulları'nın Son Padişahı Sultan Vadideddin Mütareke Gayyasında*, 297.

120. Birinci, *Hürriyet ve İtilaf Fırkası*, 238–39.

121. "Badema-Şahit olsun işte cihan/Yalnız Müslüman ve insan/Olarak kalmak üzere Türklükten/Şeref ve izzetimle istifa/Ediyorum Allahın huzurunda . . . ," *Yarın* 29 Temmuz 1927; the entire poem was also published in Karaca, *150'likler*, 222–35.

122. *TBMM Gizli Celse Zabıtları*, 439.

123. Ibid.

124. See Başbakanlık Cumhuriyet Arşivi, 30.10.0.0/106.695.21, a letter dated May 15, 1925; see also DGSA 12222-11/A 10; for another request, see 12222-11/C 13, in Bingöl, "Yüzellilikler Meselesi," 136. The full letter of Cemal Bey to Mustafa Kemal for forgiveness is included in Bingöl, "Yüzellilikler Meselesi," appendix 17.

125. See Hakan Özoğlu, *Kurdish Notables and the Ottoman State* (Albany: State University of New York Press, 2004), 81.

126. DGSA 12222-12/B 13, in Bingöl, "Yüzellilikler Meselesi," 137.

127. See Cemil Topuzlu, *Operatör Cemil Paşa: Hatıraları* (İstanbul: Türkiye yay, 1945), 134, 136–37; for his explanation of why they were not included on this list, see p. 147.

128. The National Pact was discussed and approved in the Ottoman parliament on January 28, 1920, in a closed session with the efforts of the proxies of the Anatolian movement.

129. *TBMM Gizli Celse Zabıtları*, 440.

130. After the Ottoman parliament was closed down by the occupying Allied forces in İstanbul, Sultan Mehmet Vahdettin VI formed a council to discuss the Treaty of Sevres on July 22, 1920. This was in fact the second such council; the first one dealt with the occupation of İzmir on May 16, 1919. This second Imperial Council included the sultan, Crown Prince Abdülmecit, Grand Vizier Damat Ferit, and several other members of the Ottoman high bureaucracy. After the voting, all but one member (Artillery General and member of the Ayan Council Rıza Pasha) decided that there was no alternative to accepting the treaty. Consequently, they recommended that the Treaty of Sevres be accepted.

131. The town he was born in, Mustafa Pasha, is now part of Bulgaria and was renamed Tsaribrod.

132. Birinci, *Hürriyet ve İtilaf Fırkası*, 242.

133. Syed Tanvir Wasti, "Feylosaf Rıza," *Middle Eastern Studies* 38 (2002): 83–100. One can also find information about him in Refik Halit Karay, *Minelbab İlelmihrab* (İstanbul: İnkilap, 1992) and *Bir Ömür Boyunca* (İstanbul: İletişim, 1996); Munise Başikoğlu, "Babam Rıza Tevfik," *Tarih ve Toplum* 1988–1989: 57–63; see also Rıza Tevfik's memoir, *Biraz da Ben Konuşayım* (İstanbul: İletişim, 1993).

134. Tevfik, *Biraz da Ben Konuşayım*, 52–53.

135. He suggests that Britain was trying to diminish the authority of the sultan/caliph out of fear that the caliph would instigate Indian Muslims against the British Empire. To eliminate this threat, Britain circulated rumors that nationalists would enter İstanbul any day and harm the sultan, a propaganda strategy that worked well and led to the abolition of the sultanate and later caliphate; see ibid., 188–91.

136. She must be one of the daughters of Abdülhamit II.

137. Süleyman Şefik Paşa published his memoirs under the title of *Hatıratım, Başıma Gelenler ve Gördüklerim: 31 Mart Vak'ası* (İstanbul: Arma, 2004).

138. DGSA 12222/18/1. This document, prepared by the office of personnel in the National Defense Ministry, lists his official appointments with exact dates. Some dates given by Şerife Özkan, "Yüzellilikler and Süleyman Şefik Kemali," about Süleyman Şefik do not correspond to this list.

139. This year was different in Şerife Özkan's work on Süleyman Şefik (1913); see "Yüzellilikler and Süleyman Şefik Kemali," 66. However, I found an archival document from the DGSA (12222/18/1) that indicates the year for his first retirement as 16 Teşrin-i Evvel 330, which corresponds to November 1, 1914, in the Gregorian calendar.

140. See DGSA, 12222/18/1.

141. Göztepe, *Osman Oğulları'nın Son Padişahı Sultan Vadideddin Mütareke Gayyasında*, 300.

142. Süleyman Şefik claimed that Anzavur did not obey his orders and act independently; see ibid., 300–301.

143. Özkan, "Yüzellilikler and Süleyman Şefik Kemali," 76, fn.

144. Göztepe, *Osman Oğullarının Son Padişahı Sultan Vadideddin Mütareke Gayyasında*, 208.

145. Ali Fuat Türkgeldi, *Görüp İşittiklerim* (Ankara: Türk Tarih Kurumu, 1987), 234–35.

146. *İkaz*, August 11, 1919, as cited in Özkan, "Yüzellilikler and Süleyman Şefik Kemali," 73.

147. Özkan transcribes the full text of the telegram in ibid., 81, fn.

148. Atatürk, *Nutuk*, vol. 1, (Ankara: Başbakanlık Basımevi, 1984), 98.

149. Ibid., 88–89.

150. The document is not clearly numbered; DGSA 2 D1, 2 D2, 2 C8. Although it is not marked as such, it is possible that these documents are the extension numbers for file 12221.

151. DGSA 12222/18.

152. DGSA 12222/18. "Türkiye uçurumun kenarındadır. Mahvolacaktır. Türkiye'yi parçalayacaklar, Cumhur ricali de birer tarafa kaçacaklardır.Çantaları hazır ve paraları Avrupa bankalarında mevdudur. Ağabeyleri İttihatçılar öyle yapmadılar mı?"

153. Ibid.

154. Başbakanlık Cumhuriyet Arşivi, 30.10.0.0/107.698.7.

155. For more information, see Tunaya, *Türkiye'de Siyasi Partiler*, 340–58.

156. Karaca, *150'likler*, 69.

157. Among those, e.g., are *Osmanoğulları'nın Son Padişahı Vahdettin Mütareke Gayyasında* and *Osmanoğulları'nın Son Padişahı Vahdettin Gurbet Cehenneminde*. Because of his Circassian origin, he was also interested in Circassian history and published *İmam Şamil: Kafkasya'nın Büyük Harp ve İhtilal Kahramanı* (İstanbul: İnkilap, 1961).

158. Erdeha, *Yüzellilikler Yahut Milli Mücadelenin Muhasebesi*, 176.

159. This court later in 1919 tried the CUP members for crimes during World War I.

160. Karaca, *150'likler*, and Erdeha, *Yüzellilikler Yahut Milli Mücadelenin Muhasebesi*, indicate that he died in Egypt. Bingöl, "Yüzellilikler Meselesi," in reference to DGSA 12222-22/A 1, claims that he died in Nice. Since the other authors do not give any reference for their information, I rely on Bingöl's reference.

161. Erdeha, *Yüzellilikler Yahut Milli Mücadelenin Muhasebesi*, 188. I do not have any corroborating information for this claim.

162. See the list of 150ers who were not alive in 1933 in Bingöl, "Yüzellilikler Meselesi," appendix 20a.

163. *TBMM Gizli Celse Zabıtları*, 440. Ali Rıza Bey of İstanbul particularly insisted on his inclusion.

164. DGSA 12222-22/A4 and C12, in Bingöl, "Yüzellilikler Meselesi," 142.

165. DGSA 12221-2/B1-B2-B6-B7; the complete list is also in Bingöl, "Yüzellilikler Meselesi," appendix 22.

166. Göztepe, *Osman Oğulları'nın Son Padişahı Sultan Vadideddin Mütareke Gayyasında*, 135–42; Erdeha, *Yüzellilikler Yahut Milli Mücadelenin Muhasebesi*, 189; Karaca, *150'likler*, 70–71.

167. Halıcı, "Yüzellilikler," 105.

168. DGSA 12222-27/D2-C14-B2, in Bingöl, "Yüzellilikler Meselesi," 146.

169. Fanizade Mesut, *Atatürk'ün Hayat Felsefesi* (Antakya: n.p., 1938); for the review of the book and information about Fanizade Mesut's life, see İsmail Arar, "Bir 150'liğin Kitabı," *Tarih ve Toplum* 10 (1989): 318.

170. Karaca, *150'likler*, gives the year as 1980.

171. Birinci, *Hürriyet ve İtilaf Fırkası*, 243.

172. Tunaya, *Türkiye'de Siyasi Partiler*, 463–80.

173. Birinci, *Hürriyet ve İtilaf Fırkası*, was incorrect in claiming that he remained in Romania for 22 years (243). We know that he died in İstanbul in 1940, making his exile 16 years.

174. For this family, see Malmisanıj, *Cızira Botanlı Bedirhaniler ve Bedirhan Ailesi Derneğinin Tutanakları* (Spanga: APEC, 1994), and Özoğlu, *Kurdish Notables and the Ottoman State*.

175. Atatürk, vol. 1, 80, 86, 92.

176. Edward W. C. Noel, *Diary of Major Noel on Special Duty in Kurdistan* (Baghdad: n.p., 1920); David McDowell, *A Modern History of the Kurds* (London, New York: I. B. Tauris, 1996), 128–29.

177. *TBMM Gizli Celse Zabıtları*, 446.

178. DGSA 12222-29/F9, in Bingöl, "Yüzellilikler Meselesi," 149.

179. Erdeha, *Yüzellilikler Yahut Milli Mücadelenin Muhasebesi*, 188.

180. DGSA 12222-29/B13, in Bingöl, "Yüzellilikler Meselesi," 149.

181. DGSA 12222-31/D10-D3-D14, in ibid., 150.

182. DGSA 12222-32/E12, in Halıcı, "Yüzellilikler," 116.

183. Durmuş Yalçın, "Milli Mücadele'de İdareciler, Günümüzün ve Geleceğin İdareciliği" *Atatürk Araştırma Merkezi Dergisi* 7, no. 21 (1991), electronic version, http://www.atam.gov.tr/index.php?Page=DergiIcerik&IcerikNo=602.

184. DGSA 12222-32/E 13, in Halıcı, "Yüzellilikler," 118.

185. DGSA 12222-36, in ibid., 118–24.

186. See Shaw, *From Empire to Republic*, 628–38.

187. Halıcı, "Yüzellilikler," indicates that he died on March 7, 1925, in Silistre (125).

188. Atatürk, *Nutuk*, suggests that his rank was full colonel (27); however, Erdeha, *Yüzellilikler Yahut Milli Mücadelenin Muhasebesi*, disputes this claim based on Ali Galip's file in the Interior Ministry Archives, (175).

189. Atatürk, *Nutuk*, 81–95.

190. DGSA 12221-1/A1-13 and G11, G13; also 12221-2/B1, 2, 6, 7, as printed in Bingöl, "Yüzellilikler Meselesi," appendix 20.

191. Republican Archives, 30.10.0.0/107.698.9.

192. Ibid. I refer to this document when I state the year of someone's death as before 1933.

193. DGSA 12222-42, in Halıcı, "Yüzellilikler," 136.

194. *Tan*, May 31, 1938, "Yüzellilikler Kimlerdir Ne Yapmışlardı?," cited in Karaca, *150'likler*, 268.

195. DGSA 12222-44, in Halıcı, "Yüzellilikler," 136.

196. Erdeha, *Yüzellilikler Yahut Milli Mücadelenin Muhasebesi*, 198. There is a novel by Tülün Yalçın, *Osmanlı'da bir İngiliz Gelin* (İstanbul: Can, 2004), about the wife of Mehmet Ali, Eleanor Loisa Bendon or Nellie.

197. See Cemal Kalyoncu, "Atatürk İle Paşaların Arasını Açmak İstediler," *Aksiyon*, September 12, 2005, http://www.aksiyon.com.tr/detay.php?id=22484.

198. Tunaya, *Türkiye'de Siyasi Partiler*, 469, fn. 28.

199. Bingöl, "Yüzellilikler Meselesi," 151.

200. Telegrams that were sent to Mustafa Kemal by Mehmet Ali were printed in Bingöl, "Yüzellilikler Meselesi," 151–56.

201. See Mete Tunçay, "Zincire Vurulmuş Cumhuriyet" *Toplumsal Tarih* 91 (July 1991): 6.

202. DGSA 12222-45-3/G11, as cited in Bingöl, "Yüzellilikler Meselesi," 156.

203. Erdeha, *Yüzellilikler Yahut Milli Mücadelenin Muhasebesi*, 214.

204. DGSA 12221-1/A1-13, G11, G13, in Bingöl, "Yüzellilikler Meselesi," appendix 20.

205. *75.inci Yıldönümünde Polis Arşiv Belgeleriyle Gerçekler*, 6.

206. DGSA 12221-1/A1-13, G11, G13; also B1-2, B6-7.

207. Erdeha, *Yüzellilikler Yahut Milli Mücadelenin Muhasebesi*, claims that he left for Italy. Police reports do not corroborate this account; cf. DGSA 12221-1/A1-13, G11.

208. We know that he was in communication with Turkish authorities in 1944. We also know that his family returned to Turkey in 1945. He must have died around this time. DGSA 12222-51, G5, G6, in Halıcı, "Yüzellilikler," 158.

209. DGSA 12222-55, in ibid., 160–62.

210. Falih Rıfkı Atay, *Çankaya* (İstanbul: Pozitif, 2004), 276–77. In this source, the author relays the reason for Ethem's brother Tevfik's objection to join in the regular forces as the following: "Our irregular forces do not like officers from the regular army. When they see an officer, they rebel as they rebel against the Angel of Death."

211. TGNA Archives, Ankara İstiklal Mahkemesi, T. 2, folder 27-4, as cited in Erdeha, *Yüzellilikler Yahut Milli Mücadelenin Muhasebesi*, 234, appendix 7.

212. Among others, see Çerkez Ethem, *Anılarım* (İstanbul: Berfin, 1998), and Cemal Kutay, *Çerkez Ethem Dosyası* (İstanbul: Boğaziçi, 1990).

213. In TGNA, Ferit Bey, the prime minister, stated that "we do not have the confidence that we could convict [Çerkez Ethem], TGNA, *Gizli Celse Zabıtları*, 452.

214. In reference to Yaşar Bağ, *Çerkezlerin Dünü Bugünü* (İstanbul: Kafkas Derneği, 2001), 93, Şerife Özkan claims that Ethem left the country on January 22, 1921; see Özkan, "Yüzellilikler and Süleyman Şefik Kemali," 31.

215. DGSA, 12222-57-1/A2, A10, cited in Bingöl, "Yüzellilikler Meselesi," 159. No corroborating information exists for this claim.

216. Another controversial account was made by Stanford Shaw when he pointed out a document indicating Ethem's request for pardon in 1922; see Shaw, *From Empire to Republic*, 1105. This is an interesting finding since, in 1938, Ethem did not accept the pardon.

217. Detailed biographical information exists in Philip H. Stoddard, "The Ottoman Government and the Arabs, 1911 to 1918" (PhD diss., Princeton University, 1963), 161–72.

218. Başbakanlık Cumhuriyet Arşivi, 30.18.1.1/3.29.16. The document states that Eşref and his associates were released because of lack of evidence.

219. Bingöl, "Yüzellilikler Meselesi," points out that Eşref was shot by one of Ethem's associates in Greece (165).

220. DGSA 12222-60-6/D1, D3-5, cited in Bingöl, "Yüzellilikler Meselesi," 165. He also sent letters to Refet Bey; see Republican Archives 30.10.0.0/ 107.702.2

221. Karaca, *150'likler*, 76. Erdeha, *Yüzellilikler Yahut Milli Mücadelenin Muhasebesi*, claims that after this event, Sami joined his brother in Greece (196).

222. Karaca, *150'likler*, 77.

223. There is no supporting evidence for the claim of Karaca, *150'likler* (77). However, Karaca is correct in raising the question that Sami had no contact with the Allied Powers until his residence in Greece in 1924, which was after the declaration of the 150ers.

224. Ibid., 77.

225. The regulation of this society contains eight articles and was published in ibid., 119–21.

226. There were also pro-Ankara Circassian organizations; see Tunaya, *Türkiye'de Siyasi Partiler*, 585.

227. "Çerkes Milletinin Düvel-i Muazzama ve Alem-i İnsaniyet ve Medeniyete Umumi Beyannamesi" published in ibid., 587–91. Tunaya warns that not all revolts by Circassians, such the Anzavur and Çerkes Ethem, could be labeled as Circassian nationalist movements; ibid., 586–87.

228. Some Circassian rebellions, such as Düzce and Bolu, created trouble for the Ankara forces. See Rüknü Özkök, *Milli Mücadele Başlarken, Düzce-Bolu İsyanları* (İstanbul: Karacan, 1970).

229. For available information, see Halıcı, "Yüzellilikler," 196–202.

230. DGSA 12222-84, F1, F11, in ibid., 203.

231. DGSA 12222-92/E 6, E 9, F 2, cited in Bingöl, "Yüzellilikler Meselesi," 169–70.

232. Halıcı, "Yüzellilikler," 202–10.

233. This event, known in Turkish history as the "31 Mart Vakası," on April 13, 1909, was regarded as the reactionary, pro-Abdülhamit counterrevolutionary uprising against the CUP regime.

234. This organization was established by another anti-CUP figure, Şerif Pasha; see Özoğlu, *Kurdish Notables and the Ottoman State*, 110–13; for Rıfat's life, see also Rohat Alakom, *Şerif Paşa: Bir Kürt Diplomatının Fırtınalı Yılları* (İstanbul: Avesta, 1998), 75–80, and Metin Martı, ed., *Mevlanzade Rıfat'ın Anıları* (İstanbul:Arma, 1992).

235. Halil Menteşe and İsmail Arar, *Halil Menteşe'nin Anıları* (İstanbul: Hürriyet Vakfı, 1986), 77, as cited in Alakom, *Şerif Paşa*, 74.

236. Mevlanzade Rıfat, *İttihat Terakki İktidarı ve Türkiye İnkılabının İçyüzü* (İstanbul: Yedi İklim, 1993).

237. Özoğlu, *Kurdish Notables and the Ottoman State*, 83.

238. Martı, *Mevlanzade Rıfat'ın Anıları*, 6.

239. DGSA, 12222-97/C 9, cited in Bingöl, "Yüzellilikler Meselesi," 172. This document was a letter from the Ministry of Interior to the Foreign Ministry dated September 13, 1930. The letter states that Mevlanzade Rıfat should refrain from writing an open article and continue to collect information on the opponents of Turkey. The Turkish consulate should evaluate this information and give him cash for valuable information.

240. These letters were published by Atatürk, *Nutuk*, vol. 1, 201–7.

241. Fethi Tevetoğlu, *Milli Mücadele Yıllarındaki Kuruluşlar* (Ankara: TTK, 1988), 141–43.

242. This letter, footnoted as C O, 67/216/3 of the British archives, was printed in "Kıbrıs'ta Bir 150'lik: Sait Molla," see http://www.biyotarih.com/?p=46.

243. Tarık Zafer Tunaya, *İslamcılık Akımı* (İstanbul: Simavi, 1991), 113.

244. There are different days mentioned for his birth. However, I took March 2 simply because it was the date given in his memoir, *Minelbab İlelmihrab*, 98. Another useful memoir is his *Bir Ömür Boyunca*.

245. Nihat Karaer, *Tam Bir Muhalif: Refik Halid Karay* (İstanbul: Temel, 1998), 22.

246. This post was previously a cabinet-level appointment.

247. *Alemdar*, January 3, 1920, for the copy of the article see Karaer, *Tam Bir Muhalif*, 175. For a collection of references criticizing Mustafa Kemal, see ibid., 70–87; Toker, *150'liklerden Portreler*, 171–72.

248. Erdeha, *Yüzellilikler Yahut Milli Mücadelenin Muhasebesi*, 210; Karaer, *Tam Bir Muhalif*, 104–7.

249. In his memoirs in 1923 (*Minelbab İlelmihrab*), this sentiment is clearly demonstrated. In a telegram published in the daily *Tan* on June 2, 1938, Refik Halit exclaims, "Long live Atatürk who made us all proud in exile."

250. Book review by Roland Belgrave and Stefano Taglia, "Through Ottoman Eyes," *Cornucopia* 36, http://www.cornucopia.net/aboutdrs.html.

251. *Adalet*, March 20, 1922. The full article was transcribed and published in Karaca, *150'likler*, 125–28; this article is full of ad hominem attacks on Mustafa Kemal.

252. Erdeha, *Yüzellilikler Yahut Milli Mücadelenin Muhasebesi*, 177.

253. Karaca, *150'likler*, 128. I failed to confirm these claims.

254. Başbakanlık Cumhuriyet Arşivi, 030.18.01-26/21, as cited in Hikmet Öksüz, *Batı Trakya Türkleri* (Çorum: Karam, 2006), 180.

255. Muhittin Birgen, a CUP member, claims that Kadri was jailed before for the killing of his neighbor and was released thanks to the amnesty after the declaration of the second constitutional era in 1908. Birgen, without elaborating, claims that Kadri became the first opponent of CUP in his neighborhood; see *İttihat ve Terakki'de One Sene: İttihat ve Terakki Neydi?*, vol. 1 (İstanbul: Kitap, 2006), 516.

256. The other two were Fanizade Zeynelabidin (thirty-seventh in the list) and Fanizade Mesut (twenty-seventh). This family also produced a member, Dr. Baki Bilgili, who received the Medal of Independence from the Ankara government.

257. İsmail Tevfik (Okday), *Adana Vilayeti Matbuatı* (Ankara: Hariciye Vekaleti Matbaası, 1932), 24.

258. Erdeha, *Yüzellilikler Yahut Milli Mücadelenin Muhasebesi*, 207.

259. The entire letter was published by Sedat Bingöl under the title of "Ömer Fevzi Bey'in Müdafaanamesi ve Mesut Fani'nin Hoybun'a İlişkin Bilgileri: İki 150'lik Üzerine Notlar ve Belgeler" in *Toplumsal Tarih* 62 (February 1999): 41–48.

260. Even the objectivity of this could be debated since there were previous international agreements, such as the Armistice of Mudros in 1918, which could be construed as treason. Rauf Orbay, who was one of the leaders of the nationalists, signed it.

261. For more information on these personalities and their political activities, see Özoğlu, *Kurdish Notables and the Ottoman State*.

262. Uluğ İğdemir, ed., *Sivas Kongresi Tutanakları* (Ankara: TTK, 1986), 2–3.

263. Second session, September 5, 1919; ibid., 17–23.

Chapter 3

1. A portion of the research in this chapter was published in Hakan Özoğlu, "Exaggerating and Exploiting the Sheikh Said Rebellion of 1925 for Political Gains," *New Perspectives on Turkey* 41 (Fall 2009): 181–210.

2. Halide Edib Adıvar, *The Turkish Ordeal* (New York: The Century Co., 1928), 355.

3. Some modern scholars compared the nature of early Turkish republican history to fascism. For example, in his article, Fikret Adanır tackles the issue

of similarities between fascism and Kemalism and concludes that fascist elements did certainly exist in the regime but that one cannot convincingly make the case for equating Turkey's one-party regime to fascism in Italy; however, it is fair to state that both are parallel developments; Fikret Adanır, "Kemalist Authoritarianism and Fascist Trends in Turkey during the Inter-War Period," in *Fascism outside Europe: The European Impulse against Domestic Conditions in the Diffusion of Global Fascis*, ed. Stein Ugelvik Larsen (New York: Columbia University Press, 2001), 313–61.

4. Later in the Eastern Independence Tribunal, when the Islamist Eşref Edip, the editor of the daily *Sebilürreşat*, was asked what his opinion regarding the abolution of the caliphate, he responded, "It is forbidden [by law] to comment on the decisions taken by the TGNA. Therefore, I would much prefer that you do not ask me this question, sir"; in Eşref Edip, *İstiklal Mahkemelerinde Sebilürreşad'ın Romanı*, ed. Fahrettin Gün (İstanbul: Beyan, 2002), 53. Although this specific case took place in 1925, it is a good example for the fear that the law on the high treason triggered.

5. For a comprehensive study, see Ahmet Demirel, *Birinci Meclis'te Muhalefet: İkinci Grup* (İstanbul: İletişim, 1994).

6. The Nine Principles (*Dokuz Umde Beyannamesi*) was published in Tarık Zafer Tunaya, *Türkiye'de Siyasi Partiler* (İstanbul: Doğan Kardeş, 1952), 580–82; see also Mete Tunçay, *Türkiye Cumhuriyeti'nde Tek-Parti Yönetiminin Kurulması 1923–1931* (İstanbul: Tarih Vakfı Yurt Yayınları, 1999), 366–68, especially the second article.

7. Michael M. Finefrock, "From Sultanate to Republic: Mustafa Kemal Atatürk and the Structure of Turkish Politics 1922–1924" (PhD diss., Princeton University, 1976), 195–97; see also Ali Fuat Cebesoy, *Siyasi Hatıralar*, vol. 1 (İstanbul: Doğan Kardeş, 1960), 316.

8. Tunçay, *Türkiye Cumhuriyeti'nde Tek-Parti Yönetiminin Kurulması 1923–1931*, 46. See, e.g., a letter by Alevi leader Veliyeddin Çelebi asking his followers to vote for the candidates whom Mustafa Kemal supports; ibid., 47–48.

9. Ibid., 49.

10. A good example for this claim could be the election of Nurettin Pasha, who was elected despite Mustafa Kemal's opposition. See Tunçay, *Türkiye Cumhuriyeti'nde Tek-Parti Yönetiminin Kurulması 1923–1931*, 124–27.

11. 867.00/1737, a report titled "Political Situation in Turkey" by Maynard B. Barnes, dated October 15, 1923. This particular report also contains very useful observation of its author concerning the political opposition in Turkey in 1923.

12. For a fair account of this party, see Erik Jan Zürcher, *Political Opposition in the Early Turkish Republic: The Progressive Republican Party 1925–1925* (Leiden: E. J. Brill, 1991), and Ahmet Yeşil, *Türkiye Cumhuriyeti'nde İlk Teşkilatlı Muhalefet Hareketi: Terakkiperver Cumhuriyet Fırkası* (Ankara: Cedid, 2002).

13. Mete Tunçay rightly observes that Mustafa Kemal's position before and after 1923 shows great difference regarding following or leading the masses;

see *Türkiye Cumhuriyetinde Tek-Parti Yönetiminin Kurulması 1923–1931*, 219. For Mustafa Kemal's relevant speech in Konya Türkocağı, which was originally published in *Hakimiyet-i Millliye* on March 26, 1923, see *Atatürk'ün Söylev ve Demeçler*, vol. 2 (Ankara: Türk Tarih Kurumu Basimevi, 1959), 140–41.

14. Rauf Bey never admitted that he was Mustafa Kemal's rival but maintained that he was opposed to the methods employed by Mustafa Kemal, not to his leadership. However, Mustafa Kemal and especially his nervous close associates always regarded him as a rival, able to form a stiff political opposition. Maynard B. Barnes, a delegate of the U.S. high commissioner in Turkey, observes that "I am also inclined to believe that Raouf Bey has never been a through supporter of Moustapha Kemal Pasha and that Kemal has always been suspicious of him." See 867.00/1740, by Maynard B. Barnes, dated October 4, 1923.

15. See "Sabık-ı Heyet-i Vekile Reisi Rauf Bey ile Mühim Bir Mülakat," *Vatan*, November 1, 1923. The full text was also published in the minutes of the group discussions of the RPP on October 22, 1923; *CHP Grup Toplantısı Tutanakları 1923–1924*, ed. Yücel Demirel and Osman Zeki Okur (İstanbul: Bilgi Üniversitesi Yayınları, 2002), 23–30.

16. Ibid., 15–111.

17. Ibid., 78.

18. "The Ghazi's Speech," *The Times*, November 2, 1927, 8, issue 44728, column C.

19. *CHP Grup Toplantısı Tutanakları 1923–1924*, 102.

20. *Ankara İstiklal Mahkemesi, Ankara İstiklal Mahkemesi'nde Cereyan Eden Su-i kasd ve Taklib-i Hükumet Davası'na Ait Resmi Zabıtlar*, ed. Selma Ilıkan and Faruk Ilıkan. (İstanbul: Simurg, 2005), 699.

21. On September 9 and 24, 1924, two meetings took place in İzmir and İstanbul, respectively, among Rauf, Kazım, and Ali Fuat. In these meetings, the formation of an opposition party was discussed; see Zürcher, *Political Opposition in the Early Turkish Republic*, 165. Ahmet Emin Yalman claims that the news of a possible new party was first published on November 6, 1924, in *Son Telgraf*. See *Yakın Tarihte Gördüklerim ve Geçirdiklerim*, 135.

22. Hulusi Turgut, ed., *Atatürk'ün Sırdaşı Kılıç Ali'nin Anıları* (İstanbul: İş Bankası Kültür Yayınları, 2005), 231.

23. PRO, E 10619/32/44, 25.11.1924, as quoted in Zürcher, *Political Opposition in the Early Turkish Republic*, 61. The same file was quoted in Tunçay, *Tek-Parti Yönetiminin Kurulması 1923–1931*, 109, fn. 162, as "Lindsay to Chamberlain," FO 424/261, E 10619/32/44. This is indeed the full citation. In the same folder, one can see the unmodified version of the article; see Zürcher, *Political Opposition in the Early Turkish Republic*, 155–58

24. For the full text, see Zürcher, *Political Opposition in the Early Turkish Republic*, 158, appendix A.

25. See Tunçay, *Türkiye Cumhuriyeti'nde Tek-Parti Yönetiminin Kurulması 1923–1931*, 109, and Zürcher, *Political Opposition in the Early Turkish Republic*, 61.

26. "The Ruler of Turkey," *The Times*, December 18, 1924, 15. The name of the reporter did not appear in the piece. The newspaper used the generic signature "From our special correspondent, Angora." Yet clearly the piece was written by Macartney.

27. The speech was published by *Hakimiyet-i Milliye*, September 23, 1924. The translation was Zürcher's; see Zürcher, *Political Opposition in the Early Turkish Republic*, 127. The same text was also published in Ahmet Emin Yalman, *Yakın Tarihte Gördüklerim ve Geçirdiklerim*, vol. 3 (İstanbul: Rey, 1970), 132–33.

28. According to the U.S. military attaché in İstanbul, the group numbered around 100,000 people. See file number 867.00/1782; U.S. Department of State, "Records of the Department of State Relating to Internal Affairs of Turkey, 1910–29" (microfilm collection).

29. Dini veya mukaddesat-ı diniyeyi siyasi gayelere esas ve alet ittihaz maksadıyla cemiyetler teşkili memnudur. Bu kabil cemiyetleri teşkil edenler ve bu cemiyetlere dahil olanlar hain-i vatan addolunur. Dini veya mukaddesat-ı diniyeyi alet ittihaz ederek şekl-i devleti tebdil ve tagyir veya emniyet-i devleti ihlal veya mukaddesat-ı diniyeyi alet ittihaz ederek her ne suretle olursa olsun ahali arasına fesat ve nifak ilkası için gerek münferiden ve gerek müçtemian kavli veya tahriri veyahut fiili şekilde veya nutuk iradı veyahut neşriyat icrası suretiyle harekette bulunanlar kezalik hain-i vatan addolunur.

30. Metin Toker, *Şeyh Said ve İsyanı* (Ankara: Akis, 1968), 44.

31. Ibid.; Robert Olson, *The Emergence of Kurdish Nationalism* (Austin: University of Texas Press, 1991); Behçet Cemal, *Şeyh Said İsyanı* (İstanbul: Sel, 1955); Aziz Aşan, *Şeyh Sait Ayaklanması* (İstanbul: n.p., 1991); Martin van Bruinessen, *Agha, Shaikh and State: The Social and Political Structures of Kurdistan* (London: Zed Books, 1992); Wadie Jwaideh, *The Kurdish National Movement: Its Origins and Developments* (Syracuse, NY: Syracuse University Press, 2006). Many Turkish daily newspapers at the time described the rebellion as both a Kurdish nationalist and an Islamist/reactionary movement. See Ebbuziyazade, "Hadisenin Ehemmiyet ve Fecaati," *Tevhid-i Efkar*, February 25, 1925, as printed in Nurer Uğurlu, *Kürt Milliyetçiliği: Kürtler ve Şeyh Said İsyanı* (İstanbul: Örgün, 2006), 536. Ahmet Emin Yalman, in his article "İsyanın Saikleri," claims that this movement was a feudal and reactionary (*irticai*) movement and that Kurdish nationalism was not a primary motivation; see *Vatan*, May 15, 1925, in Uğurlu, *Kürt Milliyetçiliği*, 577. Uğurlu collected and published newspaper clips related to this rebellion in 1925; see 519–612. For a literature review of the nature of the rebellion, see Yaşar Kalafat, *Şark Meselesi Işığında Şeyh Sait Olayı, Karekteri, Dönemindeki İç ve Dış Olaylar* (Ankara: Boğaziçi, 1992), 179–289. TITE archives also have some documents on the subject, particularly report number K23G64B3, which is noteworthy in that it claims that the Diyarbakır post office received catalogs addressed "to the Foreign Minister of Kurdistan in Diyarbakır." The document has no date or signature and bears the title "copy" (*suret*). In my judgment, it was produced

(printed) later to support the claims that Great Britain incited the rebellion. Yet no such claims were proven in Sheikh Said's trial later. The exact wording of the section is as follows: "Bugün Diyarbakır postanesine dahil olan mektuplar meyanında İngilizlerden Diyarbakır'a gönderilmiş bazı fabrika ilanları üzerinde atideki adresler görülmüştür: 1) Diyarbekir Kürdistan Hariciye Nazırı Efendiye, 2) Diyarbekir Kürdistan . . . Nazırı Efendiye." Another related document in TITE is K24G143B2.

32. Mete Tunçay has quoted Abdurrahman Chassem Lou (Gassemlou), who gives a figure of £20 million, and a Kurdish prince (Süreyya Bedirhan), who gives a figure of 60,000,000 Turkish lira. See Tunçay, *Türkiye Cumhuriyeti'nde Tek-Parti Yönetiminin Kurulması 1923–1931*, 143, fn. 16. Judging from the estimates on the loss of Turkish lives, which these authors give as 20,000 and 50,000, respectively, Tunçay has correctly concluded that these figures are gross exaggerations. Robert Olson has misquoted the figure of 20 million as £20,000; see Olson, *The Emergence of Kurdish Nationalism*, 126.

33. See report number 867.00/1863 by Bristol to the Department of State, dated March 13, 1925, in U.S. Department of State, "Records of the Department of State Relating to Internal Affairs of Turkey, 1910–29."

34. Ibid., file number 867.00/1866.

35. Ibid., file number 867.00/1864.

36. 867.00/1852.

37. 867.00/1889, from Sheldon Levitt Crosby to the Secretary of the State, August 27, 1925.

38. 867.00/1889, "General State Budget, 1925–1926—Turkey," # 4471, July 21, 1925.

39. 867.00/1889, "Cost of Suppression of Kurdish Rebellion," # 4515, August 14, 1925.

40. For Bedirhan's claim, see Tunçay, *Türkiye Cumhuriyeti'nde Tek-Parti Yönetiminin Kurulması 1923–1931*, 143, fn. 16. For Bozarslan, see "Les Revoltes Kurdes En Turquie Kemaliste (Quelques Aspects)," *Guerres Mondiales at Conflits Contemporains* 151 (1988): 121–36, particularly fn. 3 on p. 121; see also "Türkiye'de Kürt Milliyetçiliği: Zımni Sözleşmeden Ayaklanmaya (1919–1925)," in *İmparatorluktan Cumhuriyet'e Türkiye'de Etnik Çatışma*, ed. Erik Jan Zürcher (İstanbul: İletişim, 2005), 90.

41. Another report also in 867.00/1853 mentions the belief that the Ottoman dynasty supported the rebellion. This claim was also not substantiated.

42. The word "Turkish" is inserted in the document by handwriting.

43. "Memorandum: The Kurdish Revolt," by James Morgan, March 4, 1925. FO 371/10867, E 1360/1091/44.

44. A cover letter by D. A. Osborne in the same file disagrees with James Morgan's speculation. Another interesting British memorandum by Sir H. Dobbs suggests that the Turks are interested in breaking down "the Kurdish wall between herself and the Turkish population" in Iran; FO 371/10826-033, September 12, 1925.

45. See Ahmet Süreyya Örgeevren, *Şeyh Sait İsyanı ve Şark İstiklal Mahkemesi* (İstanbul: Temel, 2002), 171–280. These pages were devoted entirely to the trial and based on the court documents.

46. FO 371/10867, E 1360/1091/44. Osborne goes on to disagree with the claim that the uprising was entirely fictitious.

47. The government received the first report on February 14; see Örgeevren, *Şeyh Sait İsyanı ve Şark İstiklal Mahkemesi*, 52 (for the declaration of the state of emergency, see 48).

48. It was first Cemil Bey, the minister of internal affairs, who informed the TGNA about a rebellion in Kurdistan on February 18, 1925; this report described the rebellion as the activities of brigands headed by Sheikh Said. Hence, the first assessment of the revolt did not categorize it as either a religious or a Kurdish uprising. Örgeevren, *Şeyh Sait İsyanı ve Şark İstiklal Mahkemesi*, 46–47.

49. U.S. Department of State, file number 867.00/1852.

50. Örgeevren, *Şeyh Sait İsyanı ve Şark İstiklal Mahkemesi*, 48.

51. Kazım Özalp, *Atatürk'ten Anılar* (Ankara: Türkiye İş Bankası Yay., 1992), 38.

52. An often-cited story narrates that when the news of the rebellion came to Ankara, Fethi Bey was in Çankaya, the president's residence, playing a card game. After reading the telegram, Mustafa Kemal, at another table, asked his aide to pass it on to Fethi, who, after looking at the news in only a cursory manner, continued playing cards. Then Mustafa Kemal forwarded the message to İsmet Pasha (İnönü) at the third table. İsmet's reaction to the telegram was in stark contrast to that of Fethi. İsmet immediately stood up and looked very nervous. Then Mustafa Kemal turned to the guests at his table and pointed out the difference between the two men in regard to their attentiveness to the problems faced by the country. One of the men at the table was Yakup Kadri Karaosmanoğlu, *Politikada 45 Yıl* (İstanbul: Bilgi, 1968), 78. See also Toker, *Şeyh Said ve İsyanı*, 48–49. Needless to say, this is a very crude and incorrect observation but an important one to show Mustafa Kemal's favoritism of İsmet Pasha. For the criticism of Fethi Bey, see Örgeevren, *Şeyh Sait İsyanı ve Şark İstiklal Mahkemesi*, 45–46.

53. Rıza Nur, *Hayat ve Hatıralarım*, vol. 4 (İstanbul: Altındağ, 1968), 1324.

54. For the full text of Fethi Bey's report to parliament, see Örgeevren, *Şeyh Sait İsyanı ve Şark İstiklal Mahkemesi*, 49–55.

55. See file number 867.00/1852.

56. U.S. Department of State, file number 867.00/1864.

57. FO 371/10867, E 1360/1091/44.

58. Cebesoy, *Siyasi Hatıralar*, vol. 2 (İstanbul: Doğan Kardeş, 1960), 146–47.

59. Feridun Kandemir, *Siyasi Dargınlıklar*, vol. 3 (İstanbul: Ekicigil, 1955), 70.

60. Ibid., 71.

61. The article was published in ibid., 85–87.

62. Avni Doğan, *Kurtuluş, Kuruluş ve Sonrası* (İstanbul: Dünya, 1964), 165–66.

63. Ibid., 166.

64. Fethi Bey asked Şükrü Bey (Kaya), the minister of foreign affairs, to carry out the invitation. Ali Fuat Bey was not able to go to the meeting; instead Dr. Adnan Bey (Adıvar) participated in the meeting; Cebesoy, *Siyasi Hatıralar*, vol. 2, 143.

65. Ibid.

66. Ibid.

67. Ergün Aybars, *İstiklal Mahkemeleri 1920–1927* (İzmir: 9 Eylül Üniversitesi Yay., 1988), 359. See also Toker, *Şeyh Said ve İsyanı*, 47.

68. Cebesoy, *Siyasi Hatıralar*, vol. 2, 143.

69. This point was also subscribed by İsmail Göldaş, a Kurdish researcher, as he suggests that the main reason for the support Kazım Karabekir gave to the government regarding law number 556 was to keep the moderate wing of the Kemalists in power. Another reason would be that the PRP equally feared the use of religion for political gain. See İsmail Göldaş, *Takrir-i Sükun Görüşmeleri* (İstanbul: Belge, 1997), 402.

70. Unless otherwise indicated, the text of the discussions comes from TGNA, *Zabıt Ceridеleri*, vol. 15, 131–49, and the translation is mine.

71. *Zabıt Ceridеleri* 15, 131; I utilized Zürcher's translation of this text from his *Political Opposition in the Early Turkish Republic*, 160.

72. Quoted in Örgeevren, *Şeyh Sait İsyanı ve Şark İstiklal Mahkemesi*, 60.

73. Kemal Atatürk, *Mustafa Kemal—Eskişehir-İzmit konuşmaları, 1923: İlk Kez Sansürsüz, Tam Metin* (İstanbul: Kaynak, 1993).

74. Örgeeveren's memoir can be considered as an example for those which described the rebellion as an urgent danger to the republic; see Örgeevren, *Şeyh Sait İsyanı ve Şark İstiklal Mahkemesi*, 47–48.

75. Quoted in Tunçay, *Türkiye Cumhuriyeti'nde Tek-Parti Yönetiminin Kurulması 1923–1931*, 145.

76. For the text, see ibid., 146, fn. 19. Later the Ankara tribunal was also granted the right to carry out the capital punishment without the TGNA's approval.

77. On March 31, 1925, a proposal empowered even the lowest-ranked field commanders to execute death sentences without delay and appeal. See law number 595.

78. See Örgeevren, *Şeyh Sait İsyanı ve Şark İstiklal Mahkemesi*, 132–49.

79. The rebellion region tribunal consisted of the following names: chair: Mazhar Müfit (Kansu) of Denizli, later replaced by Ali Saip (Ursavaş) of Urfa; prosecutor: Süreyya (Örgeevren) of Karesi; member: Ali Saip (when he became the chair, he was replaced by İbrahim of Kocaeli); member: Lütfi Müfit (Özdeş) of Kırşehir; and substitute: Avni Doğan of Bozok. The Ankara Independence Tribunal was chaired by Ali (Çetinkaya) of Afyon. He was responsible for the killing of Halit Pasha in the corridor of the Assembly at

the beginning of February 1925. Ali Bey emerged from the incident without prosecution. The prosecutor of this court was Necip Ali (Küçüka) of Denizli, and the members were Kılıç Ali of Gaziantep and Ali (Zırh) of Rize. The substitute was Dr. Reşit Galip of Aydın. The tribunal is also known as the "*Dört Ali'ler*" (Four Alis); for the members of the Ankara and Diyarbakır Independence Tribunals, see TITE Archives, K24G109B109.

80. Tunçay, *Türkiye Cumhuriyeti'nde Tek-Parti Yönetiminin Kurulması 1923–1931*, 149, citing *Vatan*, April 17, 1925.

81. Ahmet Emin Yalman gives the date of March 9, 1925, for the following papers: *Presse du Soir, Sada-yı Hak, Kahkaha,* and *İstikbal*; see Yalman, *Yakın Tarihte Gördüklerim ve Geçirdiklerim*, 164.

82. U.S. consular reports include a particular entry dealing with the former CUP members of the RPP. On October 15, 1923, Maynard B. Barnes, a delegate of the U.S. high commissioner in Turkey, observes the following: "In truth, it is the People's Party which does not actually exist. It is purely a fictitious organization built upon the popularity of Moustapha Kemal Pasha. The rank and file of the party are still Unionists who will revert to their original party as the popularity of Kemal wanes and when strong Unionist leaders openly enter the political arena"; file number 867.00/1737, "Political Situation in Turkey," by Maynard B. Barnes, dated October 15, 1923. The same file predicts "that the Unionists will return to power seems inevitable." This document confirms that the former CUP members were part of the RPP, whose leadership clearly did not want to alienate them.

83. Yalman, *Yakın Tarihte Gördüklerim ve Geçirdiklerim*, 164.

84. For a brief but accurate description, see Tunçay, *Türkiye Cumhuriyeti'nde Tek-Parti Yönetiminin Kurulması 1923–1931*, 168–73.

85. See Mete Tunçay, *Türkiye'de Sol Akımlar* (Ankara: Bilgi, 1967), 188.

86. "Kominstlik teşkilat ve propagandası yapmak suretiyle emniyeti dahiliyeyi ihlal ve binnetice şekli hükümeti tağyire matuf efal ve harekatta bulunmak."

87. For a more complete treatment of Hüseyin Cahit's defense at the trial, see Kandemir, *Siyasi Dargınlıklar*, 88–116.

88. *Ayın Tarihi* 14 (1925), as referenced in Tunçay, *Türkiye Cumhuriyeti'nde Tek-Parti Yönetiminin Kurulması 1923–1931*, 152.

89. In this article, Cevat Şakir used his alias Hüseyin Kenan.

90. See Yalman, *Yakın Tarihte Gördüklerim ve Geçirdiklerim*, 165, and Tunçay, *Türkiye Cumhuriyeti'nde Tek-Parti Yönetiminin Kurulması 1923–1931*, 152.

91. Yalman, *Yakın Tarihte Gördüklerim ve Geçirdiklerim*, 165.

92. Örgeevren, *Şeyh Sait İsyanı ve Şark İstiklal Mahkemesi*, 247. Sheikh Said later adds the name of the newspaper *Tevhid-i Efkar* to *Sebilürreşat*.

93. In his memoir, Yalman states that his refusal was a mistake, for the Independence Tribunal had extraordinary power and could do whatever it wished. See Yalman, *Yakın Tarihte Gördüklerim ve Geçirdiklerim*, 168, 170. He also informs us that his paper bought an airplane for the military and

contributed 500 lira to the Aviation Society (168). Clearly, all this was not enough to escape the Independence Tribunal's wrath.

94. Hükümetin manevi nüfuzunu kırarak isyana sebep olmak; Yalman, *Yakın Tarihte Gördüklerim ve Geçirdiklerim*, 171.

95. Doğan, *Kurtuluş, Kuruluş ve Sonrası*, 173.

96. Ibid., 174. Here it should be noted that Tunçay, in *Türkiye Cumhuriyeti'nde Tek-Parti Yönetiminin Kurulması 1923–1931*, 151, publishes a letter by Avni Doğan written on September 9, 1925, to Cemil Bey, the minister of the interior. In this letter, Avni Bey certainly does not sound like someone who was in favor of the journalists.

97. Edip, *İstiklal Mahkemeleri'nde Sebilürreşad'ın Romanı*, 64–65.

98. Toker, *Şeyh Said ve İsyanı*, 133. Toker also comments on how calmed Sheikh Said looked until he was sentenced to death (128).

99. Örgeevren, *Şeyh Sait İsyanı ve Şark İstiklal Mahkemesi*, 132.

100. Ibid., 133.

101. Ibid., 135.

102. See the copies of the telegrams in ibid., 140–43.

103. Edip, *İstiklal Mahkemelerinde Sebilürreşad'ın Romanı*, 175. We know that Ali Saip, by using his influence on the Eastern Independence Tribunal, became rich but later was accused of a plot to assassinate Mustafa Kemal. The charge was false but resulted in his removal from the inner circle. See Sami Önal, ed., *Hüsrev Gerede'nin Anıları: Kurtuluş Savaşı, Atatürk ve Devrimler* (İstanbul: Literatür, 2002), 284–85, and Yalman, *Yakın Tarihte Gördüklerim ve Geçirdiklerim*, 183.

104. For interesting developments regarding the letter and Velid Ebüzziya's first objection to and later compliance with the request, see Edip, *İstiklal Mahkemeleri'nde Sebilürreşad'ın Romanı*, 185–97.

105. Staying true to the spirit of the letter, I translated it liberally. For comparison, I am adding the text of the letter as published in Eşref Edip's memoir (*İstiklal Mahkemeleri'nde Sebilürreşad'ın Romanı*, 192). The letter was signed by 10 journalists who were tried in the Independence Tribunals:

Ankara'da Reisi Cumhur Gazi Mustafa Kemal Paşa Hazretlerine:

> Şark İstiklal Mahkemesi karşısında sorgulanmalarımız icra ve ikmal olunduğu şu günlerde tahdis-i nimet kabilinden bir hareketle huzur-u ulviyenize çıkmayı vecibeden addettik. Cumhuriyetin sadık bir amelesi, inkilabın samimi bir hadimi olduğumuzu isbat etmiş olmak kanaatiyle bipeyan bir fahr ve gurur hissederek zat-ı riyasetpenahilerine bir kerre daha arzederiz ki, bu kanaat şu dakikada vicdanlarımızı müsterih etmekle beraber bundan daha çok güvendiğimiz nokta asalet-i kalbinizin lütf-ü hatapuşanesidir. Bu lütfun y[ed]d-i imtinankaranesiyle ve zeval-i napezir bir kalbi irtibatla bundan sonra vazifemize devam edebilmek, vicdanlarımızda hasıl olan intihabı müstakbel hareketlerimize rehber

edinerek yüksek gayemize doğru temiz nasiye ileyürüyebilmek için feyz-i enzar-ı itimadınızın bizden diriğ buyrulmamasına pek muhtaçtır.

Huzur-u mahkemede taayy[ü]n eden masumiyetimiz için Büyük Münci'nin yüksek vicdanından duyacağımız afv ve müsamaha müjdesi iledir ki, bizim için kıymetdar olur, [b]u lütfu bizden esirgemeyeceğinizi uluvv-u kalbinizden ümid ederek en derin tazimatımızı arz ve takdim ederiz, Muhterem Reis-i Cumhur Hazretleri.

106. "Şark İstiklal Mahkemesi Savcılığına: Gazetecilerin mahkemeye celbinden sonra Anadolu'da ve isyan sahasındaki meşhudatları üzerinde hata ettikleri ve nadim oldukları hakkındaki telgraflarını evvelce mahkemenin adalet nazarına takdim etmiştim. Bu defa yine müştereken yukarıdaki telgrafla müracaat ediyorlar. Bunu da nazar-ı insafa almak muvafıktır, efendim"; Edip, *İstiklal Mahkemeleri'nde Sebilürreşad'ın Romanı*, 193.

107. Ibid., 194–97.

108. Ibid., 185.

109. 867.00/1872, Bristol to the Secretary of State, May 6, 1925.

110. Yeşil, *Türkiye Cumhuriyeti'nde İlk Teşkilatlı Muhalefet Hareketi*, 323. The author has examined the TGNA Archives for the accusation files; hence, his statements certainly carry authority. However, for this particular conclusion, Yeşil does not offer any specific reference.

111. 867.00/1745, Bristol to the Secretary of State, entry dated October 23, 1925. Mr. Scotten's first and middle names are not clear, but they could be R. M. Scotten.

112. TGNA Archive, T 3 D 22 (Tasnif # 28), in Yeşil, *Türkiye Cumhuriyeti'nde İlk Teşkilatlı Muhalefet Hareketi*, 322, n. 41.

113. Ahmet Yeşil gives very detailed and well-documented information about the closing of the PRP based on the TGNA Archives (see particularly 321–76). For information about the TGNA Archives, I rely on Yeşil.

114. Aybars's *İstiklal Mahkemeleri 1920–1927* is a good source on these infamous tribunals, even though it is biased. For the Ankara Independence Tribunal, see 353–474.

115. The branches were Eminönü, Galata, Erenköy, Beykoz, Makriköy (Bakırköy), Rami, Kağıthane, Samatya, Arnavutköy, and Şile. Ahmet Yeşil also indicates that this list was taken from the İstanbul governor Süleyman Sami's letter to the tribunal. In the daily newspapers, these branches were slightly different; see Yeşil, *Türkiye Cumhuriyeti'nde İlk Teşkilatlı Muhalefet Hareketi*, 339, fn. 92.

116. Yeşil implies that there existed a bias in court against the arrested Beykoz members, for the date of their departure to Ankara coincides with that of the confiscated documents. In other words, the tribunal jumped to conclusions without examining the documents. However, Yeşil does admit that the initial contact with the members of the PRP was not an official arrest since the police only took them into custody for questioning. The actual arrest came

after their court appearance; see Yeşil, *Türkiye Cumhuriyeti'nde İlk Teşkilatlı Muhalefet Hareketi*, 339–40, fn. 93.

117. Only Hüseyin Bey was acquitted. The verdict is in the TGNA Archives T-3, Dosya 22, Karar 24, as quoted in Aybars, *İstiklal Mahkemeleri 1920–1927*, 363, and as referred to in Yeşil, *Türkiye Cumhuriyeti'nde İlk Teşkilatlı Muhalefet Hareketi*. The date given by Aybars is May 3, 1925, yet Yeşil gives the date as May 4, 1924.

118. TGNA Archives, T. 12, D.3. These proceedings have been examined by Ahmet Yeşil, whose text includes some of the original documents; see Yeşil, *Türkiye Cumhuriyeti'nde İlk Teşkilatlı Muhalefet Hareketi*, 356–76.

119. Ibid., 356–57, fn. 129.

120. Ibid.; see also fn. 130, 131, 132.

121. TGNA Archives, T-12, D.3, 3-4. The interrogation is quoted in Yeşil, *Türkiye Cumhuriyeti'nde İlk Teşkilatlı Muhalefet Hareketi*, 366–67.

122. Contradicting this account is the memoir of Süreyya Bey, the prosecutor of the Eastern Tribunal. Süreyya Bey claimed that Fethi Bey did not favor Article 6 of his party program and that he clearly stated this view in court. See Örgeevren, *Şeyh Sait İsyanı ve Şark İstiklal Mahkemesi*, 130.

123. For a more complete treatment, see Yeşil, *Türkiye Cumhuriyeti'nde İlk Teşkilatlı Muhalefet Hareketi*, 370, n. 160.

124. Ibid., 369, n. 157.

125. Karar No. 24/ Esas No. 3, in TGNA, T-3, D.22. The full text can be found in Yeşil, *Türkiye Cumhuriyeti'nde İlk Teşkilatlı Muhalefet Hareketi*, 482–84.

126. Karar No. 30/Esas No. 32, in TGNA, T-12, D.3. The full text can be found in Yeşil, *Türkiye Cumhuriyeti'nde İlk Teşkilatlı Muhalefet Hareketi*, 485–87.

127. For the full text in English, see Zürcher, *Political Opposition in the Early Turkish Republic*, 160–62; for the Turkish text, see Tarık Zafer Tunaya, *Türkiye'de Siyasi Partiler, 1859–1952* (İstanbul: n.p., 1952), 621–22, and Yeşil, *Türkiye Cumhuriyeti'nde İlk Teşkilatlı Muhalefet Hareketi*, 488–90.

128. Dr. Tevfik (foreign minister), Rüştü Recep (minister of defense), Dr. Tevfik Rüştü (minister of justice), Mehmet Sabri (naval minister), and Ali Cenani (minister of commerce).

129. I use the English translation by Zürcher in his *Political Opposition in the Early Turkish Republic*. I have corrected the mistranslation of the word *takibat* from "persecution" to "prosecution."

130. For example, in reference to the alphabet reform, Falih Rıfkı Atay, a close friend of Mustafa Kemal, claims, "This was a top-down (*tepeden inme*) surprise. The TGNA did not even know about it. There is no doubt that the method [of implementing this reform] was dictatorial"; Falih Rıfkı Atay, *Atatürkçülük Nedir?* (İstanbul: Ak, 1966), 34.

131. Mark L. Bristol to the Secretary of State, 867.00/1870.

Chapter 4

1. Mahmut Gologlu, *Devrimler ve Tepkileri* (İstanbul: Türkiye İş Bankası Yayınları, 2007), 237–38.

2. Osman Selim Kocahanoğlu, *Atatürk'e Kurulan Pusu* (İstanbul: Temel, 2005); Sümer Kılıç, *İstiklal Mahkemeleri Adil miydi: İzmir Suikastı* (İstanbul: Emre, 1994); Azmi Nihat Erman, *İzmir Suikastı ve İstiklal Mahkemeleri* (İstanbul: Temel, 1971); Cemal Avcı, *İzmir Suikastı: Bir Suikastin Perde Arkası* (İstanbul: I. Q. Kültür Sanat, 2007); Uğur Mumcu, *Gazi Paşaya Suikast* (İstanbul: Tekin, 1992).

3. The minutes for the Ankara trials are not fully available but can be followed by U.S. consular reports.

4. Chief among them is Erik Jan Zürcher, *The Unionist Factor: The Role of the Committee of Union and Progress in the Turkish National Movement, 1905-1926* (Leiden: E. J. Brill, 1984).

5. Zürcher's *The Unionist Factor* is a solid piece of scholarship. However, since its publication, many other primary sources have become available.

6. *British Documents on Foreign Affairs: Reports and Papers from the Foreign Office*, Confidential Print, Part II, Series B, Turkey, Iran and the Middle East 1918–1939, vol. 30, Turkey, July 1923–March 1927 (Frederick, MD: University Publications of America, 1985), 404.

7. From the microfilm collection "Records of the Department of State Relating to Internal Affairs of Turkey, 1910–29," document number 867.001K31/8.

8. Unless otherwise indicated, information presented in this section comes from Kocahanoğlu, *Atatürk'e Kurulan Pusu*; Kılıç, *İstiklal Mahkemeleri Adil miydi*; Erman, *İzmir Suikastı ve İstiklal Mahkemeleri*; Zürcher, *The Unionist Factor*; Kılıç Ali, *İstiklal Mahkemesi Hatıraları* (İstanbul: Sel, 1955); Avcı, *İzmir Suikastı*; and Mumcu, *Gazi Paşa'ya Suikast.*

9. İsmet İnönü, *Hatıralar*, vol. 2 (Ankara: Bilgi, 1987), 210.

10. Kocahanoğlu, *Atatürk'e Kurulan Pusu*, 149–67, where he published the memoirs of Faik Günday, brother of Ziya Hurşit, originally published in daily *Dünya* (September 3–13, 1956). See also the prosecutor's indictment for the İzmir trial, published in Kocahanoğlu, *Atatürk'e Kurulan Pusu*, 173–84; the same indictment was also published in the original language in Kılıç, *İstiklal Mahkemeleri Adil miydi*, 83–99.

11. Kocahanoğlu, *Atatürk'e Kurulan Pusu*, 171–84; Kılıç, *İstiklal Mahkemeleri Adil miydi*, 83–112.

12. We have reliable primary sources for this section. Late Uğur Mumcu, a Turkish journalist, had rare access to the Presidential Archives in Ankara, where telegrams between Mustafa Kemal and İsmet Pasha were housed. The collection also includes interrogation records that were vital to the case. Mumcu published this collection in his *Gazi Paşa'ya Suikast*. In addition, Mustafa Kemal Atatürk, *Mustafa Kemal'in Bütün Eserleri*, vol. 18 (İstanbul:

Kaynak, 2006), printed these telegrams. Kocahanoğlu, *Atatürk'e Kurulan Pusu,* without any reference, makes use of the police interrogation records as well. For the related information, I rely on these sources.

13. Mustafa Kemal Atatürk, *Atatürk'ün Bütün Eserleri,* vol. 18 (September 27, 1925–October 12, 1927) (İstanbul: Kaynak, 2006).

14. "İzmir Suikasti Hakkında Başvekil İsmet Paşa'ya," June 16, 1927; *Atatürk'ün Bütün Eserleri,* 222. The original was stored in the Presidential Archives, vesika # 1019, A V-2, D: 79-5, F: 11.

15. Ibid., 223. Mustafa Kemal also informs İsmet Pasha of his request from the İstanbul Police (225).

16. "Suikastin geniş bir tertibata dayalı olacağına ihtimal vermiyoruz"; ibid., 226.

17. Ibid.

18. The Turkish newspapers *Milliyet, Cumhuriyet, İkdam, Akşam,* and *Anadolu* published the statement on the first page; ibid., 229.

19. "Benim naçiz vücudum elbet birgün toprak olacaktır; fakat Türkiye Cumhuriyeti ilelebet payidar kalacaktır"; ibid.

20. The telegram was dated June 18, 1926; ibid., 233.

21. This is the crux of Mustafa Kemal's attempts to remove military from politics.

22. The telegram was sent from İzmir; ibid., 234–35.

23. Giritli Şevki informed the authorities about his decision to inform Mustafa Kemal directly in which he stated: "I planned to go to Menemen [to warn Mustafa Kemal directly] and not to inform the Government at all. Because I heard that the whole People's Party apparatus was in this plot. [Bütün Halk Fırkası bunlardanmış]. Even the speaker of parliament Kazım Paşa." Kocahanoğlu, *Atatürk'e Kurulan Pusu,* 56–57.

24. Ibid., 71.

25. *Atatürk'ün Bütün Eserleri,* 236–37.

26. For İsmet Pasha's telegram, see ibid., 239.

27. Kocahanoğlu, *Atatürk'e Kurulan Pusu,* 80; Erman, *İzmir Suikastı ve İstiklal Mahkemeleri,* 36–39.

28. Kocahanoğlu, *Atatürk'e Kurulan Pusu,* claims that Recep Peker (acting interior minister) secretly informed Mustafa Kemal of the release of Kazım Karabekir (80). For Recep Bey's telegram, see Mumcu, *Gazi Paşa'ya Suikast,* 21–22. According to Erman, *İzmir Suikastı ve İstiklal Mahkemeleri,* Police Chief Dilaver Bey informed the court of the situation (37).

29. Kocahanoğlu, *Atatürk'e Kurulan Pusu,* 81; Erman, *İzmir Suikastı ve İstiklal Mahkemeleri,* 39.

30. It was interesting to note that this letter, written to the Independence Tribunal on June 22, 1926, by İsmet Pasha, acknowledges the authority of the court, not the guilt of Kazım Karabekir. We know that İsmet Pasha sent a telegram to the Interior Ministry seemingly accepting all the accusations leveled against the PRP; see Kocahanoğlu, *Atatürk'e Kurulan Pusu,* 84–86.

31. The tribunal consisted of the chief judge, Ali (Çetinkaya); the prosecutor, Necip Ali (Küçüka); and members Kılıç Ali, Ali (Zırh), and Reşit Galip, all of whom were close associates of Mustafa Kemal.

32. Kocahanoğlu, *Atatürk'e Kurulan Pusu*, 171; *New York Times*, June 20, 1926, reported that over 40 people of the PRP background were arrested (22).

33. 867.001/K31/14. The list seems to be reliable despite the fact that there is no other list with which to compare. The names and occupations of those arrested are as follows: "Arif Bey, a retired Colonel and Deputy from Eski Shehir; Ali Fuad Pasha, a retired General and Deputy from Angora; Abeddin Bey, Deputy from Sarouhan; Beker Samy Bey, Deputy from Tokat; Bahaeddin, Military Reserve Officer; Chahin Tchaoush [Şahin Çavuş?], who was connected to a farm belonging to Edib Bey; Djemal Pasha, aretired General and ex-Deputy from Mersina; Djambolat Bey, ex-Minister of Interior, ex-Minister to Sweden, ex-Mayor of Constantinople and Deputy from Constantinople; Djavid Pasha [Bey?],ex-Minister of Finance; Djafer Tayar Bey [Pasha], ex-Minister of Finance[?] and Deputy from Adrianople; [Sarı Efe] Edib Bey, a retired Major of Gendarmerie; Faik Bey, Deputy from Ordou; Feridun Fikri Bey, Deputy from Dersim; Fazil [Faik] Bey, a brother of Zia Hourchid; Gurdji Youssuf; Ghirali Chevki Bey; Hafuz Mehmed, ex-Deputy from Trebizand; Hussein Avni Bey, ex-Deputy from Erzeroum; Halis Tourgoud, Deputy from Sivas; Hussein Riza, a brother-in-law of an ex-Deputy from Lazistan; Hilmi Bey, ex-Deputy from Erdehan; Haalet Bey, Deputy from Erzeroum;Ishan Bey, Deputy from Ergoni; Idris, a gardener at Cordelio [Karşıyaka]; Kezini Bey, Deputy from Trebizand; Kiazim Kara Bekir Pasha, a retired General and Deputy from Constantinople; Kiamil Effendi, Deputy from Afion Karahissar; Kara Vasif Bey, ex-Deputy from Constantionople; Laz Ismail; Latif, a clerk; Mouhtar Bey, Deputy from Trebizand; Moustafa Shevket, a dentist; Moustafa, a companion of Hussein Riza; Mehmed Kelesh, a boatman at Constantinople; Muammer Bey, ex-Vali of Sivas; Nedjati Bey, ex-Deputy from Lazistan; Nedjati Bey, ex-Deputy from Erzeroum; Nedjati Bey, Deputy from Broussa; Reefet Osman Noury, Deputy from Broussa, Refet Pasha, a retired General and Deputy from Constantinople; Rahmi Bey, Deputy from Trebizand; Rushdi Pasha, a retired General and Deputy from Erzeroum; Rassim Bey, a retired Army Colonel; Shukri Bey, ex-Minister of Education and Deputy from Ismid; Sabit Bey, Deputy from Erzeroum; Tchopur Hilmi; Tcholak Selaheddin Bey, a retired Colonel; Tourbali Emin Bey, a farmer; Vehab, a nephew of Hafuz Mehmed; Zia Hourshid, ex-Deputy from Lazistan; and Zeki Bey, Deputy from Gumush-Haneh."

34. Instead, the court mistakenly arrested Casım Bey (Duray), an independent deputy from Erzurum; see Kılıç, *İstiklal Mahkemeleri Adil miydi*, 51–52.

35. Rauf Orbay, *Cehennem Değirmeni: Siyasi Hatıralarım*, vol. 2 (İstanbul: Emre, 1993), 197–99.

36. Article 55 stated the following: "Persons who attempt to alter by force partially or in entirety by the Organic Statues of the Republic of Turkey; and

persons who endeavor to abolish the Grand National Assembly or to prevent it from performing its duties shall be condemned to death and executed. Individuals who instigate the foregoing offences shall also be executed, provided that the attempt actually takes place. If the offences should consist only of an attempt, the instigator shall be imprisoned for a minimum period of seven years. Persons who attempt to abolish the Council of Ministers or to attempt to prevent its functioning shall be imprisoned for life"; Article 57 stated, "If a group of persons engage collectively in a conspiracy to commit the offences mentioned in Article Fifty-five, the leaders and the members, as well as the instigators, shall be executed" (as translated in the report by Samuel W. Honaker, 867.00/K31/14, 60).

37. In the courtroom, there were also foreign journalists, one of whom, the *Times* correspondent, reported that Ziya Hurşit was not only frank in his testimony accepting the responsibility but also exaggerated his role in the plot;; *The Times*, "The Turkish Plot," June 29, 1926, 15.

38. Mumcu, *Gazi Paşa'ya Suikast*; 39; see also 867.00/K31/14, 13.

39. There were also considerations for Bursa as an alternative location for a plot.

40. *The Times*, "The Turkish Plot."

41. 867.00/K31/14, 17.

42. Kocahanoğlu, *Atatürk'e Kurulan Pusu*, 231.

43. Mumcu, *Gazi Paşaya Suikast*, 14.

44. Ibid., 245–46. Kazım Karabekir flatly denied any such accusation; Kılıç, *İstiklal Mahkemeleri Adil miydi*, 122–23.

45. The piece by Faik Hurşit Günday was published in the daily *Dünya* between September 3 and 13, 1956, as cited in Kocahanoğlu, *Atatürk'e Kurulan Pusu*, 166–67.

46. As cited in Kılıç, *İstiklal Mahkemeleri Adil miydi*, 239–63. It was not explicitly stated in this source; however, this article was clearly penned by Feridun Kandemir.

47. Kılıç, *İstiklal Mahkemeleri Adil miydi*, 121–22; Kocahanoğlu, *Atatürk'e Kurulan Pusu*, 300.

48. "Ben aksi kanaatteyim. Memleket müdriktir"; Kocahanoğlu, *Atatürk'e Kurulan Pusu*, 306.

49. Ibid., 276; Kılıç, *İstiklal Mahkemeleri Adil miydi*, 102–3. Kocahanoğlu seems to shorten the text. Kılıç, on the other hand, had the full text in both Latin script and the original Arabic script.

50. The reader must be warned that unlike those in the Ankara trials, the proceedings of the İzmir trials have not been published in their entirety. We have secondary sources making use of daily papers of the time, memoirs, and summaries of the proceedings in the U.S. consular reports. They hardly contain any such information.

51. Kılıç, *İstiklal Mahkemeleri Adil miydi?*, 277–78. The copy of the original addendum given to Kazım Karabekir was published on p. 278. Because of Karabekir's handwritten notes on the document, certain sections are not legible.

52. There is no "day" mentioned in the document.

53. Kılıç, *İstiklal Mahkemeleri Adil miydi*, 110–11.

54. The court acknowledged that the CUP rendered great service to the country by relieving the despotism of Abdülhamid II and that many prominent CUP members contribute to the current nationalist government. Therefore, the CUP in general could not be held entirely responsible for the abuses of its members; see 867.001K31/14, 30. However, such tolerance was not afforded to the PRP.

55. Faruk Özerengin's interview was published in the journal *Teklif* in 1987 (issue 6), as cited in Kılıç, *İstiklal Mahkemeleri Adil miydi*, 230. Rıza Nur also mentions this rumor in his *Hayat ve Hatıralarım*, vol. 4 (İstanbul: Altındağ, 1968), 1388. A British source also reports that "the Army began to murmur, and Mustafa Kemal was fain to let [the generals] go"; E 633/633/44, received February 7, 1926, from Sir G. Clerk to Sir Austen Chamberlain, *British Documents on Foreign Affairs*, 415.

56. Fahrettin Altay, *10 Yıl Savaş ve Sonrası: Görüp Geçirdiklerim* (İstanbul: İnsel, 1970), 241.

57. Hulusi Turgut, ed., *Atatürk'ün Sırdaşı Kılıç Ali'nin Anıları* (İstanbul: İş Bankası Kültür Yayınları, 2005), 419.

58. Kocahanoğlu, *Atatürk'e Kurulan Pusu*, 8–9.

59. "The Turkish Plot: End of Kara Kemal Bey," *The Times*, July 29, 1926, 12.

60. Kocahanoğlu, *Atatürk'e Kurulan Pusu*, 791. The newspapers announced his arrest on August 23, 1926. *The Times* reported on August 24, 1926, indicating that when he was first captured, he denied that his name was Abdülkadir. He introduced himself as Nazif, a former captain in the army; see *The Times*, "Arrest of Turkish Notable," August 24, 1926, 10. For his execution, see Mumcu, *Gazi Paşa'ya Suikast*, 101; Kocahanoğlu, *Atatürk'e Kurulan Pusu*, 821; "Another Turk is Hanged," *New York Times*, September 2, 1926, 7.

61. Kocahanoğlu, *Atatürk'e Kurulan Pusu*, 443–45.

62. Mumcu, *Gazi Paşa'ya Suikast*, refers to a significant document to substantiate this claim in the Presidential Archives in Ankara (A-IV, 16-4, D. No. 67). The report indicates that Kazım Karabekir, Refet, Cafer Tayyar, Ali Fuat, Colonel Çolak Selahattin, Kara Vasıf, Bekir Sami, Feridun Fikri, Hüseyin Avni and Aliye Hanım, wife of Cavit Bey, were under police surveillance for years; see Mumcu, *Gazi Paşa'ya Suikast*, 76 fn.

63. For the full text of the verdict see Kocahanoğlu, *Atatürk'e Kurulan Pusu*, 449–63; U.S. sources add two more names to the list that were not in the original verdict: Kara Vasıf and Hüseyin Avni Beys; 867.001K31/9.

64. Unless otherwise indicated, information for this section comes from Sema Ilıkan and Faruk Ilıkan, eds., *Ankara İstiklal Mahkemesi: Ankara İstiklal Mahkemesi'nde Cereyan Eden Su-i kasd ve Taklib-i Hükumet Davası'na Ait Resmi*

Zabıtlar (İstanbul: Simurg, 2005); U.S. archival documents 867.001K31/9 and 12; Kocahanoğlu, *Atatürk'e Kurulan Pusu*; and Mumcu, *Gazi Paşa'ya Suikast*. TITE has some documents on the activities of the CUP members; see K67G142B1, K63G96B1, and K67G141B2.

65. Falih Rıfkı Atay, *Çankaya* (İstanbul: Pozitif, 2004), 468-69.

66. "Angora Trial Gives Historical Data," *New York Times*, September 5, 1926, 16.

67. For the full text of the prosecutor's plea, see Kocahanoğlu, *Atatürk'e Kurulan Pusu*, 481–85, esp. 484.

68. 867.001K31/12 misprints these articles as numbers 45 and 48.

69. There is a discrepancy in the list provided by the 867.001K31/12 and the text of the prosecutor's plea. The former adds more names to the list: Sadettin Rıza Bey, Bekir Bey of the Kantarcı Company, and Silki (Sıtkı?) Bey. *The Times* reported that 49 people were accused and that only half of them were present when the prosecutor read his plea; "The Angora Trial," August 4, 1926, 11.

70. Zürcher, *The Unionist Factor*, 160–61.

71. 867.001K31/12.

72. Ibid.

73. *British Documents on Foreign Affairs*, 415.

74. 867.001K31/12, from Sheldon Leavitt Crosby, Chargé d'Affaires, to Secretary of State, September 1, 1926.

75. Zürcher, *The Unionist Factor*, 156.

76. Kılıç, *İstiklal Mahkemeleri Adil miydi*, 7–18; see also Kocahanoğlu, *Atatürk'e Kurulan Pusu*, 43–52.

77. Avcı, *İzmir Suikastı*, among others, suggests that Mustafa Kemal's delaying the visit was a reason for Giritli Şevki's decision to expose the plot (72).

78. Mumcu, *Gazi Paşa'ya Suikast*, 7–9; Mumcu points out that the official records of police interrogations were kept by Hayati Bey, the private secretary of the president, Rasuhi, first aide-de-camp, and Kazım Pasha, governor of İzmir. These records are kept in the Presidential Archives in Ankara; Mumcu, *Gazi Paşa'ya Suikast*, 10–11 and fn. 2, has the specific file numbers for the records. I rely on Mumcu for the information in these records, as I was unable to work in these archives. Kocahanoğlu, *Atatürk'e Kurulan Pusu*, reports without any reference that in his interrogation by the İzmir Police, Giritli Şevki stated that he became afraid when he heard from other conspirators that all the members of the Republican Party and the president of the Assembly, Kazım Pasha (Özalp), were involved in the plot; therefore, he wanted to inform Mustafa Kemal directly (56–57). This does not explain why he changed his mind. In addition, we do not know the accuracy of this information, simply because Kocahanoğlu does not cite any source for a transcript of the police interrogations in İzmir; see also Erman, *İzmir Suikastı ve İstiklal Mahkemeleri*, 97.

79. Rauf and Kazım Karabekir pointed out that Sarı Edip Efe acted the same way that Mr. Templen, a government agent posing as a British representative, did to frame Seyyid Abdulkadir after the Sheikh Said Revolt; Kocahanoğlu, *Atatürk'e Kurulan Pusu*, 47, 299.

80. Kılıç, *İstiklal Mahkemeleri Adil miydi*, 118–19.

81. Mumcu, *Gazi Paşa'ya Suikast*, 15; Ali Fuat Cebesoy, *Siyasi Hatıralar*, 2 vols. (İstanbul: Doğan Kardeş, 1960). Cebesoy, *Siyasi Hatıralar*, vol. 2, 213.

82. 867.001K31/14.

83. The members of the court were so disheartened that they left the ball secretly by jumping over a balcony. There are a number of primary sources that confirmed the incident; see Altay, *10 Yıl Savaş ve Sonrası*, 420, and Atay, *Çankaya*, 469. Kılıç Ali, a member of the court, disputes the reason they had to jump from a balcony. He claims that a friend (Falih Rıfkı Atay) complained to Mustafa Kemal that members of the court were too lenient toward the accused. They were upset by this incident and needed to leave the party; see Ali, *İstiklal Mahkemesi Hatıraları*, 67.

84. *Hakimiyet-i Milliye*, June 29, 1926, as cited in Kılıç, *İstiklal Mahkemeleri Adil miydi*, 120; see also Kocahanoğlu, *Atatürk'e Kurulan Pusu*, 44. Feridun Kandemir also reports an interview by Refik Koraltan, deputy from Konya, who insisted that he informed the authorities of a possible plot by Ziya Hurşit and his associates. See Feridun Kandemir, *Atatürk'e İzmir Suikastinden Ayrı 11 Suikast* (İstanbul: Ekincil, 1955), 33–48.

85. Zürcher, *The Unionist Factor*, claims that Mustafa Kemal's popularity was shaken because of his reform policies and the harsh way he was implementing them prior to the İzmir conspiracy. The implication is that Mustafa Kemal needed something to boost his popularity (144).

86. 867.001K31/4, a telegram sent by Bristol to Secretary of State.

87. 867.001K31/6, a report sent by Bristol to Secretary of State

88. İnönü, *Hatıralar*, 212.

89. 867.001K31/8, a report sent by Bristol to Secretary of State.

90. Ibid.

91. 867.001K31/9, a report sent by Bristol to Secretary of State.

92. Ibid.

93. We do know that the Independence Tribunal was aware of the issue of the legality. Mark Bristol reports that the position of the court was that the political activities of the accused postdate the guarantees given at the Treaty of Lausanne. The court was examining the political situation in the short period immediately before and after the Armistice of Mudros in 1918 and the postguarantee period up to the İzmir plot; see 867.001K31/9.

94. 867.001K31/15, from Charles E. Allen to Secretary of State, October 22, 1926.

95. Ibid.

96. Ibid.

97. Ibid. Şükrü Hanioğlu is not convinced of Allen's conclusion. Hanioğlu suggests that Mustafa Kemal's position in the CUP is exaggerated in Turkish historiography. He was a young officer under Cemal Pasha and, in fact, was on good terms with Dr. Nazım; personal correspondence with Hanioğlu, October 7, 2010.

98. 867.001K31/14, A Report on the Smyrna Trial, prepared by Samuel W. Honeker for the State Department, Division of Near Eastern Affairs. The date of the report's mailing is August 26, 1926.

99. Ilıkan and Ilıkan, *Ankara İstiklal Mahkemesi*. The editors indicate that their work is based on the minutes that were published in the daily *Hakimiyet-i Milliye* between August 3, 1926, and October 15, 1926.

100. 867.001K31/14.

101. 867.001K31/13, from Sheldon Leavitt Crosby to Secretary of State, September 1, 1926.

102. Ibid.

103. Seyyid Mahdi Ahmet al Sanusi (1873–1933) was a sheikh of the Sanussiya order, which was active against the Italian invasion of Libya in 1911. He came to İstanbul at the invitation of the last Ottoman sultan, Vahdettin, in 1918. We know that he supported the nationalist movement later and arrived in Ankara on November 15, 1920; see Timuçin Mert, *Atatürk'ün Yanındaki Mehdi* (İstanbul: Kara Kutu, 2006), 135.

104. 867.00/1801, from Mark L. Bristol to Secretary of State, June 17, 1924.

105. 867.00/1812, from Mark L. Bristol to Secretary of State, 26 July 26, 1924.

106. These negotiations are most interesting as reported in 867.00/1812, 1844, 1859, and 1862. According to these reports, Mustafa Kemal offered Turkey's support to Seyyid Ahmet el Sanusi for the new caliphs to be elected in the pan-Islamic conference in Cairo. In return, he was asked to legitimize Ankara's stand on secularism.

107. 867.00/1859. "War Diary," Mark L. Bristol, entry dated March 9, 1925.

108. Yücel Demirel and Osman Zeki Okur, eds., *CHP Grup Toplantısı Tutanakları 1923–1924* (İstanbul: Bilgi Üniversitesi Yayınları, 2002), 23–30.

109. "The Ghazi's Speech," *The Times*, November 2, 1927, 8; see also Rauf Bey's statement in 867.00/1831.

110. İnönü, *Hatıralar*, 214. In a letter to the editor of *The Times*, Rauf Bey did not even consider himself a member of the opposition who sought the government's pardon for an offense he did not commit; see "Turkish Government and the Opposition," *The Times*, December 9, 1926, 12.

111. İnönü, *Hatıralar*, 214.

112. İnönü, *Hatıralar*, 216.

113. Şükrü Hanioğlu suggests that "Hüseyin Cahit had never been one of the most distinguished leaders of the CUP with organizational skills. He was mainly a journalist, not a conspirator. Therefore, it is understandable that his life was spared. This also helped the Court give the impression that the

verdicts were fair and the innocent ones were acquitted"; personal correspondence, October 7, 2010.

114. Zürcher, *The Unionist Factor*, 142–68.

115. Tarık Zafer Tunaya, *Türkiye'de Siyasi Partiler*, vol. 3 (İstanbul: İletişim, 1999),411, 509, 653.

116. George S. Harris, "The Role of Turkish Military in Politics," *Middle East Journal* 19: 56–57.

117. Document 184 (E8863/32/44), Mr. Lindsay to Mr. Mac Donald, October 8, 1924, in *British Documents on Foreign Affairs*, 220.

118. Ibid.

Chapter 5

1. 867.00/1737, from Maynard Barnes to Secretary of State, "Political Situation in Turkey," October 15, 1923.

2. He must mean the ulama or religious functionaries.

3. This proclamation was passed by the Ottoman parliament on January 28, 1920. It had six articles, which mainly set the territorial goals of the Ottoman state.

4. 867.00/1745, Bristol to the Secretary of State, October 23, 1923.

Bibliography

ARCHIVAL SOURCES (UNPUBLISHED)

Directorate of General Security Archives (Emniyet Genel Müdürlüğü Arşivi)

DGSA 12221-1/A1 through A14
DGSA 12221-1/G11, G13
DGSA 12221-2/B1 through B7
DGSA 12222/1 through 150

Institute for History of Turkish Reforms (Türk İnkilap Tarihi Enstitüsü [TİTE])

K23G64B3
K24G109B109
K24G109B3
K24G143B2
K58G97B4
K63G96B1
K67G141B2
K67G142B1

Great Britain Public Record Archives and Cabinet Papers

CAB 23/20
CAB 23/35

CAB 24/129
FO 371/10826-033
FO 371/10867, E 1360/1091/44
FO 424/261, E 10619/32/44

Prime Minister's Republican Archives (Başbakanlık Cumhuriyet Arşivi)

30.10.0.0/106.695.4
30.10.0.0/106.695.21
30.10.0.0/107.698.7
30.10.0.0/31.175.32
30.18.1.1/11.43.16
30.18.1.1/13.19.2
30.18.1.1/15.54.10
30.18.01-26/21
30.18.1.1/3.29.16

U.S. Department of State, "Records of the Department of State Relating to Internal Affairs of Turkey, 1910–29" (Microfilm Collection)

867.00/1737
867.00/1745
867.00/1801
867.00/1812
867.00/1852
867.00/1853
867.00/1859
867.00/1863
867.00/1864
867.00/1866
867.00/1870
867.00/1872
867.00/1889
867.001/K31/12
867.001/K31/13
867.001/K31/14
867.001/K31/15
867.001/K31/4
867.001/K31/6

867.001/K31/8
867.001/K31/9

PRINTED ARCHIVAL DOCUMENTS

British Documents on Foreign Affairs: Reports and Papers from the Foreign Office. Confidential Print. Part II, From the First to the Second World War, Series B, Turkey, Iran and the Middle East, 1918–1939. Vol. 31. Frederick, MD: University Publications of America, 1997.

British Documents on Foreign Affairs; Reports and Papers from the Foreign Office. Confidential Print, Part II, Series B, Turkey, Iran and the Middle East 1918–1939. Vol. 30, Turkey, July 1923–March 1927. Frederick, MD: University Publications of America, 1985.

Documents on British Foreign Policy 1919–1939. Vol. 18. London: Her Majesty's Stationery Office, 1972.

İçişleri Bakanlığı. *Cumhuriyetin 75.inci Yıldönümünde Polis Arşiv Belgeleriyle Gerçekler*. Ankara: Emniyet Genel Md. Araş. Planlama ve Koordinasyon, n.d.

Ilıkan, Selma, and Faruk Ilıkan, eds. *Ankara İstiklal Mahkemesi, Ankara İstiklal Mahkemesi'nde Cereyan Eden Su-i kasd ve Taklib-i Hükumet Davası'na Ait Resmi Zabıtlar*. İstanbul: Simurg, 2005.

TBMM Zabıt Ceridesi. Vol. 2, Ankara: TBMM Matbaası, n.d.

Yüzellilikler Albümü. Ankara: Vilayet Matbaası, n.d.

PRIMARY SOURCES

Adıvar, Halide Edib. *Ateşten Gömlek*. İstanbul: Özgür, 2006.

Adıvar, Halide Edib. *Mor Salkımlı Ev*. İstanbul: Atlas, 1967.

Adıvar, Halide Edib. *The Turkish Ordeal*. New York: The Century Co., 1928.

Adıvar, Halide Edib. *Türkiye'de Şark, Garb ve Amerikan Tesirleri*. İstanbul: Doğan Kardeş, 1955.

Ahmet İzzet Paşa. *Feryadım*. Vol. 2. İstanbul: Nehir, 1993.

Altay, Fahrettin. *10 Yıl Savaş ve Sonrası: Görüp Geçirdiklerim*. İstanbul: İnsel, 1970.

Arar, İsmail. *Halil Menteşe'nin Anıları*. İstanbul: Hürriyet Vakfı, 1986.

Atatürk, Mustafa Kemal. *Eskişehir-İzmit Konuşmaları, 1923: İlk Kez Sansürsüz, Tam Metin*. İstanbul: Kaynak, 1993.

Atatürk, Mustafa Kemal. *Atatürk'ün Bütün Eserleri*. Vol. 18. İstanbul: Kaynak, 2006.

Atatürk, Mustafa Kemal. *Nutuk*. 3 vols. Ankara: Başbakanlık Basımevi, 1984.

Atay, Falih Rıfkı. *Atatürk'ün Hatıraları 1914–1919*. Ankara: İş Bankası, 1965.

Atay, Falih Rıfkı. *Çankaya*. İstanbul: Pozitif, 2004.

Başikoğlu, Munise. "Babam Rıza Tevfik." *Tarih ve Toplum* 57–63 (1988–1989): 9–14.

Bilsel, Cemil. *Lozan*. Vol. 2. İstanbul: Ahmet İhsan Matbaası, 1933.

Birgen, Muhittin. *İttihat ve Terakki'de On Sene: İttihat ve Terakki Neydi?* Vol. 1. İstanbul: Kitap, 2006.

Cebesoy, Ali Fuat. *Siyasi Hatıralar*. 2 vols. İstanbul: Doğan Kardeş, 1960.

Çerkez Ethem. *Anılarım*. İstanbul: Berfin, 1998.

Demirel, Yücel, and Osman Zeki Okur, eds. *CHP Grup Toplantısı Tutanakları 1923–1924*. İstanbul: Bilgi Üniversitesi Yayınları, 2002.

Düstur. III. Tertib. Vol. 5. Ankara: n.p., 1939.

Fergan, Eşref Edip. *İstiklal Mahkemelerinde Sebilürreşad'ın Romanı*. Edited by Fahrettin Gün. Ankara: Beyan, 2002.

Grew, Joseph C. "The Peace Conference of Lausanne, 1922–1923." *Proceedings of the American Philosophical Society* 98, no. 1 (1954): 1–10.

İğdemir, Uluğ, ed. *Sivas Kongresi Tutanakları* Ankara: TTK, 1986.

İnönü, İsmet. *Hatıralar*. Vol. 2. Ankara: Bilgi, 1987.

Karabekir, Kazım. *Günlükler*. 2 vols. İstanbul: Yapı Kredi, 2009.

Karabekir, Kazım. *Nutuk ve Kazım Karabekir'den Cevaplar*. 12 vols. İstanbul: Emre, 1997.

Karay, Refik Halid. *Bir Ömür Boyunca*. İstanbul: İletişim, 1996.

Karay, Refik Halid. *Minelbab İlelmihrab: 1918 Mütarekesi Devrinde Olan Biten İşlere ve Gelip Geçen İnsanlara Dair Bildiklerim*. İstanbul: İnkilap, 1992.

Kılıç Ali. *İstiklal Mahkemesi Hatıraları*. İstanbul: Sel, 1955.

Malmisanıj. *Cızira Botanlı Bedirhaniler ve Bedirhan Ailesi Derneğinin Tutanakları*. Spanga: APEC, 1994.

Meray, Seha L., trans. and ed. *Lozan Barış Konferansı Tutanakları, Belgeler*. 1. Takım, Vol. 2. Ankara: Ankara Üniversitesi, 1969–1973.

Mevlanzade Rıfat. *İttihat Terakki İktidarı ve Türkiye İnkılabının İçyüzü*. İstanbul: Yedi İklim, 1993.

Noel, Edward W. C. *Diary of Major Noel on Special Duty in Kurdistan*. Baghdad: n.p., 1920.

Oranlı, Ziya, ed. *Atatürk'ün Şimdiye Kadar Yayınlanmamış Anıları: Anlatan Ali Metin, Atatürk'ün Emir Çavuşu*. Ankara: Alkan, 1967.

Orbay, Rauf. *Cehennem Değirmeni: Siyasi Hatıralarım*. Vol. 2. İstanbul: Emre, 1993.

Örgeevren, Ahmet Süreyya. *Şeyh Sait İsyanı ve Şark İstiklal Mahkemesi*. İstanbul: Temel, 2002.

Özalp, Kazım. *Atatürk'ten Anılar*. Ankara: Türkiye İş Bankası Yayınları, 1992.

Rıza Nur. *Dr. Rıza Nur'un Lozan Hatıraları*. İstanbul: Bogaziçi, 1999.

Rıza Nur. *Hayat ve Hatıralarım*. Vols. 1–4. İstanbul: Altındağ, 1968.

Rıza Nur. *Hürriyet ve İtilaf Fırkası Nasıl Doğdu, Nasıl Öldü*. İstanbul: Kitapevi, 1996.

Rıza Tevfik. *Biraz da Ben Konuşayım*. İstanbul: İletişim, 1993.

Şimşir, Bilal, ed. *Lozan Telgrafları*. 2 vols. Ankara: Türk Tarih Kurumu, 1990.

Soyak, Hasan Rıza. *Atatürk'ten Hatıralar*. İstanbul: Yapı Kredi, 1973.

Süleyman Şefik. *Hatıratım, Başıma Gelenler ve Gördüklerim: 31 Mart Vak'ası*. İstanbul: Arma, 2004.

Topuzlu, Cemil. *Operatör Cemil Paşa: Hatıraları*. İstanbul: Türkiye, 1945.

Turgut, Hulusi, ed. *Atatürk'ün Sırdaşı Kılıç Ali'nin Anıları*. İstanbul: İş Bankası Kültür Yayınları, 2005.

Türkgeldi, Ali Fuat. *Görüp İşittiklerim*. Ankara: Türk Tarih Kurumu, 1987.

Yalman, Ahmet Emin.*Yakın Tarihte Gördüklerim ve Geçirdiklerim*. Vol. 3. İstanbul: Rey, 1970.

SECONDARY SOURCES

Adanır, Fikret. "Kemalist Authorianism and Fascist Trends in Turkey during the Inter-War Period." In *Fascism Outside Europe: The European Impulse against Domestic Conditions in the Diffusion of Global Fascism*, edited by Stein Ugelvik Larsen. New York: Columbia University Press, 2001.

Ahmad, Feroz. *The Young Turks: The Committee of Union and Progress in Turkish Politics, 1908–1914*. New York: Columbia University Press, 2009.

Alakom, Rohat. *Şerif Paşa: Bir Kürt Diplomatının Fırtınalı Yılları*. İstanbul: Avesta, 1998.

Anıl, Yaşar Şahin. *Mahkeme Tutanaklarına Göre İzmir Suikastı Davası*. İstanbul: Kastaş, 2005.

Arar, İsmail. "Bir 150'liğin Kitabı." *Tarih ve Toplum* 10 (1989): 318.

Aşan, Aziz. *Şeyh Sait Ayaklanması*. İstanbul: n.p., 1991.

Atay, Falih Rıfkı. *Atatürkçülük Nedir?* İstanbul: Ak, 1966.

Avcı, Cemal. *İzmir Suikasti: Bir Suikastin Perde Arkası*. İstanbul: I. Q. Kültür Sanat, 2007.

Aybars, Ergün. *İstiklal Mahkemeleri 1920–1927*. İzmir: 9 Eylül Üniversitesi Yay, 1988.

Ayhan, Bünyamin. *Hakimiyet-i Milliye*. İstanbul: Zaman, 1949.

Ayhan, Bünyamin. *Milli Mücadele'de Basın: Olağanüstü Durumlarda Propaganda*. Konya: Tablet, 2007.

Aytepe, Oğuz. "Milli Mücadelede ve Gurbette Mürfit Bir Muhalif: Ömer Fevzi Eyüpoğlu 1884–1952." *Toplumsal Tarih* 53 (May 1998): 24–30.

Bağ, Yaşar. *Çerkezlerin Dünü Bugünü*. İstanbul: Kafkas Derneği, 2001.

Bardakçı, Murat. *Şahbaba*. Ankara: İnkilap, 2006.

Baykal, Hülya. *Türk Basın Tarihi 1831–1923: Tanzimat, Meşrutiyet, Milli Mücadele Dönemleri*. İstanbul: Afa, 1990.

Belgrave, Roland, and Taglia, Stefano. "Through Ottoman Eyes." *Cornucopia* 36. http://www.cornucopia.net/aboutdrs.html.

Bingöl, Sedat. "Ömer Fevzi Bey'in Müdafaanamesi ve Mesut Fani'nin Hoybun'a İlişkin Bilgileri: İki 150'lik Üzerine Notlar ve Belgeler" *Toplumsal Tarih* 62 (February 1999): 41–48.

Bingöl, Sedat. "Yüzellilikler Meselesi." MA thesis, Hacettepe University, 1994.

Bingöl, Sedat. *Yüzellilikler Meselesi: Bir İhanetin Anatomisi*. İstanbul: Bengi, 2010.

Birinci, Ali. *Hürriyet ve İtilaf Fırkası: II. Meşrutiyet Devrinde İttihat ve Terakki'ye Karşı Çıkanlar*. İstanbul: Dergah, 1990.

Bozarslan, Hamit. "Les Revoltes Kurdes En Turquie Kemaliste (Quelques Aspects)." *Guerres Mondiales at Conflits Contemporains* 151 (1988): 121–36.

Bruinessen, Martin van. *Agha, Shaikh and State: The Social and Political Structures of Kurdistan*. London: Zed, 1992.

Cemal, Behçet. *Şeyh Said ve İsyanı*. İstanbul: Sel, 1955.

Çiftçi, Ali. "Kazım Karabekir'in Siyasi Hayatı." PhD diss., Ankara University, 2005.

Demirel, Ahmet. *Birinci Meclis'te Muhalefet: İkinci Grup*. İstanbul: İletişim, 1994.

Demiryürek, Mehmet. "Kıbrıs'ta Bir 150'lik: Sait Molla." http://www.biyotarih.com/?p=46.

Doğan, Avni. *Kurtuluş, Kuruluş ve Sonrası*. İstanbul: Dünya, 1964.

Erdeha, Kamil. *Yüzellilikler Yahut Milli Mücadelenin Muhasebesi*. Ankara: Tekin, 1998.

Erman, Azmi Nihat. *İzmir Suikastı ve İstiklal Mahkemeleri*. İstanbul: Temel, 1971.

Fanizade Mesut. *Atatürk'ün Hayat Felsefesi*. Antakya: n.p., 1938.

Finefrock, Michael M. "From Sultanate to Republic: Mustafa Kemal Atatürk and the Structure of Turkish Politics 1922–1924." PhD diss., Princeton University, 1976.

Göldaş, İsmail. *Takrir-i Sükun Görüşmeleri*. İstanbul: Belge, 1997.

Goldstein, Erik. "British Official Mind and the Lausanne Conference, 1922–1923." In *Power and Stability: British Foreign Policy, 1865–1965*, edited by E. Goldstein and B. J. C. McKercher. London: Frank Cass, 2003.

Gologlu, Mahmut. *Devrimler ve Tepkileri*. İstanbul: Türkiye İş Bankası Yayınları, 2007.

Göztepe, Tarık Mümtaz. *İmam Şamil: Kafkasya'nın Büyük Harp ve İhtilal Kahramanı*. İstanbul: İnkilap, 1961.

Göztepe, Tarık Mümtaz. *Osmanoğulları'nın Son Padişahı Vahdettin Gurbet Cehenneminde*. İstanbul: Sebil, 1991.

Göztepe, Tarık Mümtaz. *Osman Oğulları'nın Son Padişahı Sultan Vadideddin Mütareke Gayyasında*. İstanbul: Sebil, 1994.

Gülmez, Nurettin. *Kurtuluş Savaşı'nda Anadolu'da Yeni Gün*. Ankara: AKDTYK Atatürk Araştıma Merkezi, 1999.

Güven, Zühtü. *Anzavur İsyanı; İstiklâl Savaşı Hatıralarından Acı Bir Safha*. Ankara: İş Bankası Yayınları, 1965.
Halıcı, Şaduman. "Yüzellilikler." Master's thesis, Anadolu University, 1998.
Harris, George S. "The Role of Turkish Military in Politics. Part 1." *Middle East Journal* 19 (1965): 56–57.
İğdemir, Uluğ. *Biga Ayaklanması ve Anzavur Olayları: Günlük Anılar*. Ankara: Türk Tarih Kurumu Basımevi, 1973.
Jwaideh, Wadie. *The Kurdish National Movement: Its Origins and Developments*. Syracuse, NY: Syracuse University Press, 2006.
Kalafat, Yaşar. *Şark Meselesi Işığında Şeyh Sait Olayı, Karekteri, Dönemindeki İç ve Dış Olaylar*. Ankara: Boğaziçi, 1992.
Kalyoncu, Cemal. "Atatürk İle Paşaların Arasını Açmak İstediler." *Aksiyon*, September 12, 2005. http://www.aksiyon.com.tr/detay.php?id=22484.
Kandemir, Feridun. *Atatürk'e İzmir Sukastinden Ayrı 11 Suikast*. İstanbul: Ekincil, 1955.
Kandemir, Feridun. *Hatırları ve Söyleyemedikleri ile Rauf Orbay*. İstanbul: Sinan, 1965.
Kandemir, Feridun. *Siyasi Dargınlıklar*. Vol. 3. İstanbul: Ekicigil, 1955.
Kandemir, Feridun. *Sultan Vahdettin'in Son Günleri*. İstanbul: Yağmur, 2008.
Karaca, Emin. *150'likler*. İstanbul: Altın, 2007.
Karaer, Nihat. *Tam Bir Muhalif: Refik Halid Karay, Yüzellilikler Meselesi*. İstanbul: Temel, 1998.
Kibar, Nizamettin. "Muhalefetten Sesler ve Nizamettin Kibar." *Birikim* 35 (1992): 87–88.
Kılıç, Sümer. *İstiklal Mahkemeleri Adil miydi: İzmir Suikastı*. İstanbul: Emre, 1994.
Kocahanoğlu, Osman Selim. *Atatürk'e Kurulan Pusu*. İstanbul: Temel, 2005.
Kutay, Cemal. *150'likler Faciası*. İstanbul: Sıralar, 1955.
Kutay, Cemal. *Çerkes Ethem Dosyası*. İstanbul: Boğaziçi, 1973.
Kutay, Cemal. *Yüzellikler Faciası*. İstanbul: n.p., 1955.
Martı, Metin, ed. *Mevlanzade Rıfat'ın Anıları*. İstanbul: Arma, 1992.
Mazıcı, Nurşen. *Atatürk Döneminde Muhalefet*. İstanbul: Dilmen, 1984.
McDowell, David. *A Modern History of the Kurds*. London: I. B. Tauris, 1996.
Mert, Timuçin. *Atatürk'ün Yanındaki Mehdi*. İstanbul: Karakutu, 2006.
Mumcu, Uğur. *Gazi Paşa'ya Suikast*. İstanbul: Tekin, 1992.
Okday, İsmail Tevfik. *Adana Vilayeti Matbuatı*. Ankara: Hariciye Vekaleti Matbaası, 1932.
Öksüz, Hikmet. *Batı Trakya Türkleri*. Çorum: Karam, 2006.
Olson, Robert. *The Emergence of Kurdish Nationalism*. Austin: University of Texas Press, 1991.
Önal, Sami, ed. *Hüsrev Gerede'nin Anıları: Kurtuluş Savaşı, Atatürk ve Devrimler*. İstanbul: Literatür, 2002.
Özkan, Şerife. "Yüzellilikler and Süleyman Şefik Kemali: A Legitimacy and Security Issue." Master's thesis, Bosphorus University, 2004.

Özkaya, Yücel. *Milli Mücadele'de Basın 1919–1921*. Ankara: Türk Tarih Kurumu, 1989.

Özkök, Rüknü. *Milli Mücadele Başlarken, Düzce-Bolu İsyanları*. İstanbul: Karacan, 1970.

Özoğlu, Hakan. "Exaggrating and Exploting the Sheikh Said Rebellion of 1925 for Political Gains." *New Perspectives on Turkey* 41 (Fall 2009): 181–210.

Özoğlu, Hakan. *Kurdish Notables and the Ottoman State: Evolving Identities, Competing Loyalties and Shifting Boundries*. Albany: State University of New York Press, 2004.

Özoğlu, Hakan. "Sultan Vahdettin'in ABD Başkanı Coolidge'e Gönderdiği Bir Mektup." *Toplumsal Tarih* 142 (October 2005): 100–106.

Özsoy, Osman. *Gazetecinin İnfazı*. İstanbul: Timaş, 1997.

Rıza Nur and Joseph Grew. *Lozan Barış Anlaşmasının Perde Arkası*. İstanbul: Örgün, 2003.

Sedat Bingöl. "Ömer Fevzi Bey'in Müdafaanamesi ve Mesut Fani'nin Hoybun'a İlişkin Bilgileri: İki 150'lik Üzerine Notlar ve Belgeler." *Toplumsal Tarih* 62 (February 1999): 41–48.

Sertoğlu, Mithat. "Amasya Protokol'ünün Tam ve Gerçek Metni." *Belgelerle Türk Tarihi Dergisi* 3 (December 1967): 9–14.

Sevim, Ali, Akif Tural, and İzzet Öztoprak. *Atatürk'ün Söylev ve Demeçleri*. 3 vols. Ankara: Türk Tarih Kurumu Basimevi, 1959.

Shaw, Stanford. *From Empire to Republic*. Vol. 2. Ankara: Türk Tarih Kurumu.

Soysal, İlhami. *150'likler*. İstanbul: Gür, 1985.

Stoddard, Philip H. "The Ottoman Government and the Arabs, 1911 to 1918." PhD diss., Princeton University, 1963.

Tahir, Kemal. *Kurt Kanunu*. Ankara: Bilgi, 1969.

Tevetoğlu, Fethi. *Milli Mücadele Yıllarındaki Kuruluşlar*. Ankara: TTK, 1988.

Toker, Metin. *İsmet Paşa'yla On Yıl*. 4 vols. Ankara: Akis-Burçak, 1966–1969.

Toker, Metin. *Şeyh Sait ve İsyanı*. Ankara: Akis, 1968.

Toker, Yalçın. *150'liklerden Portreler*. İstanbul: Toker, 2006.

Tunaşar, Seyhun. *Gizemli Bir Devrimci İsmail Canpolat*. İstanbul: Piramit, 2004.

Tunaya, Tarık Zafer. *İslamcılık Akımı*. İstanbul: Simavi, 1991.

Tunaya, Tarık Zafer. *Türkiye'de Siyasi Partiler*. 3 vols. İstanbul: İletişim, 1999.

Tunaya, Tarık Zafer. *Türkiye'de Siyasi Partiler*. İstanbul: Doğan Kardeş, 1952.

Tunçay, Mete. "Zincire Vurulmuş Cumhuriyet." *Toplumsal Tarih* 91 (July 1991): 6.

Tunçay, Mete. *Türkiye Cumhuriyeti'nde Tek-Parti Yönetiminin Kurulması 1923–1931*. İstanbul: Tarih Vakfı Yurt Yayınları, 1999.

Türker, Hasan. "Basın Özgürlüğü Tartışmaları: Cumhuriyet'in İlk Yıllarında Ankara-İstanbul Çatışması." *Toplumsal Tarih* 53 (May 1998): 15–23.

Uğurlu, Nurer. *Kürt Milliyetçiliği: Kürtler ve Şeyh Said İsyanı*. İstanbul: Örgün, 2006.

Villalta, Jorge Blanco. *Atatürk*. Translated by William Chambell. Ankara: TTK, 1979.

Wasti, Syed Tanvir. "Feylosaf Rıza." *Middle Eastern Studies* 38 (2002): 83–100.

Wright, Quincy. "The Mosul Dispute." *American Journal of International Law* 20, no. 3 (1926): 453–64.

Yalçın, Durmuş. "Milli Mücadele'de İdareciler, Günümüzün ve Geleceğin İdareciliği" *Atatürk Araştırma Merkezi Dergisi* 7, no. 21 (1991), electronic version. http://www.atam.gov.tr/index.php?Page=DergiIcerik&IcerikNo=602.

Yalçın, Tülün. *Osmanlı'da bir İngiliz Gelin*. İstanbul: Can, 2004.

Yeşil, Ahmet. *Türkiye Cumhuriyeti'nde İlk Teşkilatlı Muhalefet Hareketi: Terakkiperver Cumhuriyet Fırkası*. Ankara: Cedid, 2002.

Zürcher, Erik Jan, ed. *Political Opposition in the Early Turkish Republic: The Progressive Republican Party 1925–1925*. Leiden: E. J. Brill, 1991.

Zürcher, Erik Jan, ed. "Türkiye'de Kürt Milliyetçiliği: Zımni Sözleşmeden Ayaklanmaya, 1919–1925." In *İmparatorluktan Cumhuriyete Türkiye'de Etnik Çatışma*. İstanbul: İletişim, 2005.

Zürcher, Erik Jan, ed. *The Unionist Factor: The Role of the Committee of Union and Progress in the Turkish National Movement 1905–1926*. Leiden: E. J. Brill, 1984.

NEWSPAPERS

Adalet
Akşam
Alemdar
Anadolu
Anadolu'da Yeni Gün
Cumhuriyet
Dünya
Hakimiyet-i Milliye
İkaz
İkdam
İstikbal
Kahkaha
Milliyet
New York Times
Presse du Soir
Resmi Ceride
Sada-yı Hak
Son Telgraf
Tevhid-i Efkar
The Times
Yeni Türkiye

Index

About the Author

HAKAN ÖZOĞLU is an associate professor of Middle Eastern History in the Department of History at the University of Central Florida, Orlando. From 1997 to 2007, he was on the faculty of the Department of Near Eastern Languages and Civilizations at the University of Chicago as the Endowed Ayaslı Senior Lecturer in Modern Turkish Studies, teaching modern Turkish language, culture, and history. He also taught classes in different capacities for New York University, the University of Michigan, Loyola University at Chicago, and Ohio Wesleyan University. His first book, *Kurdish Notables and the Ottoman State* (2004, 2007), deals with the role of Kurdish notables in the emergence of Kurdish nationalism. The Turkish translation of this book was published by Kitap Yayınevi under the title *Osmanlı Devleti ve Kürt Milliyetçiliği* in 2005. His current research project deals with the tenure of U.S. High Commissioner Mark L. Bristol in Turkey, 1919–1927.

www.ingramcontent.com/pod-product-compliance
Lightning Source LLC
LaVergne TN
LVHW010739140525
811236LV00003B/27

9780313379567